WITHDRAWN

LIBRARY
Agricultural College
N. D.

NORTHCLIFFE

THE MACMILLAN COMPANY
NEW YORK · BOSTON · CHICAGO · DALLAS
ATLANTA · SAN FRANCISCO

MACMILLAN & CO., Limited
LONDON · BOMBAY · CALCUTTA
MELBOURNE

THE MACMILLAN COMPANY
OF CANADA, Limited
TORONTO

LORD NORTHCLIFFE AS HE APPEARED TO A FAMOUS CARICATURIST, "SPY", OF "VANITY FAIR", IN 1895

NORTHCLIFFE

AN INTIMATE BIOGRAPHY

BY
HAMILTON FYFE

THE MACMILLAN COMPANY
NEW YORK   1930

COPYRIGHT, 1930,
BY THE MACMILLAN COMPANY.

All rights reserved — no part of this
book may be reproduced in any form
without permission in writing from
the publisher.

Set up and electrotyped. Published October, 1930.

PRINTED IN THE UNITED STATES OF AMERICA

A LETTER FROM THE AUTHOR TO VISCOUNT ROTHERMERE

DEAR ROTHERMERE,—
Whether you will like this book I cannot tell, but I know you share the feeling which impelled me to write it.

This feeling was that the time had come to make a just survey of the personality of one who played so large a part in moulding the form and pressure of our age, and who yet remains scarcely known to the world outside a very small circle.

His motives were frequently misinterpreted, his character misunderstood. He worked always behind the scenes of public life. I am a student of letters, diaries, recollections, and I have been surprised at the very few mentions of Northcliffe to be found in them.

No, not surprised exactly, for I am aware how few saw more than the outside, which was often deceptive.

That is why I have written this book about my old Chief, and because I know what devotion you showed to him and still show to his memory I want to dedicate the fruit of my labour to you.

This does not commit you to approval of everything the book contains. As his brother, you may very likely think I have missed points or laid stress on wrong ones. Probably you will be right.

I have done my best, however, and "never anything can be amiss when simpleness and duty tender it". I did feel it a duty, and my other motive was simply—affection. No man I have known displayed it with more generosity or compelled it with more charm. Yours,

HAMILTON FYFE

CONTENTS

CHAPTER		PAGE
I.	An Opportunity and a Young Man	1
II.	The Young Man's Growth and Character	13
III.	The Young Man Makes Good	32
IV.	Widening Out	49
V.	The New Public and Its New Guides	68
VI.	A Failure Turned to Triumph	85
VII.	The Development of the Stunt	103
VIII.	The Struggle for THE TIMES	119
IX.	Newfoundland and the Conquest of the Air	134
X.	The Years Before the War	149
XI.	The Fullness of His Stature	171
XII.	"Most Powerful Man in the Country"	190
XIII.	The Mission to America	205
XIV.	Rejection of Cabinet Office	222
XV.	"A Master of Mass-Suggestion"	238
XVI.	The Years After the War	257
XVII.	The Big and the Little	283
XVIII.	Round the World	303
XIX.	"A Mind Diseased"	320
XX.	The End and After	336
	Index	355

ILLUSTRATIONS

Lord Northcliffe As He Appeared to a Famous Caricaturist, "Spy," of "Vanity Fair," in 1895   *Frontispiece*

A Letter Written by Lord Northcliffe (Then Alfred Harmsworth) in 1904   PAGE   4

                                  FACING PAGE

A Group of Bicyclists, Including Lord Northcliffe (Then Alfred Harmsworth), on the Extreme Right of the Picture   10

Mrs. Alfred Harmsworth, Mother of Lord Northcliffe   18

Lord Northcliffe As He Was When He Began Work in London   90

A Letter Written by Lord Northcliffe During an Illness He Had in 1911   PAGE 158

Lord Northcliffe in the Early Days of His Success   210

Lord Northcliffe at the Height of His Fame   260

Lord Northcliffe As He Was Towards the End of His Life Before Illness Attacked Him   310

NORTHCLIFFE

CHAPTER I

AN OPPORTUNITY AND A YOUNG MAN

I attribute my success, as you call it, to seeing ahead.
LORD NORTHCLIFFE

A GRIMY street in the grimiest part of London. A tall grimy building which seems to be falling to pieces. On an upper floor printing-machines; on a bench a man of thirty-four with a dish at his side, a plate on his lap; he is eating his midday meal.

He hears a step on the rickety stairs. He looks up to see who his visitor may be. It is a young man—a young man on the look-out for an Opportunity. His alert air proclaims this. His large, shining eye turns this way and that, misses nothing.

He is handsome. He is smartly dressed. He wears, of course, a tall hat. It is the year 1885. Not to wear a tall hat in the year 1885 proclaims a man to be of no account. This young man knows, none better than he, the value of Appearances.

Behind him enters another young man. Not so alert, not so challengingly smart in his dress; with all his wits about him nevertheless.

"What can I do for you?" asks the man with the midday meal, one George Newnes, proprietor and editor of a weekly publication called *Tit-Bits*.

The first young man does not seem to hear. He is looking about him, for an Opportunity perhaps. The second young man replies:

"We want to write articles for your paper."

The proprietor-editor looks at him doubtfully.

"What do you want to write about?" he asks.

Thus cornered, the second young man glances desperately about him. The ruinous state of the building gives him an idea.

"I should like to do an article on jerry-building," he blurts out.

"All right, send it in."

"Is it true you pay a guinea a column?"

"It is true."

The midday meal is resumed. The interview is over.

Down the rickety stairs go the visitors. In the mind of the one are thoughts of the article he has undertaken to write. He will do it competently. It will be worth the three guineas he is to receive for it. Later he will write stories for boys, workmanlike stories with no loose ends to them, no flats unjoined. He will write novels of adventure. He will start a School of Journalism. When his friend dies, he will be left a handsome income to remember him by. His name is Max Pemberton.

The other young man's thoughts go farther. They are not on the immediate future. They are not concerned with the earning of three guineas.

The sight of the printing-office has set his imagination working furiously. It was he who had proposed to climb up to it. Yet, when they arrived, he had no word to say. He had left to his friend, clearly accustomed to play Horatio against his Hamlet, the explanation of their visit. He had made no proposal, though he was so plainly the more vital of the two.

Here was a publication which could afford to pay contributors a guinea a column—handsome pay in those days: a short column, too, not more than seven or eight hundred words. There sat the man who had conceived the creation of it, who brought it out every week. What an enviable fortune! What a stepping-stone to greater things!

So thought Alfred Harmsworth as he stood in the presence of George Newnes, the Ancestor of all that will be known as the New Journalism. So he thinks as he walks along grimy Farringdon Street. His friend may plan the article on jerry-building. He will have henceforward another kind of building in his dreams.

For at last an Opportunity has presented itself. His imagination has been suddenly quickened. It has given him a glimpse into the future. He sees a world different from that which lies about him. He sees printing-presses pouring out incessant heaps of papers of every kind for the New Generation, for the millions who have just learned and are learning to read.

Around him here swirl and eddy with sluggish movement the tides of the City of London's life, its surface soiled by all manner of rubbish and filth. Around him in his Temple Chambers has flowed the dusty current of the law. In the City of London, in the Temple, men talk as if the final stage of perfection in human affairs had been reached. They cannot imagine a world different in any material element from the world they know.

Nor is it so long, he reflects (with wonder at his own foresight), since he too fancied the conditions of the moment must be immutable, fixed. He had set his ambition on writing leading articles for *Daily Telegraph,* for *Morning Post;* some day possibly for *The Times*. His eye had been on the Old Public. He had not perceived that the New Public existed. *Tit-Bits* he had looked down on as trash; was not he a contributor to daily newspapers, to those great organs of opinions which were the envy of the world?

A LETTER WRITTEN BY LORD NORTHCLIFFE (THEN ALFRED HARMSWORTH) IN 1904.

"Trash" it was called by all whom he knew. "For workmen and maidservants and office-boys," they said in their rather tired, contemptuous voices. The great majority of their country-folk they held to be beneath their notice. It did not seem to them that any class was worth considering but their class. That was the opinion in which the young man had been brought up.

He knew what they would say about Newnes, if they ever thought about him. "Vulgar," they would say; "one who made money by pandering to the low taste and the immature intelligence of the Mob." Naturally, bred in that atmosphere, he had set his mind, as soon as he began to find his feet in journalism, upon writing for the newspapers produced by and for the members of his class.

Now he has had just a glimpse into a world where these organs would be "back numbers", just a startled realization of possibilities that no one else, perhaps, is at this date foreseeing. He is not a fluent talker at any time. As a child he was precociously silent. As he walks back to Hampstead—where he shares rooms with Pemberton, preferring that to residence in the Temple—as he passes with his friend along Fleet Street and looks up at the newspaper offices, he speaks scarcely at all. He is under the spell of that vision of the Opportunity which came to him in the office of George Newnes.

Newnes—until now scarcely a name to Alfred Harmsworth with his chambers, his tail-coat, his tall hat, his right of entry to certain great newspaper offices. What interest should a young man of good social position, with connections in journalism, take in such a publication as *Tit-Bits?* It was produced for the lower orders. He disdained it. His eyes were closed to its importance as a Sign of the Times.

Now his eyes are opened. Newnes is a Social Portent. *Tit-Bits* is a finger pointing to a New Age.

He will look into its history. It was born in 1881. The popular legend speaks of its founder as a "pedlar"; tells how he kept a scrap-book and pasted into it anything which caught his fancy in the daily Press. Tells how his wife said to him: "If it interests us, George, it might interest other people. What a pity you can't print your tit-bits and make a weekly paper of them." Tells how he acted promptly upon her suggestion.

Legend, as usual, a little overdoes the dramatic value of what happened. Newnes was not a pedlar, but managed for a London firm a branch of a fancy-goods business in Manchester. He was a Congregational minister's son; had been well educated up to the age of sixteen at the City of London School, then apprenticed to a wholesale dealer's business. The scrap-book is apocryphal, but he was in the habit of reading out to his wife what he called "tit-bits" from any newspaper, magazine, or book he happened to be reading; from this grew his idea of a new kind of periodical.

He resolved, at the age of thirty, to publish a weekly collection of scraps of information, anecdotes, incidents, jokes, verses, taken from all kinds of sources, and to call it *Tit-Bits*. He had tried to induce Manchester people to invest £500 and give it a start. They declared that such a fantastic scheme was sure to fail. So he began with what money he could put into the venture, and in three years he was doing so well that he moved it to London, to the Farringdon Street Office with rickety staircase and bulging walls. Here it continued to prosper.

Newnes was the first to present buyers of a paper with insurance policies—against railway accidents. He was also the first to offer to the winners of competitions prizes of high value and of ingenious novelty. In 1883 he gave a house as a prize on condition that it should be called Tit-Bits Villa. In 1884 he offered to the solver of some puzzle or problem an engagement on the staff of the paper. This was won by an Anglican Church minister's son named Pearson; he had been at one of the great public schools, Winchester, but did not feel drawn towards any of the occupations into which Winchester boys usually drifted. He set up a rival to *Tit-Bits* called *Pearson's Weekly,* and he ended his career as Sir Arthur Pearson, owner of the *Daily Express* and other properties.

In 1891, ten years after Newnes had founded the business which Manchester called fantastic, it was formed into a company with a capital of £400,000. Four years after that the capital was increased to a million pounds. By that time Newnes's firm was publishing a number of magazines, but *Tit-Bits* was the richest of its properties as well as the foundation on which its prosperity had been built.

Newnes was, therefore, what I have called him, the Ancestor of the New Journalism; but there was one vivid difference between him and the young man who was now resolving to carry on the work begun by him: Newnes moved by instinct, Northcliffe by design. Newnes had established *Tit-Bits* because he and his wife were fond of tit-bits themselves and guessed that other people might be. He had chanced upon something which a great many wanted and were waiting for. He had blundered into it. Northcliffe saw what the success of *Tit-Bits* meant; he deliberately aimed at taking advantage of the changed conditions brought about by the teaching of everybody to read.

Newnes knew his limitations. He was enticed into daily journalism and lost a vast deal of money. He did not grumble but he knew he had made a mistake. He wrote once to W. T. Stead:

There is one kind of journalism which directs the affairs of nations, which makes and unmakes Cabinets; it upsets Governments, builds up navies, and does many other great things. That is your journalism.

There is another kind which has no such great ambitions. It is content to plod on, year after year, giving wholesome and harmless entertainments to crowds of hard-working people craving for a little fun and amusement. It is quite humble and unpretentious. That is my journalism.

It never occurred to Newnes that there were further worlds waiting to be conquered. Northcliffe sensed them at once. *Tit-Bits* had been until now beneath the notice of a young man who read Thackeray and wrote essays in the style of Defoe, who dressed fashionably and, when he could afford it, rode in hansom cabs. Suddenly he saw what its success signified, what might be gained by turning away from the old paths of journalism and exploiting the new readers, becoming more numerous yearly, and eager for "something to read".

As the young man walks back to Hampstead, and as he ponders over the revelation which has come to him—over the Opportunity which gleams before his eyes—he sees the despised publication in a new light. He studies its pages, he understands why it is bought by so many. He begins to discover how fortunate he is to be on the threshold of his career in the year 1885.

Young politicians of that date are thrilling to the excitement of the Home Rule for Ireland issue. Will Mr. Gladstone offer self-government to the Irish? Will the Conservatives forestall him and buy the Irish vote in Parliament? The young Northcliffe is no politician. True, he feels vaguely sympathetic with the idea of Ireland a Nation, as he feels vaguely sorry for the bands of white-faced, ragged unemployed who sing in the streets and try

AN OPPORTUNITY AND A YOUNG MAN

to hold meetings in Trafalgar Square and are clubbed by the police. But he is not easily moved to believe in political remedies, either then or at any time in his life.

Young engineers are talking eagerly about a tricycle with an internal-combustion engine consuming benzoline, which is being tried out. They are anxious to hear more of a submarine boat which the gun-maker, Nordenfeldt, has invented. Sensible men say it is all nonsense, but the engineers think we may be on the verge, don't you know . . . our young man is inclined to believe they may be right. A French balloon, which is steered across the Channel, excites him more. Suppose that some day—not in his time, maybe, but in the course of centuries—men should learn to fly?

Young painters and followers of art movements are interested in what they call the Impressionist Method and the founding of a certain New English Art Club. Royal Academicians smile in their lofty way. "End in smoke", they prophesy. It would amuse our young man if he could guess that the founders of the new club will be famous when the value of the canvases left behind by those Royal Academicians (and sold in their time for high prices) has gone down and down to zero almost. But "Art is not in his line", he says, so he does not concern himself with an artists' quarrel.

Uppermost in his mind is the ambition to make money. Not so much for the sake of money itself, rather because money stands as a symbol for success. There is an energy boiling up within him for which he must find outlet. Writing does not carry it off. He does not belong to the writer type. He is a man of action, although he does not yet know it. He must create material things—things that the multitude can see, and understand, and admire. And now it has been revealed to him that material things of untold worth in money are waiting to be created in this year 1885.

For fifteen years the law has ordained that every child shall go to school. It took a few years to round them all up and put them at their desks and find teachers for them. But now the system has been for a long time at work. Already a large number of children who have been to school are grown up. Each year more and more are added to the working population. They are not in any real sense of the word educated, but they can read. A large proportion of them want to read. The rest can be tempted to read if reading matter within the grasp of their intelligence and within the limits of their purse is offered to them.

Never before has the young man been conscious that there exist these possible readers, these millions who can be coaxed to buy. He is aware of the people who buy daily newspapers and weekly illustrated newspapers and Monthly Reviews. He is aware of people who read nothing at all—have no desire to read. He has not until now suspected the presence all about him of a vast army of products of the elementary school who find little or nothing to attract them in the journals for which he writes, who therefore read scarcely at all, but who could be induced, without great difficulty, to buy something of a different character, something more "popular" in its appeal.

He sees immediately possibilities which Newnes has not seen, will never see. "The man who has produced this *Tit-Bits* has got hold of a bigger thing than he imagines." Still the disdainful note in his voice. This *Tit-Bits!* A production which young men in tall hats could not be seen reading. A scrap collection which he, as one who has written leading articles for Great Dailies, can hardly contemplate without a superior smile.

A GROUP OF BICYCLISTS, INCLUDING LORD NORTHCLIFFE (THEN ALFRED HARMSWORTH) ON THE EXTREME RIGHT OF THE PICTURE

But never mind that. Here is this fellow Newnes making money, and "he is only at the beginning of a development which is going to change the whole face of journalism". He got hold of the idea first, but there is plenty of room for others in the field which he discovered.

Another paper of the same kind as his might do as well—or better. And then there will be all sorts of chances to start other kinds: a comic paper, for instance, that would not be above the heads of the simplest people; and how about a cheap paper for women, something more direct and useful than the weeklies of dignified appearance which only go into highly prosperous homes?

Once you start on the idea of exploiting the new class of readers, there is no end to it. There they are, millions of them, waiting with pennies in their hands. Anyone can get those pennies who will give them what they want. That's it, find out what the public wants. New idea that it wants anything! Easier to tell what it doesn't want. Evidently the new readers don't want the newspapers. They can't understand them. They haven't time for them. They can't concentrate their attention for long enough at a time to wade through their voluminous reports and immense three-decker articles.

The Young Man begins to look at newspapers with a fresh eye. Hitherto he has not been critical of them. They appeared to suit the people for whom they were produced. They were dull, it was true, often very dull. Page upon page of parliamentary report, column upon column of political speeches outside Parliament, Law Reports, Police Court Reports, disquisitions on Foreign Politics. Now and then a murder, a theatre fire, a wreck, a dramatic criminal trial, or a sensational divorce, but for the most part dullness, heavy, unrelieved.

Well, if that was all the newspapers received, how could

they make themselves more interesting? Weren't they dependent on what flowed into the office? Yes, but need they be? Couldn't one imagine newspapers which should create news, not, of course, by inventing it, but by hitting every day on some event, some oddity, some aspect of everyday life which would interest the mass of people, set them talking, make them shudder or smile?

It sounded fantastic. The editors whom he knew would call it absurd. Perhaps it was, and yet . . . there was that New Public—all those new possible readers who had been and were being turned out by the elementary schools. Totally different from the existing newspaper public. Their minds resembled Newnes's mind; they liked scraps, tit-bits. Well, why not give them scraps? News could be treated in a way that would please them; make them feel they knew all about everything, instead of suggesting to them, as existing newspapers did, that everything was very difficult to understand, that nothing could be discussed or reported except at very great length.

Yes, there was something in that; something in the dream of a newspaper that should be welcomed by the meanest intelligence; something in this notion of turning away from the old kind of reader and calling a new kind out of the void. But all that was in the future. No use thinking too much about it. The first thing to do was to get money together for setting up as a rival to Newnes. After that might follow—who knew what? But—first things first. Here was an Opportunity. How to make the best of it, that was the problem for to-day.

CHAPTER II

THE YOUNG MAN'S GROWTH AND CHARACTER

He seemed to be merely a careless onlooker at life.
AARON WATSON

WHENCE has this young man in search of an Opportunity sprung? What have been his birth, his upbringing, his education? How has his mind been nourished, his character formed?

Like almost all who have made revolutions, he has sprung from the middle class. Romantic popular opinion, delighted by melodramatic contrasts and surprises, likes to imagine always that the men whose careers have made history started from the lowest rungs of the ladder. That is seldom true of them—for a reason easy to understand.

To one who will require exceptional vigour, developed at an early age, it is an obvious advantage to be brought up comfortably; not to be obliged to use his strength as soon as he has it. Those who rise from the ranks of manual toilers seldom have energy enough left, after they have risen, to become innovators. Their vitality has been so largely spent, first on the hard tasks set to them at the start of their working lives; later, on the incessant, exhausting effort to exchange those tasks for others more to their taste, that, as a rule, they "take things as they find them", which means they fall into line with whatever is generally accepted, with any traditions which happen to be in vogue. From lack of resisting force they conform to the practices which are hallowed in the common mind by long usage, by convenient custom.

If Northcliffe had been forced to earn his living as a boy by selling newspapers in the streets (which most people, relying on legend, believe that he did), he would not have revolutionized the daily newspaper. He might have become a famous journalist; he certainly would have made in that or any other line of business a resounding reputation. His abounding vitality could not be checked; whatever he took up he would have done far more successfully than most other men did it. But he would not, had the popular legend been authentic, have made history.

He could not, if as a boy he had sold newspapers, have seen with clear vision at the age of twenty-one how the future of the newspaper might be shaped. He could not, by the age of twenty-three, have reached a position from which he could begin to create that future.

To his middle-class home he owed the sufficient nourishment and the leisure which allow youthful brains to brood over distant possibilities without the harsh compulsion of attending to immediate material needs. His early surroundings were favourable to the natural, unforced growth of mind and character.

Though he was born in Ireland (at Chapelizod, close to Dublin, on July 15, 1865), he was not on his father's side Irish. That strain which contributed most to his genius he derived from his mother.

There are still a few very old men and women in Ireland who remember Geraldine Maffett as a girl and a bride. No one who was acquainted with her at any period of her life could easily forget her. As an old lady she was strikingly handsome; as a young one she must have been nobly beautiful, too intelligent ever to be called "pretty". She was probably the only person whose judgment her eldest son consistently respected. She was certainly the only one whose censure he feared.

Daughter of a man of energetic character, by profession a land-agent in County Down (Ulster), she was, like all Ulster folk, partly descended from the Scottish settlers "planted" in the north of Ireland during the seventeenth century. The name of the family was no doubt a variation of Moffatt. This is common in the south of Scotland, whence the "plantation" emigrants mostly came. But there was in her veins some Celtic blood as well. To her eldest son she handed on a temperament impulsive and generous—a character marked far more by Irish impetuosity than by Scottish caution. Neither his nor her intellect had patience for the painstaking process which argues from the particular to the general (the Scottish method of deduction). They were both intuitive in their habits of thought. Instinct and imagination contributed a great deal more than reasoning to shape their decisions.

In both of them, too, there was a grimly humorous Celtic sense of reality. Neither could be drawn away by sentimentality from seeing things as they were. Northcliffe would no more shrink from admitting a failure than he would believe in the permanence of prosperity which was not continuously fostered. When he discovered that he had made mistakes, he made no effort to persuade himself that perhaps things might turn out well after all. He cut his losses without hesitation.

He was charged with fickleness, even with cruelty, because he would often, after making a man a favourite and encouraging him to hope for high advancement, cease to take any interest in him and maybe have him dismissed. Both charges were unjust. Somehow or other such men made him believe they could be useful to him. As soon as he found that he had over-estimated their ability, he dropped them. On his side it was purely a business transaction. The error on their side lay in the delusion that they had been casually picked up and as casually thrown away. He had picked them up for a purpose, they had failed him. He did not want them any more; purposely he dropped them. It was not in his nature to attempt to hide this either from himself or from them.

The relation between Mrs. Harmsworth and the most famous of her children has been likened to the tie of affection and confidence which so frequently binds French mothers and sons. The comparison is apt. The French are of partly Celtic origin. It was a Celtic trait in Northcliffe's nature which made him send off at the beginning of every day, while he was head of the British War Mission in America, a cable of greeting to Mrs. Harmsworth, giving her his news. He did this, indeed, whenever he was out of England.

If he were within telephoning distance, he telephoned, "so that we can hear each other's voices". He gave her a beautiful home on the outskirts of London, so that he could see her very often. If he were missing from his office and from his home at a moment when some difficult decision was to be made without delay, he would be found in all probability lying in a long chair before the fire by his mother's side, or arm-in-arm with her pacing garden walks and lawns.

Between them there appeared to be that complete confidence which sometimes exists between husband and wife. They seemed to know each other's minds without going through the tedious process of putting thoughts into words. She was not an adoring mother, ready to admire with enthusiasm whatever her boy might do or say. She was a critic, shrewd, kindly, frank; if speech had been required, she would have been an outspoken critic too. But whenever she had ground for censure, something in the atmosphere about her subtly conveyed to him a sense of her disapproval, so that words were unnecessary. He would begin at once either an explanation or an admission that she might be taking the correct view.

She never tried to influence him—beyond letting him know what her views might be. She was not of a controversial temperament. She formed her own opinions and was ready enough among her intimates or in general company to express but not to argue about them. A serene self-confidence upheld her. Courteously she would listen to comment or objection; seldom would she answer it.

The habit of relying upon her own judgment had been early acquired. As a girl, she was given by her father opportunities far beyond those of her friends. She read a great deal, she knew England as well as Ireland, she travelled in France and Germany. In her Irish surroundings she was something of an oracle; all through her life she spoke at times in an assured, dignified, oracular tone.

Such women usually marry men of weaker character than their own. Geraldine Maffett did so. In Alfred Harmsworth the elder there was a great deal to like and to admire. From him Northcliffe inherited that easy charm of manner, that gay irresponsible humour, that quickness to make friends which fascinated even people who approached him with strong hostile prejudice ingrained in their minds. From his father's side, too, came Northcliffe's instant sympathy with anyone in need, sorrow, sickness, or any other adversity—the instant impulse to give generous aid, if aid was required.

But in the father these pleasant qualities were not backed, as they were in the son, by the sterner virtues of perseverance, dogged industry, determination to win. Even before she married, Geraldine Maffett knew that the task of making a home and bringing up children would fall mainly upon her. She soon discovered after their marriage that her husband was without ambition. He would have been content to stay all his life in Dublin, where he practised a little as a barrister and wrote a little, without payment, for such ponderous periodicals as the *Dublin Review*. He liked the easy-going society, cultivated, unpretentious, self-indulgent, which Dublin then offered to a professional man with a genius for companionship.

His wife chafed under the limitations of what was, in essence, a provincial town. She felt certain that her husband would not much improve his position there; she made up her mind that he would be able to discover more profitable openings at the English Bar. So when her little first-born was two years old, she transported the family to London, rented a cottage in what was then the rural suburb of Hampstead, and in the style of the days of the patriarchs continued to bear children up to the number of fourteen.

Upon a small income she made for them a home on which, when they were grown-up men and women, they all looked back with delight and gratitude. She brought them up with a mixture of discipline and liberty, admirably conceived and most successful in its results. They could do more as they liked, they had a better time than most other children; in small matters they were under no strict compulsion or control. But where the larger issues of life came into play they knew they must observe the rules that had been laid down for them. It was a marvel to neighbours who saw them running wild outside their home that they should be so orderly, so polite, so amenable inside it.

The father now earned a sufficient income as a barrister to keep the household in comfort, without having much left for anything beyond daily expenses. He was regu-

Photo]   *[Mendoza Galleries, Old Bond Street*

MRS. ALFRED HARMSWORTH, MOTHER OF LORD NORTHCLIFFE

larly employed on the legal staff of a railway company (the Great Northern) and was obliged to travel up and down its line a good deal, so he was often away from home. But he was a genial companion to his elder sons. Northcliffe spoke of him always with warm affection, kept in his office a large portrait of him in wig and gown, took an abiding interest in a London Debating Society which he had helped to establish.

Sometimes he would take his eldest boy with him on his journeys and good-naturedly allow him to do "wild" things which startled his wife. Once the lad, then eleven years of age, reached home with his face like a chimney-sweep's and clothes disastrously dirty. To the cries of astonishment and alarm which greeted him he replied by explaining with pride and glee that he had ridden from Grantham, in the north of England, to London in the cab of the locomotive with engine-driver and fireman, and that it was "tremendous fun". For at least a week after this adventure he was convinced that driving a locomotive was the only occupation for him.

That was a passing fancy: there were others. But long before he left school his aptitude for journalism displayed itself; his career was fixed. His father helped to fix it by encouraging him to read, letting him read what he liked, but telling him who were the authors held in honour by the world. Thus he turned the boy's attention to Thackeray, whose novels appealed to all clever boys of that period by reason of their man-of-the-world tone, their trick of persuading readers that they were being admitted "behind the scenes" of life. All were devoured eagerly and left their mark on the young mind. Northcliffe's jovial cynicism about society, about public men and public affairs, about life in general, was not unlike that of Thackeray as the novelist appeared in his novels.

He had none of the reforming zeal of Dickens, though he was inclined to sympathize with it. He was not interested in progressive thoughts, either at that period or at any time, though certain practical movements appealed strongly to him. He was among the early supporters of Garden City schemes and a warm admirer of the framer of them, Sir Ebenezer Howard. In the humour of Dickens he revelled. Defoe and Oliver Goldsmith (both favourites of his father) he enjoyed because they were good journalists. Later on he saw that; he was, of course, unconscious of it at the time.

He delighted especially in Defoe's descriptive genius, which left out nothing that could make a scene real and vivid in the reader's imagination. He had been trained to observe for himself—all the children were. Their schoolbook education did not begin until fairly late. Northcliffe used to say that he was seven years old before he was taught his alphabet. Then he learned to read very quickly, for his intelligence had been sharpened in many ways, chiefly by observing nature. In this direction he found out so much for himself, and so often discovered that commonly held opinions were wrong, that he was all his life suspicious of what the mass of people believed.

There was not money enough in the Hampstead cottage exchequer for sending even the eldest son to one of the famous old schools. He went first to Stamford Grammar School in Lincolnshire; it was ancient enough and had a respectable history. At this time, unhappily, it was not in very good hands. Northcliffe's recollection of what he suffered there never softened. George the Third, it was said, would not live in Hampton Court Palace because he had once been caned there, by order of his grandfather. The indignity rankled to the end of his life. Northcliffe, too, smarted always under the recollection of early canings—those he got at Stamford. A school-fellow, who has kindly sent me some recollections of him, says the canings were usually the result of inattention and a preference for playing with marbles in school-hours to doing lessons which did not interest him.

He was on one occasion caned more unmercifully than usual, the dose being four on each hand—and a very tender hand (a real nice hand, too, as I remember it), though hardened considerably with periodical canings—and as many strokes from the nape of the neck to the calf of the leg as could be put in without overlapping. Now this is no exaggeration, for plenty of us saw the black and blue marks and all the black and blue stripes when we saw Dodger stripped as we were bathing at the usual place. Dodger never forgave the Rev. E. C. Musson that lot (one of many), and left soon after. Some old boy in after-life said the Rev. E. C. Musson tried to get some appointment necessitating Dodger's influence, but Dodger told him he never forgave him that thrashing and would not use his influence for him.

"Dodger" was the nickname he earned by his swiftness and slipperiness as a Rugby football player. He was an untidy boy. The Eton suit in which he appeared, neat and well-dressed, at beginning of term would soon lose its buttons, show tears and stains. In this matter of tidiness he altered; though he was never interested in his clothes, they were always trim and orderly. A characteristic more important, noted by his school-fellow, remained with him through life. This was his knack of compelling affection.

Every boy at the school liked him; I should not be wrong if I used a much stronger word and said loved him.

He was a very nice-tempered and well-mannered boy, and did not like to hurt anyone's feelings, though he was often at fault in that respect because he was very fond of bringing boys to book over some very trivial, at the time appearing senseless, thing, and was always sorry and apologetic to the one hurt; and he would be the last to fall out with another boy if it could be avoided.

That was Northcliffe's disposition always. He often did hurt people's feelings, but never because it gave him any satisfaction. He fell out with many men (scarcely ever with a woman), but he never did so "if it could be avoided".

One thing he did want to learn—the German language. This school-fellow knew it. While others teased him or made him talk so that they might be amused by his gibberish, young Harmsworth took lessons from him and found in this not less entertainment than in collecting stamps and rearing silkworms—the boyish hobbies which made special appeal to him. Also, "he was always writing little odds and ends which every other fellow who thought he knew things would call daft stuff; but he was always on the look-out to get any other fellow, if possible, to help him in his ideas".

We get the picture of a boy with lots of the usual interests, and others beside, who was certainly not unhappy and rebellious. Yet in after-life he hated all his memories of the place.

Very different were the feelings he had towards the school in Hampstead (Henley House, it was called) to which he went as a day-boy after his frequent petition to be taken away from the other had moved his parents' hearts. Here he enjoyed himself thoroughly. Whether he learned very much of what schools try to teach is doubtful. If he did he soon forgot it, for, although he had at all times a stock of odd out-of-the-way information in his head, he knew no Latin or Greek; he had very hazy notions of history; he was well acquainted with no modern foreign languages (German had been soon neglected); the interest he took in science was that of a quick-witted child. No doubt he picked up what was necessary for making a sufficiently good impression on his teachers. The head master was kindly and clever, father of A. A. Milne, known later as playwright and author of children's verse. He believed in letting a boy's aptitudes develop themselves. He had discernment enough to engage H. G. Wells as a very young mathematical master and to let him take the boys for walks in the fields, where his delight in nature taught them lessons they never forgot. Young Alfred Harmsworth may not have retained much learning from school-books, but Henley House quickened and developed his mind. It was then and always receptive far beyond the common. He could "get up" a subject very quickly and then let it slip out of his mind. He must have done that at school, for he was reckoned an exceptionally clever boy.

This reputation he owed less to industry and accomplishment in the class-rooms than to what he did out of school. He was a pioneer bicyclist, a pioneer lawn tennis player. He was chiefly admired for his enterprise in starting a school magazine. He not only edited this and wrote most of it; he also set up the type himself. A printer's shop in the district, nearer to London than Hampstead, where the family now lived, gave him the opportunity to satisfy his young ambition and to produce a journal that looked like the real thing. The hours he spent in the composing-room, in shirt-sleeves and white apron, picking the type rapidly from its slanting box with finger and thumb, putting it into his compositor's stick, were some of the happiest in his life. The magazine gave him his first incentive to put forth all the powers that were in him. He was pleased to be doing it all himself. He felt that it was worth doing. He enjoyed the praise it won. None of the triumphs of after-years (he would say) brought him quite the same elation, the same pride, the same perfect satisfaction with success won in spite of so many difficulties.

His father watched his effort with good-humoured amusement. He watched it also with some misgiving when the boy announced that he meant to be a journalist. Mr. Harmsworth had friends who were editors and leader-writers. When he asked them for their opinion, they gave it frankly. "Get the idea out of the boy's head", they advised. Later on, with the same vigour, they offered the same counsel to the boy himself.

He paid no heed to them, nor to his father pointing out the precarious nature of newspaper work and urging him to be a barrister, with the chance of succeeding to the position, now fairly comfortable, which he himself held. At fifteen Northcliffe's will was strong; he had already the quiet confidence in his own judgment and his own powers which were to carry him so far. He found an ally, too, in his mother. She had spurred him on to form ambitious plans. She had told him of her belief that he could do great things. Now she saw a line marked out for him to follow. She resolved that, if he remained steadfast to his intent, he should follow it. She was convinced that it would lead to fame and fortune, nor did she hide this conviction from her boy.

In his mind, therefore, while he was still at school, while he lived with brothers and sisters, becoming more and more numerous, in a roomy, rambling, old-fashioned house in St. John's Wood, large ideas were framing themselves. Improved though the family circumstances were, he knew that he must set about earning a living for himself as soon as possible. For the law he had no fancy. Journalism seemed not merely to offer in course of time the hope of distinction, of a good income; more important, it might be made to yield an immediate harvest. Not a rich one, but one that would support a young man with no extravagant tastes.

Of an immediate income, small though it may be, he is in need. Mother and father have debated long, over and over again, the possibility of sending him to a university, to Oxford or Cambridge. "I was against it at the time", he once told me. "I knew it would mean a pinch for the others, and I didn't think that would be fair. I wanted to help them as soon as I could rather than to be a burden on them. But I have often regretted that I had to renounce what would have been of immense value to me."

He believed fervently in the exaggerated value of a university education to young men entering journalism. I once put it to him that nearly all the most famous journalists of his time had succeeded without having had this advantage. I cited Greenwood, Stead, Garvin, Wickham Steed, Massingham, A. G. Gardiner.

"Yes, yes," he cried, "but they were men bound to make their way to the front. I am not thinking about geniuses—they can take care of themselves; but think of the social value of having been at a university. It is like being able to ride. Every young man who wants to get on ought to be able to ride—and to talk French." He over-estimated the importance of such trifles because he had missed them himself.

At fifteen, then, he leaves school, prepared to face life, not as yet asking for very much from it, believing that he can make a start, at all events, by writing for the papers.

Nor is he mistaken in this. The editor of a local paper (*Hampstead and Highgate Express*) gives him employment as a reporter. He is paid very little. The work is not inspiring. One day he reports a funeral and a flower-show: the next day a sale of poultry and a political meeting. Nothing but bald statement of fact is required—

or even permitted. But he learns a good deal. He sees that many things are not what they seem. He discovers that politicians have one voice for the platform and another for the man behind the platform, where they tell young reporters what an infernal nuisance it has been to them to come! Hence, perhaps, his lifelong distrust of politicians.

Grateful to Editor Jealous the boy will always be, but that kind of reporting is not for long congenial. He is glad to make a change, when by a piece of luck a short-time tutorship is offered to him. He accepts, is ready to try his hand at teaching or anything else, but as a tutor he is not conspicuously successful. The abilities which make a journalist seldom make a competent teacher. Still, the job brings in a little money, and then another piece of luck falls in his way. A friend of the family offers to take him abroad; he travels for some months in Europe. Thus there is planted in him that passion for wandering which becomes one of his most prominent characteristics.

Now he begins to understand for the first time what the advantages of wealth are. It gives those who are greedy for a sight of the world beyond their own doorsteps the opportunity to move about in comfort. This is a revelation to a boy who has not until now discovered the drawbacks of being poor. Money, he now sees, is a necessity if you want to make the most of life. He does not as yet fix his desire for money high, but he has learned its importance to a young man who is not going to be content to stay all his life at home.

That first taste of the amusement and the mind-stimulus of travel have another effect. They start the young man on a path which will lead him to the point at which he ceases to care about possessing a home, at which he is most content when living in hotels and continually moving about. Life suddenly widens out before him. His head is filled with new ideas. He is too busy sorting out his impressions to write them down. But they remain, fresh and vivid. Now he is inflamed by that love of France which never leaves him. Now he first feels that amused disdain towards Germans (although he has German relatives) which is to influence his attitude at a critical point in world history.

His trip over, he sets about finding employment. He cannot earn enough, as a free-lance, to keep him in silk hats, which in those days every self-respecting young journalist must wear. Now his contributions to the school magazine come in useful. He shows them to the proprietor of several weekly papers, a Mr. William Ingram, who smiles and says they are not bad, not at all bad—for a schoolboy; who thinks so well of the young writer's ability that he engages him, at £2 a week, to be assistant editor of one of his periodicals. Is it not of good omen that it should be called *Youth?*

What an answer to the croakers who have warned him against journalism! What happiness for the mother who has so firmly believed in her boy! How the mother and brothers and sisters look up to him, filled with affectionate admiration, not dreaming of what he will some day do for them—play the part of fairy godfather, endow them with opportunities and fortunes, one and all!

Off he goes every morning, in top-hat and tail-coat, to "the office", works with a will when he gets there, but cannot make much headway with *Youth*. The editor is one Edward Morton, who later attains some prominence as a critic of plays, as writer of a popular musical comedy, *San Toy;* is known as "Monkey Morton". From him the Young Man picks up a knowledge of a certain kind of journalism: is soon sharing with him rooms almost in the

Temple. Through an archway from the Strand Thanet Place was in those days approached. It has long ceased to exist. Here, in an old-world house, forming part of a quadrangle, live editor and assistant-editor, separated in age by some ten years, but inseparable in companionship. At this time, one who knew him then has written, "he had a beautiful head of light hair, almost flaxen in hue, but with a sort of sunlight in it"; often he wore no hat.

"He was a picture of radiant health, buoyant, athletic-looking, easy and graceful in all his movements. His manners, too, were very delightful. As for the rest, he seemed to be merely a careless onlooker at life. Nothing appeared to concern, or to ruffle, or greatly to interest him; but he had observant eyes, with a rather soft and caressing expression, but also full of inquiry. They were eyes that warded off inquiry from the other side. He was friendly, but aloof."[1]

This same witness, not entirely an admirer, bore testimony to Northcliffe's enduring friendliness to any he had known in these early years. An old journalist, Byron Webber, was in need, Mr. Aaron Watson recalled. Northcliffe was asked if he would contribute to a fund raised by those who had known Webber. He immediately sent £10 and promised to do, in addition, "whatever you may advise". A pound a week in Webber's pocket for some time was the result of that promise.

That air of being "an onlooker at life" is deceptive. Already he is ambitious, already hard-worked. In the evenings he almost always writes. Nothing with fresh thought in it, nor even fresh expression. Essays in imitation of familiar models. Leading articles of the three-paragraph order, three long paragraphs, each saying the

[1] *A Newspaper Man's Memories*, by Aaron Watson.

same thing in differing words, on the principle that "what I say three times is true".

Sometimes he gets a leader accepted by the *Daily Telegraph,* which he has a secret ambition to own. Long after, when he heads a deputation to Lord Burnham on his eightieth birthday, he laughingly recalls this. As a relief from heavy articles he writes stories for a boys' paper called *Young Folks,* which had published Stevenson's *Treasure Island*—and not done at all well out of it. He contributes light social paragraphs for a weekly called *Vanity Fair.*

He does them all competently; he is a useful journeyman, but he does nothing that is unlike the work of other competent, industrious young men. Unless it is in his light touch, the careful, delicate phrasing of some of his essays, giving them a note which almost recalls Max Beerbohm's early "works". No one exclaims after reading his articles: "The writer of that will go far." Nor does he show at this period any impatience with the heavy, unenterprising journalism of the time. He accepts it calmly as a condition of the trade he has entered. Not yet has the vision of the new reading public visited him. His eyes are unopened to the possibilities that lie within reach of those who can give that public what it wants.

Until the visit to the printing-office of *Tit-Bits,* he remains the capable young journalist of conventional type. That visit became, as we have seen already, one of the turning-points in his career. It showed him what was waiting to be done. It convinced him that he was the man to do it. Henceforth he concentrates his powers upon the task that has been, by a flash of insight, revealed to him. The young man and the opportunity have "clicked".

From now on he scorns delights and lives laborious days. Up to this time he has been spending a large part of his energy on amusement and exercise, chiefly on bicycling. He is the possessor of one of those risky-looking machines with one very tall wheel and one very tiny. He is a daring rider; a rider, too, of long distances. One day (he is in his twentieth year) he rides from Bristol to London, a distance of a hundred and twenty miles. The day turns wet, he keeps on through the rain. He has no food on the way. The result is an attack of pneumonia which leaves behind it weakness, susceptibility to chill.

This is the last of a whole series of madcap bicycling feats. He has ridden forty-three miles without dismounting, only stopping once to drink at a road-side fountain, steadying himself with one hand while he filled the drinking-cup with the other. He has set off late at night to ride from London to the sea-coast, arrived at Eastbourne in the morning, slept till afternoon, then ridden back.

Now there can be no more of such adventures. He must be careful. He must not risk hard exercise. He had better live out of London—for a time at any rate, the doctor says. So to his mother's sorrow, but without a word from her to influence his decision, he engages himself with a printing and publishing firm named Iliffe's at Coventry in Warwickshire to edit a bicycling paper in the first instance and to make himself generally useful.

So useful does he make himself that before two years are over he is offered a partnership. He has put many ideas into the firm's business. He has written chatty little books on such topics as *One Thousand Ways to Earn a Living* and *All About our Railways*. Clearly it appeared to Iliffe's that this was a young man who would prosper in anything that he undertook. Whatsoever his hand found to do he would do it with his might.

He has not been content merely to do the tasks set before him. He has been studying methods of publication. He is familiar with a type of printing-press more modern than that on which he produced his school magazine. It would be a pity, the Coventry firm thinks, to let a young man like this go. So the offer of a partnership is put before him.

But by this time the young man has saved money. He has managed to put by £1,000; he has the promise of as much from an old friend. He feels that he can set up in business for himself. He will soon, he feels certain, be in a position to launch a rival to *Tit-Bits,* a paper that will tickle the intelligence of the new reading class, the enormous number who have been to elementary school, who are ready to whet their brains on anything they can understand, who find newspapers and periodical literature generally far beyond them. This is the notion which he has cherished for two years. Now the time has come to try it out.

CHAPTER III

THE YOUNG MAN MAKES GOOD

You must throw your pebble into the pond every day.
A. DE VILLEMESSANT,
founder of the Paris *Figaro*

BACK to London, then, goes the young man; not now in search of an Opportunity; in search of means that may enable him to seize the Opportunity he has found.

He had tried, before he went to Coventry, to find someone who would finance his Great Idea. The answers which were made to his proposal were as discouraging as those which Newnes received when he was seeking to make a start. Now he tries again, and in the meantime busies himself with minor enterprises. With his friend Carr, an Irishman little older than himself, he sets up in business. The new firm of Carr & Co. takes a tiny office in a region hallowed for him by long association with periodicals and publishers. In Paternoster Square, almost within the shadow of St. Paul's Cathedral, he has a couple of small rooms with a dull outlook; he has a share of an office-boy; before long he has the enchanting companionship and help of a wife.

Calling at a little house in Hampstead on a Sunday just after the occupants have settled in, their honeymoon over, a friend found the Young Man with his coat off, typing vigorously; in an arm-chair sat a graceful, charming girl with brilliantly expressive dark eyes reading manuscripts. They were old friends; their marriage had for a long time been looked forward to. As soon as he could make and support a home it was hurried on.

Mary Milner was a country girl. Her father had been a West Indian planter. Her home was in an Oxfordshire village. She had been to a good school, was quick-witted, well-informed. "You can't think what a help she is to me", the young husband tells the visitor with proud enthusiasm. He will have occasion to say that at every stage of his career.

When it becomes necessary for her to manage great houses, she does it with the same quiet capability that she once put into the management of her very small one. She plays the hostess at splendid entertainments to owners of the most celebrated names, to holders of ancient and exalted titles, with the simple, unaffected ease and kindliness that she showed in welcoming early friends to a supper of coffee and sausage-rolls.

Nor will early friends be cold-shouldered either by her or by her husband when wealth has come to them. In the Celtic temperament there is no snobbery. No man ever lived who was less a respecter of persons than Northcliffe. He could no more pay honour to rich, highly placed people on account of their riches and their high place than he could slight people who were poor and unknown. As for Lady Northcliffe, her nature was so sincere, her heart so warm, her feelings so spontaneous—and her sense of humour so strong—that she could never simulate, never seem to be other than she was—a woman of delightfully vivid intelligence and sparkling charm.

She will have difficult places to traverse, griefs to endure. Mated with a genius, she will, as his fame becomes world-wide, sometimes sigh for the years when he was struggling—with her help; when he was unimportant, unknown. She will see him, disappointed in his hope of a family, turn from her and solace himself in another home. Yet she will bear all this with dignity, with patience. Her mind will not be embittered nor the gentleness of her nature eclipsed.

Happily hidden are these aspects of the future in the Paternoster Square days. Very full and very happy days they are for young husband and wife. In his thoughts are many projects. He negotiates for the right to publish in London an American open-air magazine named *Outing*. He plans a monthly to be called the *Private Schoolmaster;* he edits a series of small informative books on Iliffe lines, including one that told simpletons how to make money by bets on horse-racing—a matter in which neither at this time nor at any other did Northcliffe take any other interest whatever. But no scheme occupies his mind so constantly as that of a weekly paper for those whom he calls jestingly "my public": those who are waiting for him to exploit them, those upon whom he has something ready to be launched as soon as money can be found to launch it.

He has noticed that the papers which pay attention to their readers' tastes devote a good deal of space to answering correspondents. They are asked all kinds of questions. They are consulted on intimate and delicate problems. Why should not these numberless seekers after knowledge, these pathetic suppliants for advice, have a paper all to themselves? He has watched with envious interest the progress of a weekly called the *Bazaar, Exchange and Mart*. The founder of this saw that in many publications many people placed "Wanted" and "For Sale" advertisements. He conceived the idea of bringing together those who wanted to sell, exchange, or purchase anything, no matter what. That idea proved very profitable. The young man in Paternoster Square says he wishes it had occurred to him. No matter; he has as good a one, he fancies. But how obtain the money to try it out?

He does not worry about this. He will never in all his life worry about anything—excepting his health. There will be nothing, save health, that he will really and truly care about. "Everything counts, nothing matters", is a motto that later he will adopt and act on. He does not word his feeling thus in the years of buoyant youth, but the feeling is there. He is not discouraged, nor even impatient. He gets all the fun he can out of work and out of play. There is plenty of time before him. He can wait.

To those who wait—and work—comes in time whatever they wait for. There are people who believe in him already. One of them is named Markwick, a leader-writer for the *Daily Telegraph*. He had put into the business of Carr & Co. a little money of his own and of his sister's. Now he says there is a chance to get a fairly large sum from a retired naval officer occupying himself in the fur trade, by name Beaumont.

"Where is he?"

"He's in Italy at present. We'd better wait till . . ."

"Wait! No, we might lose him. Can you go after him?"

"At once?"

"Of course at once. Can you start to-night?"

Here is the character of the authentic Northcliffe revealing itself. In this summary fashion he will send special correspondents to the uttermost parts of the earth. With such rapidity of action he will embark in enterprises of vast extent. Mr. Markwick protested, but Mr. Markwick went. In less than a week he cabled one word, "Joy". Captain Beaumont invested £3,000 in the young man's enterprise. Very soon *Answers to Correspondents* appeared.

It is the year 1888. Chief among the subjects of interest to the world is the fatal illness of the Emperor Frederick of Germany, which must leave the throne to his son, William, of whom little is reported that is good. *Robert Elsmere* is being discussed; it has made the reputation of Mrs. Humphry Ward. The South African gold-mines have begun to boom. In London some of the more important streets are being lighted by electricity. Mr. Edison has invented an ingenious toy called the phonograph, which reproduces (at several removes) the human voice. Lord Salisbury, Foreign Secretary as well as Prime Minister, is introducing typewriters into the Foreign Office; Queen Victoria is refusing to read any typed document. Everything she reads must be written by hand. Horror is being expressed at revelations about sweat-shops in the East End of London, made in an official report.

No one chronicling the events of the year when it closes thinks of mentioning the appearance of *Answers*. No one foresees that upon it huge newspaper and other businesses will be built up. Of the first issue (June 2, 1888) twelve thousand copies were issued. No sensation was caused by them. Fleet Street either ignored the newspaper or muttered wearily, "That won't last long".

There was one man, however, who looked carefully through it and who did not prophesy its early death. The popularity of *Tit-Bits* had led to several imitations being published. Newnes had without alarm seen these appear; he had without surprise or much elation seen them vanish. Now he knew that a rival of a different calibre had taken the field. He was not apprehensive. There was plenty of room for both. But he said truly of the new-comer, "This is the first real opposition I have had to meet".

Looking through the early numbers, one can see that Northcliffe could give the new reading public what it wanted. He was already gauging pretty accurately the depth and quality of his new reading public's taste. He paid scarcely any attention to current topics. The stream of life swirling and foaming around him was dammed out of his pages, which were filled with historical anecdotes, with tales of odd characters, with humour of the boisterous or verbally facetious variety. These were what he liked himself. He could always tell what interested his public because he was, intellectually, himself a member of it. Had this not been so, he could not have done what he did. In order to purvey successfully to any section of a public "what it wants", the purveyor must be in sympathy with his customers. He cannot please it by taking thought; his action must be instinctive. A better educated Northcliffe would have been unable to produce either an *Answers* or a *Daily Mail* so exquisitely suited to the minds of those who welcomed them.

Although he intended to exploit the new readers, he did not in any direction play down to them. The paper contained nothing to outrage intelligence, little to offend taste —unless one takes a severe view of paragraphs explaining that the Prince of Wales (afterwards King Edward VII) was called "Tum-tum" by his intimate friends, and that this was on account of his "graceful rotundity of person". But if there was nothing to provoke censure in the twelve pages of harmless reading matter offered to the public for a penny, neither was there anything to cause a rush for them, anything to set people talking about the new venture.

The venturer had not yet learned what was to be the keystone of his success—the art of making people talk. He had not heard yet that phrase coined by de Villemessant, founder of the Paris *Figaro,* and quoted so often by

Northcliffe in later life: "You must throw your pebble into the pond every day." He supposed, as everyone else supposed at this time, that papers would be bought if their contents were reasonably informing or diverting. He thought it was their contents alone which decided whether they would sell or not.

That was the common opinion of the age. Northcliffe's memory is not discredited because at twenty-three he shared it. What does him credit as a pioneer is that he very soon renounced that erroneous view. He discovered before anyone else in England that few people bought papers for their intrinsic value.

"I came to this conclusion," he said once in later years, "it was necessary to get a paper talked about before the public would take any interest in it. There were only two reasons, I saw, for the purchase of papers. One was Curiosity, the other Habit. It became clear to me, as I used to sit puzzling my brains over the very slow progress my first venture made, that it was necessary for me to arouse the curiosity of the public at which I aimed, to make them talk about *Answers,* some days praising it, other days abusing it, all days wondering what it would do next.

"Everyone is aware now of the need for publicity to induce sales, whether sales of a newspaper, sales of a motor-car, sales of no matter what. Everyone knows that skilful advertising forces people to buy whatever the advertiser wants to sell. In the year 1888 this wasn't known at all. Publicity hadn't been born. The art of exciting curiosity was in its babyhood. It was considered rather indecent to advertise in anything but a quiet, unobtrusive way. To push one's wares under people's noses was reproved as undignified. To try and get one's efforts talked about was unmannerly, as bad as for a woman to attract attention by lifting her skirt and showing her ankles. The persistent prejudice against me all through the earlier part of my career was due to the shock I gave refined intellectual persons by the methods I adopted to make unintellectual, common or garden people buy *Answers,* I am sure of that."

What were these methods? How was the financial disappointment of Northcliffe's first venture during its first year turned to dazzling prosperity? At the end of twelve months the circulation with which it began had not much more than doubled. At the end of eighteen months it had gone up to nearly 200,000. It was exactly the same paper. Its contents had not been altered. What produced the change? Simply the venturer's discovery of the nature of people in the mass.

Up to now he has been an eminently respectable, conventional, top-hatted middle-class young man, with a respect for establishd institutions, including daily newspapers: with a refreshing pride in his position as a contributor to these organs of public opinion. By his editing he has proved that he possesses some ideas; he has shown commendable enterprise. He employs a special correspondent, "Mr. Answers", to go through all kinds of experiences and to describe them briskly, without the overloaded verbiage in which descriptive writing mostly abounds. He sends another correspondent round the world, thus beginning a practice which he kept up in his newspapers—the practice of continually providing travel articles: he knew these are always read with curiosity and pleasure. But by these activities he has pushed only a little ahead of current methods. Now he breaks the tradition that a journalist must be read but not heard of. Not without a severe shock do his friends, his relations, see him suddenly appear in a new character. He becomes, as they term it, a kind of merry-andrew. Not only is what they call "this rag of his" talked about; he himself is ridiculed, admired, envied, criticized, denounced.

To assert that he does not care at all would be untrue. But he consoles himself with the reflection that times are changing. In a few years his discovery will be common knowledge. All will be doing what he is doing now. How right he is in that anticipation scarcely anyone but he knows. Like all revolutionaries, he is living at the close of an era. With or without him change is coming. He does not yet understand how far-reaching that change is to be, how completely it will cut away the coming generations from those which have gone before. But he is acutely conscious of change in the air. Ever since his vision of the new reading public, of a nation which for the first time in history has been through school, he has pondered over the difference this must make. Why should he fear to advance boldly where it is plain all must soon follow? Why hesitate to play the pioneer and win a pioneer's reward?

There is another force, too, which impels him. In the flamboyant, facetious editorial which he wrote for his first number he had said, "The word 'fail' is not in our vocabulary" (already the Napoleonic touch). From the ruck of commonplace sentences, ill-constructed, uninspired, that one stands apart. Suddenly one feels a waft of sincerity. This was no boyish brag. No, it was the truth, springing from the core of his nature. Failure he cannot admit as a possibility even. People do not buy *Answers* for its contents, as he hoped they would. Very well, he will make them buy it for other reasons. No matter what friends say of him, no matter the disapproval of those whose good word he once sought to gain. At whatever cost he will justify the self-confidence which dictated in all sincerity that ringing declaration: "The word 'fail' is not in our vocabulary."

So he thinks now less about the contents of his paper than about methods of bringing it to the notice of more and more people. Once it is talked about, they will buy it. He knows that. And having bought one copy they will like it; buying it every week will then become a habit with them. But first they must hear about it, they must know it is there. Ideas jostle one another in his quick-thinking brain. From the crowd of them two emerge. He will offer a larger, more sensational prize than has ever been dangled as a bait before. A pound a week for life shall be secured by the competitor who comes nearest to guessing what on a certain date is the value of the bullion in the Bank of England vaults. Each guess must be written on a post card; five persons must witness each competitor's signature. Thus every entry will give assurance that at least six persons have heard of *Answers* and its astonishing enterprise. They will talk of their astonishment and so advertise the paper still more widely.

Nor do the authorities fail to add their quota to the mass of publicity thus accumulated. When it is announced that another prize for a guess will be offered, the police interfere. This is illegal, it is a "lottery". To one infringement of the law they have benevolently closed their eyes, but it must not occur again. Which sets everyone talking once more. Some think the police are right, some blame them. More and more copies are bought every week.

The guessing competition and the popularity into which an *Answers* puzzle is cleverly pushed are sufficient to transform the paper into a profit-maker. It becomes known all over the country. The ingenious puzzle gives opportunity to organize local competitions; for the final stages, town halls or other large buildings are hired. Local newspapers are compelled to report the excitement caused.

Circulation goes up and up and up. At the end of its first year it was selling 78,000 a week. A month and a half after the competitions were started the circulation had jumped to 205,000.

Almost the puzzle turns out a failure. As it is brought to the office and bought for a small sum, it consists of a small flat box with marbles in it and a glass top. The marbles are to be moved about by tilting the box this way and that so that they may form a word (the word to be formed is, of course, *Answers*). But the marbles are heavy; when the boxes come to be packed for sending away, many glass tops are broken. Northcliffe walks home one day dispirited. He has been told that the puzzles will not pack. As he walks he glances at shop-windows; in one he sees a dish of sweets about as large as the marbles and, as he guesses, very much lighter. He goes into the shop: his guess is proved to be correct. He buys the sweets; next day places an order for a very large quantity. The puzzle is now perfect for its purpose; it has an enormous success.

The sun of prosperity ripens the young man's character. He is sure of himself now. Sometimes he talks grandiosely about coming to grief in a magnificent manner. "If I fail, it will be one of the biggest failures ever known." But he is certain in his heart that he cannot fail. He may, for effect, declare that he is haunted by the fear of dying a pauper. Some of his friends may think that he is in earnest. They are wrong. He has now a Napoleonic belief in his destiny. Frequently he is told of his likeness to Napoleon. He is pleased by this. He begins to collect portraits and small possessions of the Emperor. He starts a Napoleon Cult. Later he will sign himself with a single initial which is not unlike the imperial "N".

He is, in truth, far more handsome than the young Bonaparte ever was, even in the eyes of that adoring yet critical parent Letizia. ("Curious that I should have a mother critical and adoring too.") The novelist, Helen Mathers, has described him at sixteen as "a young Apollo". Now Dame Nellie Melba first encounters him, a fair-haired young man, very striking in appearance. His blue eyes are brilliant, his resolute features are at the same time charming. The singer thinks—or pretends to think—that this flashing youth cannot be the founder of a flourishing business. "I wanted to see your father", she says prettily. Gravely he explains to her. A lifelong friendship is begun.

The business expands rapidly. Other papers are started; all are aimed at the same kind of reader. A paper for the women who couldn't afford to buy elaborate weeklies; a comic paper which contains "just the humour that office-boys love"; a sentimental story paper; a paper for schoolboys (he recollects the lessons learned from old James Henderson in Red Lion Square). Soon there are six weekly publications being prepared in a larger office over a hosier's shop in Fleet Street. Here gather and work young men who will in time be making fortunes out of these papers, as yet feeble and despised. For to those who aid him faithfully the proprietor will always be loyal, will always be grateful. Already he shows that kindly forbearance, that attachment to the men about him, which remains a characteristic all his life.

"Sutton has made big mistakes," he tells a visitor one day with irritation in his tone, "but," he adds, "he's been with me two years. If he hadn't, I should sack him." He who escapes the sack will become a very rich man and receive a title. Sir George Sutton, Baronet, he will be.

As the staff expands, there becomes evident the proprietor's genius for using each member of it to the best advantage, for drawing out their ability. One man is tried in editorial jobs, and fails. "Well now, what can you do?" "I can write short stories", is the reply. "Go ahead, then. I'm glad you've told me." The editorial failure turns out to be a success at short-story writing.

Before long, expansion of staff made another move necessary. Now a whole building is occupied, a building in Tudor Street, forerunner of the immense block which the Amalgamated Press afterwards builds in Farringdon Street.[1] In this building there now sits a man with power equal to that of the founder. This is the founder's brother Harold, third eldest of the family. He had entered, on leaving school, a lower branch of the Civil Service. He had the reputation of being good at figures; on the financial side the firm was weak. Some little persuasion was needed to induce him to join it. As soon as he had settled down he displayed a gift for finance equal to his elder brother's gift for undertaking, for exploiting the mass of people who could just read. Soon he was installed as financial dictator, and now, as a very young man, he begins that surprising career which will make him, even before Northcliffe's death, by far the richer of the two.

For Northcliffe it was a piece of wonderful luck that he happened to have a brother supremely talented in this direction. Ability so transcendent in the handling of money, foresight so piercing into obstacles and opportunities, are impossible to buy in the open market. Northcliffe might have searched all his life, and searched in vain, for a partner endowed with just the characteristics he lacked himself, yet able to understand and appreciate him at his real value. He was fortunate enough to find in his own family the man he required.

[1] There *Answers* and other of the original little papers are still published, together with a host of others, though they have passed into other hands, those of the Berry Brothers.

Never were two brothers less alike. One lived by imagination, the other by his calculating faculty. One had every charm of appearance and manner; the other, though kindly at heart, was not prepossessing. While Alfred had the Celtic Irishman's quick apprehension and sunny, though slightly malicious, humour, Harold's dour temperament was that of the Ulster Scot. His seriousness was grim; in his lightest moment he was never gay. Alfred's interest began and ended with the publications of all kinds that he had brought into being. He began as a journalist, he remained a journalist to the end. Harold cared little for the papers themselves; he cared for what they could be made to produce.

He had at times larger ideas than his brother's. Once, when he was launching the Newfoundland enterprise which put them in possession of a large territory where they could cut down their own trees, make their own pulp, and turn it into paper, he sketched its future at Elmwood between two sets of lawn tennis. "I can foresee the time", he said, "when this Newfoundland colony of ours will be one of the greatest business organizations in the world. We shall own cities, railroads, harbours, mines, huge mills. We shall have to provide a big population with everything they need. And attached to this tremendously successful colonizing experiment will be a little newspaper called *The Daily Mail*. People will ask how on earth the connexion between them was established. And we shall discuss the question of cutting ourselves away from it. It will be a nuisance, a hindrance. Eventually we shall let it go."

Brother Alfred listened to this with frowning brow, with angry eye. He said irritably: "You're talking nonsense. Let's get on with the game." He was annoyed, hurt even, that *The Daily Mail's* importance should be underrated.

To him the territory he had bought in Newfoundland represented so much "news-print" for his newspaper. He saw it dispatching each year so many thousands of rolls across the Atlantic. Nothing more was required of it than that. It was to serve *The Daily Mail,* not to supplant it. Brother Harold's more ample vision did not even amuse him. He had not created Newfoundland; he *had* created *The Daily Mail.*

Northcliffe's interest being limited in this fashion, he was never tempted into financial ventures outside the range of his business. He did not set any store by money as money. He wanted as much as would buy him the things he desired, which were simple enough; he wanted to have some put away in case anything happened. Beyond that he was as little inclined to amass money as to save used postage stamps or treasure nutshells.

He had no illusion about money giving him power. If he sought power—not until the war did he seek it—his newspapers would provide him with influence far more effective than money could bring to bear. Nor did it please him to juggle with the knives and dinner-plates and glass balls of finance; to make a fortune double, treble, quadruple itself by prudent speculation; to watch the value of investments shrewdly chosen creep up and up with the advance of a new country or the displacement of one industry by another. He was more delighted if a paper of his could in some way get ahead of its competitors than by figures showing that he was richer this week than last. He would be more truly glad to hear that a special correspondent had bought an expensive automobile or at great cost leased a telegraph wire than to be told of reductions in expense.

Northcliffe was thus exclusively a journalist. His brother Harold was a master of finance as well. There are some gardeners born with lucky fingers; they can make everything grow. What they do which others neglect to do they cannot tell you. They follow some instinct, some predisposition, about which they know nothing themselves. So it is with some who cultivate, not flowers and vegetables, but money. They have the Midas touch. Whatever they handle turns to gold. It seems to be as impossible for them to go wrong in placing their capital as it is for the ordinary investor to go right.

No sooner has Harold Harmsworth joined his brother (he was created in 1913 Viscount Rothermere) than he is seen to be among the very small number of people endowed at birth with this mysterious faculty. No sooner does he take hold of the business side of Carr & Co. than substantial profits begin to be shown. He watches every penny. He discovers ways of doing things more cheaply. He stands out doggedly against the extravagances which his brother would like to commit. Throughout life this is to be Rothermere's function. Northcliffe will try continually to rush into adventures without counting the cost. He will admit this failing. He will boast with wry humour that he employs a number of Scotsmen "whose hearts are as hard as their heads" to keep him in check. There are times, however, when he will admit no check from anyone except Rothermere. All other opposition to some large spending on which he has set his heart he will sweep tempestuously aside. To Rothermere he will listen always, and almost always take his advice.

He knows that in matters which concern money "Harold has a knack of being right". He cannot understand this. As a journalist, he says, Harold would be worth little to him. Yet he can be trusted without hesitation when he deals with finance. It is a combination miraculously fortunate. Brother Number One knows how to catch the attention of the new reading public, how to entertain it, how to make it form the habit of reading his papers. Brother Number Two knows how to extract from this exploitation the largest possible profit. Their gifts are wide apart. They have little in common save the determination to make their business a winner. They supplement each other to perfection. Antiquated persons predict their approaching downfall and bankruptcy. No one who knows them doubts their going a very long way.

CHAPTER IV

WIDENING OUT

When Alfred Harmsworth founded The Daily Mail *and sold it at a halfpenny, I doubt whether a dozen men in Fleet Street foresaw the revolution that was beginning.*
WICKHAM STEED

"WE are now in Hampstead society. I hope we shall soon be in St. John's Wood society."

So speaks the wife of the new Successful Young Man after his earlier triumphs. Half in earnest, half in jest, she looks forward to following the upward movement of his family from one suburb to the other. No ambition, as yet, for a more aspiring thrust. Neither in her mind nor in his. Those who go farther seldom see how far or in what direction they are going. Vague notions are often forming and dissolving and reforming in his imagination, as they do in the imaginations of all clever young men. He speaks sometimes of the possibility of catching his 250,000 *Answers* public with a daily newspaper "which they could understand". This project is born of a fear that a rival may spring up and choke his weekly venture. Many rivals do appear, but they have no enduring strength in them. They lack the essential; they do not make people talk.

"Throwing the pebble into the pond" is profitable when there is a Brother Harold to handle finance; but it is exhausting. Perhaps it is the daily care and labour of the business which hinder him from thinking much about future plans. He watches, corrects, criticizes all that his staff are doing. He is their inspiration, he provides them with ideas. His is not the type of organizing mind which selects its instruments and leaves them alone to perform their allotted tasks. He must be at the centre of everything. He must be the driving-force, the fount of energy. This explains why he never trains his officers to become generals.

Often in later days men will rise high in his service, will be deemed capable of great achievements, will be tempted away, or will of their own accord strike out for themselves. They will grotesquely disappoint themselves and all who have believed that "Northcliffe picked their brains", that they were the creators of his prosperous enterprises. They will be exposed as merely subalterns who have carried out instructions and received credit which truly belonged to him. Of all who for long periods were retained by him in posts of great emolument and, in appearance, great responsibility, none will make any individual mark, acquire any personal distinction. Apart from the organization in which he gave them their places, for which he provided the motive-power, they can do very little.

Those who serve him and yet preserve an identity of their own, who prove their competence in other fields, stay with him in executive positions for but a short while. They learn much from him, without subordinating their wills entirely to his. A clash comes, cannot be avoided. With reluctance, it may be, on both sides he and they part. Already in these early days he chooses men for his purpose who will always acknowledge that he knows best. He wants subordinates, satellites, rather than colleagues.

This is temperamental; nor does it arise from any defect of disposition. So fierce his vigour, so abounding his vitality, he can endure no check. There is no touch of meanness in his dislike of opposition; there is no conceit, no overbearing, hectoring impatience. He is so sure of himself, so convinced of having received a revelation and therefore of "knowing best", that he cannot, for the sake of efficiency, forgive any hesitation to do what he wishes to be done. With those who set up their judgment against his he does not argue, he sends them away.

If he can, he finds some employment for them in which conflict cannot arise. He may engage them as writers, then all is well. For, when he has decided that a man can write in a manner likely to attract readers, he leaves him alone. He admires and respects good writing, in spite of being at first afflicted with a commonplace style himself. He never acquires a mastery of language, though he does later on express himself with a plainness, an emphasis, which arrest attention. In these early years he writes much, but he has no illusions about himself.

"I could turn my hand to anything, as every capable journalist should be able to. I could produce passable verse even. But I do not think I ever, after I left school, took any pleasure in writing for its own sake. I liked to turn out whatever I did in a workmanlike manner, but I very soon knew that writing was not to be the occupation of my life."

Perhaps it is the strain of much writing, added to the toils and anxiety of controlling six papers, which accounts for his uncertain health at this period. There was a delicate look on his face with its "clear pale skin, well-cut features, light golden hair, and large clear blue eyes". So a contemporary described him, and added: "To some he seemed almost girlish; there was, indeed, a feminine softness in his contours as if he would have been all the better for rough exercise." This was after he had given up bicycling. Football he never played after leaving school. "Too little exercise and fresh air, too many large Egyptian cigarettes", say the doctors. They advise him to live in the country, so he buys a house and garden on the coast of Kent; at Elmwood he passes years that he will afterwards look back on as the happiest of his life. He is strong and well. His papers are becoming more and more popular, bringing in larger and larger profits. The future is before him, with its visions so bright, if not very clearly defined. Partly for its memories, partly because he loved the place for its own sake, Elmwood remains his favourite house, the only one to which he was attached by any affection. None who visited him in it can ever feel surprised at this.

Life there was simple, as he liked it to be. It was an open-air, out-of-door life, which suited him exactly. The house was not large, therefore the number of guests had to be small; all were friends or people whom he really wished to entertain. Any new member of his staff whom he liked was invited to stay at Elmwood, and would generally find one or two interesting visitors there. Northcliffe never at any time had many friends, but those he had, and their adoption tried, he "grappled to his soul with hoops of steel." The men on whom he depended for friendship at the end of his life were men he had known for the greater part of it.

They were men, too, whom he knew to be incapable of "wanting to get anything out of me". A staunch, affectionate nature he possessed, which was steadfast in its loves and in its hates (though that is too strong a word to use for the half-joking dislikes he took to certain people, women as well as men). When he had once made friends, he was unvarying towards them. He was fascinating, kindly, thoughtful; he chaffed them (but did not often care to be chaffed in return). He was carelessly happy and did all he could to make them happy. One thing he never forgot and never forgave: an attempt to use intimacy with him as a means to obtain personal advantage.

So the years of early triumph are passed between the new offices in London and Elmwood in Kent, with its pleasant gardens, ancient shady trees, lawn tennis courts, hot-houses; with North Cliff and sands and sea close by. To the mass of people the name Harmsworth now suggests youthful adventure, daring enterprise. By the cultivated few it is sneered at, especially by those engaged in the solid, stolid journalism which not long ago was revered by the Bold Youth himself, and which pursues its dull path without suspecting the revolution imminent that will upset long-established newspaper theories, set up new dictators and dynasties, change the whole newspaper business from top to base.

Often in later years Northcliffe would describe the journalism of that age with genial sarcasm, with comic exaggeration. He would make fun of the immense importance which was attached to the leading articles of immense length, to reports of speeches that covered as a rule almost a page. He would quote a saying of the famous editor of *The Times,* John T. Delane, "that he would rather have crawled from Scotland to London on his hands and knees than that, during his absence, a certain leading article on the Eastern Question should have appeared". He would ridicule the notion that opinions expressed by newspapers had in ordinary times any influence upon events. When he became chief proprietor of *The Times* himself, he was more concerned to make the leaders readable than to make them weighty.

The effort to secure weightiness led leader-writers to take themselves very seriously indeed. Northcliffe never forgot a passage in the *Life of James Macdonell,* a journalist of mark in his young days, who was employed at a salary large for those days to contribute to the *Daily Telegraph* four or five articles a week during ten months in the year; the other two were his holiday months. This passage described Macdonell's method of work. He was, to begin with, very particular about his pens, ink, and paper. The ink must be thin, new, and blue-black. The paper must be unruled, thin, and smooth. Even when these requirements were satisfied, he found it very difficult to get started. He would write a few lines, tear up the sheet, begin again. This he might repeat several times. At last he would find an opening which contented him, and would write on "hour after hour", filling "sheet after sheet". It was at another period Macdonell's duty to revise articles which others had written. "Often", he said, "they have to be so altered, added to, subtracted from, sentences being struck out, others put in, sometimes the half of an article rewritten, and often every second sentence recast", so that "the revision of four leaders frequently takes five hours". On which Northcliffe's comment was that "they didn't know their business. To employ men to write articles and to employ other men to rewrite them was stupid waste."

Another famous writer of leading articles, Russell, editor of the *Scotsman,* was accustomed to pace the floor furiously, waving his arms in a frenzy of composition. Northcliffe liked the story of a guest in the same house with him whose window happened to overlook that of the room in which one day he was writing. She gave an imitation in his presence that evening of a leader-writer at work, jumping up and sitting down again, scratching his head, biting his pen, shrugging his shoulders, jerking his body about. Even the butt of her sarcasm was compelled to smile.

"And to think", Northcliffe would say, "that they took

all this trouble and went through all these contortions for something that would be read by very few people and in a few hours would be as dead as Queen Anne!"

He would rightly describe the newspaper of that day as "unreadable". Its news pages were as tedious and as unattractive to the eye as its leading articles. "It was made up of parliamentary reports at great length; of speeches outside Parliament reported word for word; of the proceedings in law courts, police courts, criminal courts; of long dissertations on foreign politics from correspondents abroad, who thought it no part of their duty to describe the life of the people they were living amongst. The result of all this dullness was that newspapers had small circulations. One boasted that it sold 250,000 copies a day and advertised this as the largest circulation in the world, which it probably was." Why so many people bought the *Daily Telegraph* of those days Northcliffe never understood.

Yet although his discovery of the new reading public has revealed to him the possibility of far larger sales for the right kind of newspaper, he does not in 1894 yet know what description of newspaper that must be. He fancies that something in the nature of a daily *Answers* might do. He has, in truth, a great deal to learn about the newspaper business.

Methods of pushing his weekly venture he was able to teach himself. He was exploring a new country then. He knew as much as anybody about it; he picked up fresh knowledge far more quickly than anybody else could. In the newspaper field experience counts for much. There is ample room for an innovator, but there is need also for a practised hand. A tutor is now required. Again luck favours the Fortunate Young Man.

Opposite his office was the office of an evening newspaper, the *Sun*. This was edited by T. P. O'Connor, who employed for reporting and odd jobs a fellow-Irishman named Kennedy Jones, already known in Fleet Street as "K.J." and reckoned as one who "might do much better for himself if he chose". In 1894 he did choose. He looked back over his life, saw little that pleased him. He had gained no reputation, he had made no money. An unwise marriage had clouded his prospects, embittered his soul. In and out of the office across the road he sees the handsome, smartly dressed young man who is so much talked about. No doubt he has ability, but K.J. feels that he could show as much, and attract as much attention, if he got into the right surroundings. These, he knows, will not be made for him. Very good, he will make them for himself.

In this hour, with energy and ambition spurring him on, he hears that another evening paper, the *Evening News,* is for sale. It is a derelict property; it has been mismanaged. "What a chance", thinks K.J., "to get hold of it, to put it back on the map, and myself with it!" If only he could induce some man of means to buy it and make him editor! Well, why not try? No harm, at any rate, in finding out what the price would be and, with daring bluff, in asking for the refusal of it.

He does not make the application himself. He suggests to a fellow-reporter, an amiable, personable, well-dressed young man named Louis Tracy, with ambitions in the novel-writing line, that he should make the needful inquiries. He is to secure, if he can, an option, and then propose to the Harmsworths that they should produce the money and become the owners. The price asked is not high. For £25,000 cash the property will be handed over. Tracy is given an option for two weeks.

At once he goes to the office across the road. It is not difficult to see the chief proprietor of all these little papers which are making so much money; he laughs at the tradition which makes editors shut themselves up in their offices, never to be seen without an appointment, granting audiences to very few. Tracy is admitted; he tells his business. The brothers hesitate; they are not satisfied that it is his own idea. He seems too simple. Soon he lets out that the project is really K.J.'s. So K.J. is asked to come himself. Rather grandiloquently, because he is nervous, he explains what he would do with the *Evening News*. He makes an immediate impression on Alfred. Harold is more cautious. What does K.J. want out of it? For a few moments K.J. does not reply. Then he says quietly, out of the side of his curiously twisted mouth, in his Glasgow-Irish accent: "This option is practically mine. I can take it elsewhere and sell it, for a certainty. What I propose is that I shall transfer it to you without any payment and that you shall make me editor."

Follows much debate, much careful calculation by Harold, but in a few days the purchase has been completed, the Harmsworths have invaded the daily newspaper territory. When the story leaks out, Fleet Street gossips about it. Fleet Street says sardonically, "It will finish those young fools", then goes on reporting speeches at enormous length, concocting those portentous leading articles. No public interest is taken in the transaction. Not a word is vouchsafed to the public about it. Newspapers and their proprietors are not considered at this date to be "news". No solemn daily journalist would demean himself by allowing a purely private matter like the sale of a newspaper to be alluded to.

That will all be changed; many other things as well. A new combination has been formed; it will have results not less striking than the combination of Alfred and Harold five years ago. Results that will make more noise and stir will echo round the globe. Results that will affect the national character, the characters of nations in many lands. As yet no one, not even those who are preparing them, can foretell what those results are to be.

K.J. will laugh in later years over the engaging innocence of "Alf", his total lack at this time of that knowingness, that cynical disbelief in everything and everybody, which marks "men of the world". "He was dead right about one thing. He said from the start that we must make people talk about the *Evening News,* and keep them talking. But he seemed to think the stuff he put in *Answers,* piffling little articles about Beau Brummel and Mary Queen of Scots, would please readers of a daily."

The change in newspapers since that time has proved that Northcliffe knew more than his partner about what the mass of people liked to read. He gave them new features in the evening paper which certainly helped to make it successful. T. P. O'Connor, starting the *Star,* relied upon clever writing—writing by Shaw, Walkley, Le Gallienne, Charles Hands. Northcliffe was wiser "in his generation". The *Star* might appeal to a few. The *Evening News* must be bought by the many.

Still the "magazine features" would not by themselves have won the favour of the multitude. K.J. knows what will get readers and make them talk about the paper. "Crime," he says, "that's our game. A real good mystery murder trial would be the making of us." And so it turns out.

A murder is committed, just the sort of crime K.J. has been hoping for. There is mystery in it, there is a female interest. When an arrest is made and the prisoner put on trial, K.J. sees that it will be easy to create a sensation. He orders special reports. He has "descriptives" written to supplement the question and answer report of the trial. Arrangements are made to send supplies of the paper far into the country. The good will of newspaper sellers is aroused; if necessary, purchased. Success crowns the effort. The sale of the *Evening News* leaps up.

Sometimes these young men are luckier than they deserve to be. A man is charged with certain squalid crimes, thefts from girls and such-like, committed by a certain John Smith. The prisoner declares his name is Adolf Beck, and that he had nothing to do with the offences. Nevertheless he is convicted, serves a term of imprisonment. Soon after his liberation crimes of the same nature are committed. He is again arrested. Again he offers to prove an alibi, asserts that he is wrongly accused. The police press hard for conviction, the judge is almost persuaded.

One morning K.J. says, "We aren't making enough of this case. It's tremendously interesting. Everyone can imagine himself in the position of a person falsely accused." The editor shrugs his shoulders. He has no doubt about the so-called Beck's guilt. Still, he has a vivid account of the case written up. The man has been found guilty, but not yet sentenced. The judge has asked the police to make further inquiries. Days go by. Nothing turns up. The editor says, "I told you so." K.J. admits that he was wrong. Then suddenly the news flashes in that the real John Smith has been caught—caught in the act of pawning rings stolen from two silly women. What a sensation! And the *Evening News* alone among the papers had been playing Beck's story up.

Crime and sport, lots of football and racing and cricket in season, lots of crime, if it is readable, if there is a mystery in it—that is the line K.J. takes; doesn't bother about anything else. "Alf", as K.J. calls him, does not altogether like it (he does not altogether like being called "Alf" by this unabashed, hard-bitten Scottish-Irishman). He says little; he is learning. But the lesson is not entirely to his taste. By nature he is fastidious. He has never talked schoolboy smut. As a man he never tells "men's stories". He has a clean mind, a mouth unstained by foul or obscene language. Many years later, when a sex film of a nasty character is being shown in London, he sends his staff the laconic instruction: "Kill it." He is interested in murder cases, keeps the *Newgate Calendar* near his bedside; but he shrinks from what K.J., with brutal outspokenness, calls "sex stuff". However, he is new in the newspaper business. Success is what counts. If people want this sort of thing, says K.J., they must have what they want. In the two years which pass between the purchase of the *Evening News* and the founding of *The Daily Mail,* he learns from K.J. and from others a great deal. He becomes a first-rate daily newspaper man of the new kind.

He discovers how easy it is to work up public interest. He notes that the mass of people have no tastes of their own; they will adopt any that fall in their way. Give them a great deal to read about any topic within their comprehension: they will think they are getting what they want, will ask for more. Their most unswerving attention is paid to what they read about "love", about crime, about sport, about food. These must be subjects never absent from his newspapers, which must send out and collect the material they require. They must not be content, as newspapers have been until now, to print merely the best of what is sent in to them. News is a commodity like any other; it can be obtained by those who go the right way to work. The new kind of newspaper, K.J. declares, is going to create its own kind of news.

A new idea to "Alf", this; he turns it over; his quick mind assimilates it, sees more ways to do what K.J. is suggesting than K.J. sees himself. Of him is true what has been written of Mirabeau: "He neglected nothing that was of interest to his contemporaries, and what he learned he assimilated so quickly that he seemed to have known it all his life."

What he and K.J. have discovered, what they are exploiting, is the docility of the public, its lack of ideas. They can give it ideas, a daily dose of them, perfectly safe, agreeably soothing. They can compel it to be interested in this or in that. Football, for example. That has been an interest for a small number, for those who could go to see matches played, for staunch supporters of the various teams. The newspaper can make football interest an enormous number. Not only by printing a great deal of news and gossip about the game, but by competitions for money prizes.

Another illustration: flying. When automobiles were struggling into use, Northcliffe had little newspaper influence. He did his best to make England realize that the invention and perfection of the gasolene motor would change all problems of transport and road-making; that the automobile was not a toy. England was obstinate. England lagged behind France and America, only later made up for lost time. When flying begins, he is at the top of his power. He forces everyone to follow what is being done. He speeds up the improvement of machines by giving prizes for notable flights. Flying makes rapid headway. England has been forced to take interest in it. England is in the van of progress.

Northcliffe's quickness to learn is proved by this illuminating fact. The modernized *Evening News* was in the main of Kennedy Jones's making. When *The Daily Mail* is started, two years after the other had been transformed, it is seen on every one of its pages to bear the impress of Northcliffe's mind. Something he has learnt from America. He paid his first visit to the United States in 1895. There he talked with newspaper owners and editors, went through newspaper offices, studied printing-plants. He saw the value of making editorial persons, and even contributors, acquainted with the mechanical processes of newspaper production. When he went to see Charles Dana Gibson, he was taken to a machine-room and there found the famous artist arranging the stereotypes of his own illustrations. He also found much to admire in the American presentation of news, but he did not think British readers would care for it.

The idea behind *The Daily Mail* was that it should appear to be a penny paper sold for a halfpenny. Other halfpenny papers had been on the market for some little time before it; they had devoted their front pages to news instead of advertisements, thus making a difference plain at sight between themselves and the "heavies". Northcliffe would not do this. He made his front page resemble as closely as possible those of the old-established papers. Nor was there much novelty at first in the appearance of the other pages. He did not want to startle people, to suggest to them that they had got hold of something to which they were altogether unaccustomed. *The Daily Mail* had a lighter, brighter look than the older journals, for the reason that the matter was broken up and shorter; it seemed to have more in it than they contained. But it was only when the pages were looked into that the far-reaching nature of the experiment could be grasped.

Now at last Fleet Street does get a shock. The 4th of May, 1896, becomes a leading date in newspaper history. The new venture does not have to fight its way. Of its first number, 367,215 copies are bought; the demand is not satisfied even then. When the paper has gone to press in the early morning, K.J. goes home to bed. In the afternoon he returns to the office. "How goes it?" he inquires of his partner. "Orders still pouring in", replies "Alf", and then adds with enthusiasm, "We have struck a gold-mine." And they had struck it cheaply. Not more than £13,000 was spent on the production of *The Daily Mail;* the sum seems incredibly small to-day. Twenty-one years later Kennedy Jones was asked to take part in founding a new daily paper. He asked what capital it was proposed to start with. He was told £300,000. He said no newspaper could hope to succeed without a capital of half a million. All newspaper authorities agreed with him. He had helped to bring about the change himself.

The Daily Mail settles down with a circulation of 170,000 a day during its first months. During the first year its daily sale averages 202,000. Then it increases steadily week by week. There is prejudice to be overcome. It is usually spoken of by educated persons as "that rag". It is sneered at by the Marquis of Salisbury, Prime Minister of the day, as "a journal produced by office-boys for office-boys". The Conservatives, his followers, applaud—without a suspicion that the day is coming when they will be truckling to these "office-boys", begging for their support. In the variety theatres jokes are made about it. A song, "By kind permission of *The Daily Mail"*, is sung. All the better; good advertisement. "Of course, I don't believe a word I read in it", say solemn and ponderous pillars of society, but they continue to read it—furtively, perhaps, poking it into their pockets until they are at home.

Here is something that the chief proprietor has not understood until now, though K.J., in his ruthless, cynical way, has dropped hints for him: Those who have been the supporters of the older journalism do not really like it. They find it dull. They are glad to get a paper that is more lively than any they are accustomed to—though they dare not as yet confess this. They can read the whole of *The Daily Mail* in a short time and be entertained by all of it. Flitting from one topic to another, running their eyes over informative headlines, finding subjects for conversation, knowing more about events because they are explained, they soon get the habit of looking through it. If they do not see it, they feel they may have missed something of interest. That is exactly what the proprietors aim at making everybody feel. The result is in three years a daily sale of 543,000. It is advertised as The Busy Man's Paper. Eight pages only, not so unwieldy in size as the old-established sheets. It claims as a merit, in its first issue, that it has not so many advertisements as the other dailies. Strange, when we recollect how it came to have more than any! But this is before the Advertising Age. The Store announcements covering whole pages will not begin for many years yet. Publicity is still an infant. Far distant the time, not even to be imagined, when there will be twelve, sixteen, twenty, even twenty-four pages, when the Busy Man will have to hunt for his reading-matter through acres of advertisement.

Just at the right moment to catch the new reading public comes the New Journalism, as it is slightingly, sarcastically spoken of among the high-priests of the Old. Not one of these has made any move to provide what that public has been waiting for. Not one of them has given any sign of being aware even that such a public exists.

Just at the right moment, too, for another reason. The number of men who now travel to and fro, between suburban homes and offices, out in the morning, back at night, has been growing with the growth of cities. Farther and farther out the small householder must go. And to the troops of men who are daily travellers by train or omnibus or street-car are beginning to be added women—not in troops as yet, though before long they will be equalling and then outnumbering the men. These travellers want something to read in the morning, something of a lighter, more diverting character than the news which the old-established pages contain. The new daily gives them exactly what they require. It amuses them, they can get through it during their journey, they are satisfied they have got all the news of the day. And men take it home in the evening so that their wives can glance over it and read the serial story.

Always convinced of the value of women's support, Northcliffe has insisted on following the example of French newspapers and printing every day an instalment of a tale calculated to carry all who have begun to read it along with it until the end. He argues that this will do more than add an interest and increase the numbers of "readers per copy". It will also lengthen the life of each day's issue. Most morning newspapers, he has noticed, are dead before the morning is through. This one will not be dead until night. It will live for twelve hours instead of two. That must be brought to the notice of advertisers. They will appreciate his reason for including a serial story.

In his hands this feature gains an importance it has never enjoyed before. He founds a Serial Department which supplies fiction to all his publications. He lays his finger on the weakness of serials written by novelists. "They are stories cut up into lengths. They have not the continuous but jerky interest which a story published by instalments ought to possess. They flow along with unbroken current, instead of rising to a climax at the end of each day's chapter, leaving a situation which makes the reader long to know what happens, and then beginning again and working up to a fresh climax on the following day." Serials, he says, must be manufactured. Writers must be trained to produce them. This branch of the business is important, must be put on a sound footing. So the Serial Department is established, under his close personal control.

Unimportant in itself, that is an example of his policy of Thorough. No detail is too small for his attention. He will examine it, lay down a policy, select instruments to carry out that policy, and see that it is carried out. He must inspire them, they must act under his direction; if they do not, he will get somebody else. Yet he never spends time on working out details, on doing routine work, himself. In that he was unlike and had the advantage over the man who sought to be his rival. Arthur Pearson was a victim to that bustling temperament which afflicts a man at the head of a business with an itch to do everything himself. He would sit in the editorial chair and expose himself to ridicule by his impatience, his inconsistency, his inability to explain how he wished things to be done. When his newspaper was published for the first time, he was to be seen in the packing-room, with his coat off, shouldering parcels, hurling them on to vans. Northcliffe was in *The Daily Mail* office throughout the ordeal of the first issue, while it was being prepared, printed, published. But he did nothing himself, save give decisions, swift and satisfying, when matters in dispute were put before him. He moved about quietly, encouragingly, smoothing away difficulties, letting his presence be felt.

It is felt by this time over a wider range than that of his office. At thirty-one he is the owner of newspapers which exceed in circulation any others in Britain. In eight years he has built up an organization which is earning vast profits. By swift successive steps, without seeing for some time whither they might lead, he has moved to this commanding position. That hope of rising into "St. John's Wood society" is now scarcely remembered. He has a town house by this time in Berkeley Square, the most fashionable quarter of London, next door to Lord Rosebery, of late Prime Minister, with whom he and his wife have quickly made friends. Hampstead is far behind them. St. John's Wood they have taken in their stride. They are in Society with a big S.

CHAPTER V

THE NEW PUBLIC AND ITS NEW GUIDES

> *Northcliffe was immensely important, however much solemn people might try to blink or evade the fact. He and his imitators influenced the common mind more than all the Education Ministers put together.*
>
> J. ALFRED SPENDER
> in *Life, Journalism, and Politics*

HERE, then, is the New Reading Public awaiting its Daily Press, ready to be instructed, ready for a view of life to be put before it by guides who will have an influence vastly more powerful than that of moralist, philosopher, or pulpiteer.

Britain is approaching a critical passage in its history. One year after *The Daily Mail's* appearance it will celebrate Queen Victoria's Diamond Jubilee, which means celebrating the end of an epoch. In the year before its appearance (1895) those who see the necessity of preparing for the next epoch have had to confess themselves divided and feeble; the Liberal Party claiming to represent them has resigned office, discredited, disheartened. The Conservatives have begun a period of rule which will last for eleven years.

After Britain had adopted democratic government, when in 1867 the system of Votes for All began to be set up, a politician wiser than most exclaimed, "Now we must educate our masters!" In the schools a process called education has since then been going on. This has produced a nation which can read. Now its real education is beginning. The question to be decided is: What *will* it read?

Not a question to which much attention is paid. In

effect, no attention is, visibly or audibly, being given to it. Nothing much is doing in the political line. Allayed are the excitements that were stirred up by the intervention of President Cleveland in the Venezuela difficulty, by the foolish Jameson Raid in South Africa and the German Emperor's haste to congratulate the Transvaal Republic on bringing it to nought. The Anglican Church is as usual chiefly interested in the age-long dispute as to whether its doctrine is Protestant or Catholic. No one seems to have noticed this new reading public—no one, that is, but these young men who have launched their *Daily Mail*.

Very busy they are; high-spirited, thoroughly enjoying themselves. "A great lark" the chief among them calls it. He is, in mind and heart, a schoolboy still. He recaptures the fun of bringing out that Hampstead school magazine. Early and late he works, sometimes too long and too hard. He begins to have trouble with his eyes, goes to the famous Pagenstecher in Germany, fears he will go blind. He suffers strange discomfort—torture sometimes—from dyspepsia. For a number of years the energy with which he uses his brain leaves not enough for the digestive organs. He turns from this remedy to that, adopts one treatment after another, takes advice from many physicians. Now he "stokes abundantly", now he starves. At one period he eats no meat, then nothing but meat. He jumps from hot bath into cold bath at nights to induce sleep. In the end he discovers for himself the way of life which suits his constitution and habits. This is based on the old proverb:

> Early to bed and early to rise
> Makes a man healthy, wealthy, and wise.

He is ready at six o'clock in the morning to look through newspapers, his own and the rest. In his bed, with a secretary sitting beside it, he turns over the pages, scowls at them, utters cries of exultation, pounces upon ideas, pours out instructions. "Ha," he says proudly, "do you see that? No one else had the gumption to go after the story behind that question in Parliament" (or that suicide, or that murder, or that rise in the price of hairpins). "We got it. I told them it was there. I always have to keep prodding them." Or else he thumps his fists on some newspaper crumpled against the bed-clothes. "I warned them, I warned them. They will not listen. Here is the very thing in *The Times* that I was talking about yesterday. The *Mail* could have got it—by worrying. We could have made far more of it. Get me the News Editor. What? Won't be up! Why not? I'm up, or at any rate I'm at work. Get him. Pull him out of bed if necessary."

When he goes to his office he carries with him a sheaf of complaints, congratulations, suggestions. His arrival sends a current of activity, at times a tremor of apprehension, through the whole place. He has a marvellous gift for drawing the best out of those who serve him—if he does not by some outburst of caustic irritation scare them out of his service before they have learned to know him.

Even the fits of irritation are as likely as not to be cleared off in an instant by a sunny smile, a quick thrust of humour, a lightning turn to some entirely different theme. He is inclined to browbeat those who allow themselves to be browbeaten. He will make a butt of stupid men, keeping them in his employment and paying them well mainly in order that he may chaff them, ridicule them, use them as laughing-stocks. Not viciously, not unkindly, but with an impish delight in their dullness, with sardonic pleasure at their clumsy efforts to follow the workings of his restless brain.

It is this restlessness which often makes his tone sharp

and peremptory when he gives orders or complains. He does not care to have about him as subordinates men who will not endure that tone. He reads character at a glance, with an insight that borders on the uncanny. He knows whether he can give rein to his explosive humour, whether the person exploded against will resent it, decline to risk further discharges, or whether the indignity will be swallowed, as many swallow it who amass fortunes in his employ. To them he makes amends, as he believes, by showing a real solicitude for their comfort and well-being. He compensates them by material advantage for treatment which men of spirit could not suffer.

Thus the magnetic, handsome man with the large brilliant eyes and the wave of fair hair falling over the left side of his forehead is regarded by most of his staff with a mixture of adoration and alarm. He is now "particularly fresh and wholesome-looking". His grey eyes are "kind but penetrating", records a woman who applied, as a girl, for employment as secretary, noticing especially his "chiselled features, finely shaped nose, determined mouth, and strong, square jaw." She was impressed by his "lack of affectation and snobbishness".

To a few he shows always his fascinating side. These are writers mostly. Those who have to carry out his instructions, in printing or publishing offices, never know whether they are to be purred over or scratched and bitten. On occasions when they are conscious of having blundered they may find either that he has overlooked their errors or that he is disposed to treat them leniently, even as a joke. At other times, when they confidently expect commendation, they are met with a storm of invective.

One thing they quickly learn. Alfred (so he is called in the office) is a famous bluffer. He will pretend that some fact he has learned a few minutes ago is so well known that not to know it is disgraceful. He will assert that a number of people at a dinner-party have offered him the same adverse criticism of some feature in the paper which he dislikes, the party and the conversation having both been invented by him on the spot. He is capable of clever acting whenever he thinks it will produce the right impression and so improve the paper. Pretending to know all about everything is necessary, he maintains, for the creation of the belief in the office that he cannot be deceived.

Not less necessary, in his view, to keep editors and managers up to the full pitch of their activity by making them uncertain of their jobs. He allows, indeed encourages, competition for the highest executive posts. At one period there are two men, each claiming to sit in the chair of editor-in-chief. When one goes out, the other seizes it. Victory falls at last to him who can for the longest time resist the imperious demands of his physical nature. Alfred watches these combats with amusement; he is convinced that the paper benefits, that each combatant shows more enterprise, more fertility in ideas. At moments he is hated, but none who have known him at close quarters cherish their ill will for long. He is so schoolboy-like, so freakish in his ways; they speak of him with a laugh and shrugged shoulders, half in affection, half in frank inability to understand.

Now and at all times it is he who supplies the dynamic force that drives his newspapers and keeps people talking about them. He can let the weeklies run without constant supervision. They have conquered their public; it has formed the habit of buying them. They have settled down. It is with fresh ventures in the making that he delights to concern himself.

Nothing has drawn out his daemonic energy as *The Daily Mail* does. Since he widened out, since he bought the *Evening News,* since he entered the territory of news, that energy of his has marvellously swelled. He has a bigger arena to perform in. He knows that he is, in the phrase of Wickham Steed, beginning a revolution. He feels himself to be what Sir William Robertson Nicoll later called "a transforming force".

He transformed the daily newspaper into something totally different from what it was before. Not immediately, not at one stroke. He was too well acquainted with his public for that. He took care not to startle them at first. Later his policy was to startle them every morning, if possible. But to begin with he walked warily.

Everyone knew that *The Daily Mail* office was unlike any of the old newspaper offices. In it there was no hierarchy. Anyone might rise to any position. The young were encouraged to make suggestions. Ideas that found favour were richly rewarded. This plan he kept up all his life. A man who hit upon a happy heading for extracts from letters to the editor was promptly rewarded by a cheque for £100. A young member of his staff noticed during a week-end visit to a popular resort that contents bills were poorly displayed there. He brought this to the notice of a manager, who mentioned it to Northcliffe. "Send him his expenses for the week-end", Northcliffe said. By such wise generosity he stimulated the flow of notions for the benefit of his newspapers.

"Alfred", as everyone called him, was on the look-out for genius. He would use talent if he could not find the more precious quality. He laughed at the old methods of looking for likely recruits at Oxford and Cambridge. He had not at this period the respect which he afterwards conceived for the ancient Universities. He looked for his recruits in the columns of contemporaries. Whenever he noticed a good feature, a clever piece of reporting, a touch of humour in an article, he made inquiry: "Who did it?" and very likely asked the author to call. He breathed into journalism a life which had not been in it for two generations, and which began to fade away again as soon as he was dead. He had imitators, but no successors.

Throwing his pebble every day into the pond, he makes *The Daily Mail* both interesting and powerful. His eye ranges over the whole field of human activities. Now he dispatches correspondents to China, to Peru; now he works up agitations for a larger Navy or reduced taxation. One day he decides that the public shall know all about the marvellous German progress in industry, due to qualities which he unrestrainedly admires; the next day he warns the Foreign Office of some French intrigues that have been discovered for him in Africa. For the first time his vigour, enterprise, initiative have sufficient scope. He rises to the height of his opportunity. He directs and urges forward a newspaper as no one, not even James Gordon Bennett, has done before him. Wisely he keeps himself still free of any definite, regular participation in the work of the paper. He does not attempt even to play the part of editor. He has seen what makes the older journals dull, monotonous. Those who produce them are not in touch with life at many points, only at one or two points which have no strong continuous interest for the mass of people.

"A newspaper", he says, "cannot be kept in contact with realities, and with everything big and little that is happening day by day, unless it has someone watching, listening, going about, picking up, like the elephant, now a huge tree-trunk of news, now a few pins of gossip. Men who have to be at their desks for a number of hours a day cannot do this. Nor can they see how the paper looks from outside; what impression it makes on those who have not produced it. The most valuable work I do is done away from the office. If I were there always, I should not be able to look at the paper with a detached eye, I should not see where effort was misplaced, sense of proportion warped and judgment clouded."

So he calls himself the Elephant, and what he picks up helps notably to make the paper readable, to give its readers every day something to talk about. "The talking-point", upon that he is ever insistent. "What is your talking-point to-day?" he will demand at the afternoon conference of editorial chiefs which he has instituted. In early days he sits at his table while this exchange of views, this exposure of plans, goes on. Later he will lie back in a deep, low, and softly padded chair. Now he asks in a dangerously quiet tone why the importance of some event was not appreciated, and, when he gets no satisfaction from the reply, turns the full glare of his eyes on the stammering culprit and shouts at him, "But you ought to have known!" Now he sarcastically taxes someone with coming to the office to sleep and smoke a pipe. "I can hear you snore as soon as I get into the street", he declares. "Some of you keep him awake." Pipe-smoking he dislikes. It makes men lethargic, he says. He smokes cigars himself: German cigars mostly, large ones, mild ones, with the Kaiser's picture on their coloured bands and box-lid.

Much discussion daily on this "talking-point". Old journalists hear of it with puzzled surprise. They have always thought it enough to "give the news". Never mind whether it makes people talk or not: that's not our business. "Now understand", says Alfred to one who argues thus (for in the beginning the New Journalism must make a shift with some of the old journalists), "your business is to do what I tell you, and I tell you that if *The Daily Mail* doesn't decide for the people of this country what they are to talk about, *The Daily Mail* will go into bankruptcy, and you'll be hunting a job. Talking-points every day! Every day our pebble must be thrown into the pond. You old stagers thought that 'news' was what you got sent in to you, the routine stuff, the ordinary. I tell you that the only 'news' worth the name is what you send out and gather."

It is this conception of a newspaper, a conception to the British mind entirely new, which sends *The Daily Mail* circulation up and up and up. Even K.J. has been doubtful of the advantage to be gained from departing so far from the normal. "We ought not to go too fast", he counsels, out of the side of his queer mouth. "If we make the paper look like the other papers," retorts Alfred, "no one will be startled. They will only notice that they find ours more interesting. They won't have any idea what we are up to." This proves itself to be substantially true.

Of all who abuse them, ridicule them, praise them for their enterprise, admire them for their pluck, none seem to discern just exactly "what these young men are up to", nor what the result of their efforts is likely to be. As to result, they do not themselves speculate beyond the wealth they will gain, the power they will exercise. Alfred in Berkeley Square muses now and then on social advancement. Not that he cares for the company of the titled and rich, nor wishes to be invited to their week-ends, to sit at their tables. Once he had his fancies of that nature; by a short realization of them he was cured. Boredom and annoyance assailed him. Never will he run that risk again. Yet the value of a title, he reflects, might for him be worth thinking about. He knows that the English are, to the core of their character, snobbish. They rate a man more highly if he has "a handle to his name", no matter how he got it. Yes, it is worth consideration. Peerages are known to be for sale.

K.J. smiles a trifle sourly when he notices the wind blowing from this quarter. He has no such ambition for himself. "Alf can have the limelight", he says; "there isn't room in it for two." Had he made a different marriage, had he been prudent enough to wait, he might not have practised this self-effacement. Things being as they are, he will remain in the background, pulling the strings. While Alfred comes and goes, listens, watches, learns what people are saying, plays "the Elephant", K.J. is the man always on the spot. Morning, afternoon, very often evening too, he sits in his swivel-chair, usually with his feet on the table, smoking cigarette after cigarette, up to eighty, ninety, a hundred a day. He will see anybody, he will hear any suggestions, but most of his visitors leave his room with the feeling that they have been insulted. As for the staff, a summons from him is obeyed with trepidation. They do not know which is worse, his contemptuous, quiet, cross-examining manner, or that sudden swing-round in the swivel-chair which is followed by an outburst of savagely impatient indignation.

A man more bitterly hated Fleet Street has never known. Numbers who work under him will speak of him with a curse throughout their lives. His method is to give all who ask for work a trial. He remembers how hard he found it to get his foot into newspaper offices. He will not inflict on others the contemptuous indifference under which he suffered. "Come for a month", he tells all likely applicants. "We'll see whether you are any good." The greater part of them go when their month is up, and they go with execrations on him who gave them the opportunity which they have failed to seize. Hence the legend that *The Daily Mail* sucked the brains of promising young journalists or experienced old stagers and then threw them away. A legend without truth, the truth being that the proprietors prize brains too highly ever to let them go, if they can by any means keep them.

On this, as on other matters important to the success of the paper, there is agreement between "Alf" and K.J. Their coming together has made their venture prosperous; one completes the other. They are invincible as a combination. Yet they are never more than partners in a business. They never become friends. There is always just a hint of hostile criticism in their tone when they speak of each other. Those who know both well and have learned the finer qualities of either see that they will walk divided paths until the end, though it is not so easy to understand why this must be. They are so far apart in character that there might be the closest intimacy between them. What prevents this is a difference of fibre and an odd little consciousness of it which they cannot suppress.

K.J. had none of Alfred's early advantages. He was born to very poor parents in the same Glasgow street which housed Sir Thomas Lipton's father and mother: "only we lived at the better end of it", K.J. used to remark, with his twisted yet charming smile. As a lad, he hung about a theatre; being employed in that, he formed humble connections with the Press, became a reporter, left Glasgow for Birmingham, married there, invaded Fleet Street. At twenty-nine he saw his chance and took it, was henceforward a made man, but never a contented one.

Life had presented itself to him as a brutal fight for existence. He has been acquainted with ignoble poverty. While Alfred has pushed aside obstacles with the ease of a young Samson, built up his organizations out of nothing, K.J. has had to lift himself out of the gutter by painful exertions. Perhaps as a result of these he suffers the misery of a stomach constantly disordered. There is in him a kindly affectionate spirit. He can be the pleasantest, the most considerate of companions. His intellect is strong as well as quick. He is endowed with a native wit which lends to his comment on men and things an original, amusing flavour. Few, however, are able to view him in this light. To nearly all he seems coarse-grained, intentionally ungracious, by temperament a boor.

He has soon learned that Alfred's nature, its delicacy, more like a woman's than a man's, shrank from this rough side of him. For some reason (disorder of stomach maybe) he enjoys rasping his partner's nerves. To Alfred obscenity is an offence; foul language disgusts him. K.J. is clean-minded, but his tongue has not lost its readiness to slip into the speech of the slums. He is cynically amused to see Alfred wince or betray annoyance when he drops some expression that is more emphatic than refined. He cannot help feeling, too, that in this newspaper business he is the professional, "Alf" the amateur. Perhaps he never fully realized that the revolution in journalism which he supports warmly and helps so valuably to carry out could not have been conceived but by this "amateur". Without K.J.'s professional knowledge, his skill in picking useful men, his ruthless discard of those who are not useful, *The Daily Mail* could not have won its immediate and permanent success. But he had not even been aware of the new reading public; he had never imagined a newspaper that should impose itself on its flaccid mind. He was no revolutionary. He had seen much in the newspaper world that could be improved, speeded up, modernized; but he was first led to think of radical innovations when he discussed with Alfred the policy they should follow in the *Evening News* and *The Daily Mail*.

Their policy, we have seen, is, in a sentence, to give the public every day something to talk about. If possible, something, as a rule, that they are inclined to talk about already. But now and then something that will startle them, something that will set them asking: "Isn't that just like *The Daily Mail?*" This aim K.J. approves heartily, after his early misgivings have disappeared. He who once held that "a good meaty crime" was the strongest possible attraction a newspaper could offer, who ranked politics next in importance, and after politics sport, is to be discovered arguing the relative value as "talking-points" of "Do we eat too much?" and "Is church-going out of date?" He will be heard asserting that the only good thing in a certain issue is a set of diagrams illustrating the method by which Mr. Alexander, the American evangelist, conducts hymn-singing so as to make everybody sing! "The only thing that will cause the paper to be handed about", he declares.

The props of Old Journalism feel bewildered. Their task, they believe, is to enlighten such of the public as can profit by enlightenment on political questions, on foreign policy. Their duty, they maintain, is to guide opinion concerning matters which may affect national well-being, cause changes of Government, raise the issue of peace or war. They have nothing to do with increase of circulation. They call this "pandering to mob interest in trivialities" commercial, undignified. Their standard of importance is set by the chiefs of Political parties, Foreign Office and the Treasury; by the famous clubs (Reform, Carlton, Athenaeum); by the great country houses, the country rectories; by the Universities, by Bench and Bar. Now the standard is to be set by the mass of people; the New Journalism will put in the foreground whatever is of interest to them, whatever will make them "hand the paper about".

"Our policy of twenty years ago", Northcliffe said in 1920, "was to do big things big, and little things little."

So long as we keep up to that, he added, we shall do well. He did not say then that the cause of his revolution in journalism was a difference of opinion between him and the directors of the old-established newspapers. He did at other times discuss this with a just appreciation of what had happened. "Values", he said, "had been changed by the social reform which taught everyone to read. The newspapers had up to this time been published for a small number, and out of that small number a tiny class set the standard at which the newspapers should aim.

"The tiny class was the class which ruled the British Empire, and it was, in the jargon of the day, 'highly educated', which means, in the literal sense, that it once had a smattering of Latin and Greek; it had also learned to shoot and ride and play cricket.

"In another sense, however, this tiny class could rightly be called educated, for it had studied in the school of life. Its members had few ideas, no ideals; but they did possess an understanding of the nature of things, rough and ready perhaps, but based on accumulated experience and what they would have called 'common knowledge'.

"For them the big things were politics and money. They did not expect to find in newspapers anything much besides. They certainly did not look for light reading, entertaining scraps. If they had a taste for gossip, they got it at their clubs, at their dinner-tables. Their 'talking-points' were made for them in social intercourse. They did not read, though they always glanced at their newspapers (it seems unlikely that anyone really read them!); they were satisfied, they did not want anything different.

"If you had said that a class was growing up which had no use for that kind of newspaper, which would welcome one that told what was going on in the world, not merely what politicians were saying and how the money market had been, they would have looked blankly at you, without knowing what you meant.

"For this tiny class the big thing of one day would be a speech foreshadowing a change of Government or some new combination in politics; of another day a rise or fall in stocks and shares. The new sort of newspaper reader cares little about Governments, nor is he excited about investments; he has none. Most of the things that interest him are things which the pre-*Mail* newspapers never used to mention. The reason why the *Mail* caused such a sensation was that it dealt with these things, played them up, increased the interest in them a hundred-fold.

"You could search the Victorian newspapers in vain for any reference to changing fashions, for instance. You could not find in them anything that would help you to understand the personalities of public men. We cannot get from them a clear and complete picture of the times in which they were published, as one could from *The Daily Mail*. Before that was published, journalism dealt with only a few aspects of life. What we did was to extend its purview to life as a whole.

"This was difficult. It involved the training of a new type of journalist. The old type was convinced that anything which would be a subject of conversation ought to be kept out of the papers.

"Did you know there was a sub-editor on *The Times* who once spiked an elephant? Yes, an elephant escaped from a circus in South London and went careering about the streets. When this sub-editor received an account of the incident, he stuck it on the waste-file with other rejected copy. It was too interesting!

"Most journalists of that time had that kind of mentality, though perhaps not quite so pronounced. Or else they thought that the way to sell a newspaper was to have first-class criticisms of books and pictures and music and plays. The only thing that will sell a newspaper in large numbers is news, and news is anything out of the ordinary. You know, of course, the great American editor's definition? Dana said, 'If a dog bites a man, that's nothing, but if a man bites a dog, that's news.' In *The Daily Mail* we paid little or no attention to the dogs which bit men—and the dogs didn't like it—I mean the politicians, the bigwigs, the people who laid foundation-stones and presided at banquets and opened Church bazaars. On the other hand we gave the men who bit dogs such prominence as they never had before, and we were accused of lowering the dignity of journalism!"

That reproach leaves the new guides unruffled. Alfred smiles in that delightfully confidential, inscrutable way of his. K.J., twisting his mouth, says, "Hell! They've got so much dignity they've no room for anything else." Brother Harold, busy with accounts, finance, expenses, balance-sheets, growls out, "What does it matter?" Dignity? Their business is to show increasing profits. Commercial? Of course they are. They are the first in Britain to see that a daily newspaper can be made to earn a great deal of money.

Those in existence have never made much. They have not studied to make much. Newspapers have not been put on a level with other kinds of business which exist only to make as much profit as possible. Not even the Levy Lawsons, who long ago built up the prosperity of their *Daily Telegraph,* had made dividends their principal aim. Here is the real nature of the revolution now in progress. A newspaper is to be made to pay. Let it deal with what interests the mass of people. That will send its sale up—up to a point hitherto unimagined, undesired even. Then it can sell its advertisement space at prices which at first may sound absurd. Advertisers will be shrewd enough to take advantage of a medium for getting into touch with the mass of people. As the circulation rises, they will pay more and more. Brother Harold foretells possibilities unlimited. The other two nod approvingly. This, then, is the motive impelling the new public's new guides.

CHAPTER VI

A FAILURE TURNED TO TRIUMPH

Anybody may make a mistake—once.
Lord Northcliffe

For seven years *The Daily Mail* occupies all the time, all the energy, of the man who, by means of it, has changed the face of British journalism. He has made it what he planned it to be; it is more talked about than any other newspaper in the world. It has fought down the ill feeling, the scorn, which it aroused in its early days. During the South African War its special correspondents have been more numerous, their dispatches have attracted more attention, than those of any other journal. Also a special train, the South African Express, has been chartered to carry the papers filled with war news to the north, arriving long before the other London journals and competing with local organs. This was first of many newspaper trains loaded with early editions for the country which soon became a feature of newspaper distribution.

The war, too, gave occasion for the first of *The Daily Mail* Funds by which vast sums were raised and which helped so much to increase the influence of the paper, proving to advertisers that it went among readers with money. The object in this case was to provide comforts for the troops. To give it a good start Northcliffe instructed the editor to ask Mr. Rudyard Kipling for a poem. When he sent several verses of doggerel entitled "The Absent-minded Beggar", the office was in despair. How could prominence be given to such stuff? K.J. pronounced it "rot". "Alf" shrugged his shoulders. He had ordered £250 to be paid for the effort. Never mind, let it go. Print the verses inconspicuously among the war news.

However, an order had at the same time been given to Sir Arthur Sullivan for a setting to music of whatever Mr. Kipling should write. The composer had expected something like "Recessional". When he read "The Absent-minded Beggar" he was in despair. Forcing himself to attempt his task, he failed over and over again. There was no inspiration in the lines. So he went to Kennedy Jones to confess himself beaten. K.J. would not admit this to be possible. "There is a lilt in the lines", he said, and then he asked suddenly, "Do you know 'Soldiers of the Queen'?" a favourite song of that time. Sullivan did not; K.J. whistled it to him. He went away happier, and next day sent in a setting which instantly caught the public fancy, made "The Absent-minded Beggar" a success, and helped to collect £100,000.

This South African War was of service to *The Daily Mail;* its supremacy over the other newspapers in circulation and enterprise was established; it conquered not only a place, but the leading place, among them. Yet it suffered heavily by the loss of one of its most vivid and original writers, George Steevens, who, leaving Oxford with a reputation for wit as well as scholarship, had found these qualities hard to market in London and had applied for a leader-writer's position on *The Daily Mail*. He was given a trial. His leaders were unconvincing. "Let him try something else", the chief proprietor said. He was sent to a Horse Show, which he described in so vivid a manner as to make all the readers of his report feel as if they had been there. Henceforward his line was "star-reporting".

Soon he was sent abroad, wrote *The Land of the Dollar,*

contrasted the competence of German methods with the slackness of British, became a national figure—and one of the very small circle of Northcliffe's close intimates. Each enjoyed the other's slashing humour; both delighted to poke fun at anything pompous, old-established, solemn. The schoolboy in Alfred went out to meet the schoolboy in Steevens. Together they provided rare entertainment. None who saw Northcliffe saddened by the loss of his companion could concur in the verdict that he was "a genius without a soul". At once, on receiving the news, he went to Merton Abbey, where Mrs. Steevens was living. She was an old woman, her husband a young man, yet the marriage had been a very happy one. Wildly Northcliffe accused himself of responsibility for Steevens's death. He told the widow she was to have a pension of £500 a year so long as she lived. She described him as "distraught with grief".

As in the first years, he still provides most of the driving-force for the *Mail*. Whatever interests the nation, or can be made to interest it, he pushes into prominence, skilfully whips up attention day after day, then turns suddenly, as a big fish turns with a whisk of its tail, to some newer "talking-point". His discreetly magnificent room in the new offices he has built is visited now by notable people from all over the world. Everyone with a project to push, a scheme to finance, a charity to assist, thinks first of *The Daily Mail*. Political parties intrigue to receive his support—without success. Once he had a view of politics at close range. He offered himself as one of the two Conservative candidates for the town of Portsmouth at the General Election of 1895. His campaign was unlike any other before or since. He bought a local newspaper and published in it a serial story which he employed a naval historian of some eminence (Sir William Laird Clowes) and a young man on his staff to write. He had always believed, he said, that a powerful piece of fiction published day by day would be valuable in an election. Whether *The Siege of Portsmouth* was not powerful enough—or too powerful—it had small value. The idea was to alarm Portsmouth with a description of what might happen to it in the event of the Navy being unable to meet an enemy attack in war-time. Posters showing the Town Hall square strewn with dead and dying, women and children among them, the victims of shells and bombs, were put up in large numbers. Electors were urged to read "the most astounding and sensational story of the day" and to vote for the Conservatives, who were pledged to keep up a strong Navy.

Unfortunately for the younger candidates the electors treated this as a joke. He and his fellow-Conservative, an old person of aristocratic lineage and no brains, were beaten—not badly beaten, another five hundred votes and Northcliffe would have been elected. But even so he would not have stayed in political life more than a very short time. He was not a ready platform speaker; he did not enjoy making speeches, as most politicians do. The memory of that election was like a nightmare, he said. He nodded with sympathy when he heard in 1914 that Lord Kitchener, soon after being made a Cabinet Minister, wrote to a friend pathetically inquiring: "Did you know the sort of people these politicians are?" Never will he consent to link his newspapers with any political cause.

It is this unconcern with the parliamentary combat, this refusal to take part in public life, which keep his mind entirely on journalism. He has no regular hobby, no vivid interest apart from his work. He is a keen fisherman; goes to Spain for trout, to Florida for tarpon; rents reaches of different rivers in England. But that is a seasonal sport.

He has no daily spare-time occupation. He strums on the piano at odd moments; his fondness for music never went beyond light opera, now he cares little for that. He drives an automobile, less for the pleasure of it than for the convenience of getting from one place to another. When for health reasons he is induced to play golf, he plays it as a duty, though later on he does become eager to improve and shows schoolboy elation when he has made a respectable score. For a long time he gibed at the game, couldn't believe good of anyone who played it. The topic had to be avoided at family gatherings. Then one day a brother indiscreetly spoke of golf; an explosion was expected, but Alfred listened with interest. He had taken his first few lessons under his doctor's order. Soon he was recommending everyone to follow his lead.

In order to entertain more guests than Elmwood will hold, he rents an ancient and beautiful house, Sutton Place, in Surrey: it is his wife who delights in its restful, stately charm, in its gardens, in filling it with beautiful things. He admits that he is happier in his office. He is fond of quoting, with playful reference to himself, the reply of a Scot when asked how he came to hit upon some invention: "Ah thocht o' naething else."

As soon, therefore, as he has leisure to think of anything outside the *Mail* office, and the office where he houses all his "little papers", he begins to turn over the idea of a daily journal for women. Where this came from is never certainly known. He vehemently denied the conception of it himself. He takes it up, however, with a firm belief in its possibilities. "Look at the number of weekly papers women buy", he argues. "Why shouldn't they be glad to have a daily which gives them the same sort of matter, and the news in a brief, intelligible form as well? Of course they'll welcome it—and we shall get the advertising which now goes into the sixpenny weeklies." That was the thought behind the notion of the *Daily Mirror,* wherever it came from. Later on he secured this class of advertising for his other papers; in 1903 they had next to none of it. It was almost the monopoly of the weeklies. Hence his conviction that, if a daily is founded with the same class of contents and a very large circulation, it is bound to secure all that advertising aimed at women which he cannot bear to see going elsewhere.

So a staff of women is engaged—women who know how to write for the women's weeklies. The "high-class" weekly is taken as a model; the new journal must, Alfred insists, be "high-class". Here he displays his accurate analysis of the lower middle-class mind. "These people," he says, "women especially, like to read papers which seem to be intended for persons of superior social standing. We have always assumed that readers of the *Mail* are interested in whatever interests the class at the top. You must make the *Mirror* suggest that it is produced for people in Society; for those who first adopt new fashions; for those who have leisure and large means. Nine women out of ten would rather read about an evening dress costing a great deal of money—the sort of dress they will never in their lives have a chance of wearing—than about a simple frock such as they could afford. A recipe for a dish requiring a pint of cream, a dozen eggs, and the breasts of three chickens pleases them better than being told how to make Irish stew."

As much as £100,000 is spent on publicity for the new venture, on telling the public what the novelty will be like. Curiosity is inflamed, the mere repetition of the name makes almost everybody want to see it. Of the first number 400,000 are printed—and sold. It is a greater success, cry Alfred's flatterers and satellites, than was *The Daily*

LORD NORTHCLIFFE AS HE WAS WHEN HE BEGAN WORK IN LONDON

Mail. Of course they knew it would be. How could anything that he launched fail?

But in a few days come gloomy reports from the publishing office. Orders are being cut down in all parts. Newsagents report that they cannot sell it. Enormous numbers of copies will be returned. "Give them away", goes forth the order. They are not wanted, even as gifts. What is wrong? "The public taste", chorus the satellites. Women are so difficult to understand, declare the flatterers. Alfred brushes aside their fatuities, sends his wife to ask women who will speak frankly what is the matter with the thing; begs his wife to tell him as brutally as she likes where she thinks it is wrong. He is given a shock such as he has never felt before. "It is all wrong." He has made a huge blunder. He has produced something laughably inept. He has spent £100,000 on advertising a colossal failure.

For a week or two he is paralysed by this blow, the first he has had to suffer. He spends hours looking at the paper. What could be done to make it more attractive? "I don't know", he groans. "That is my difficulty. *I don't know*. I left it to these clever, experienced women editors and writers because I thought they knew what women readers would like. How can I tell? I haven't the beginning of an idea."

His knowledge of women is truly of the slightest. He went through boyhood and early manhood as a young Galahad. His strength was as the strength of ten because his heart and his life were pure. He had not even made friends among women. By those whom he employs and who come into personal contact with him he is liked. He calls them "my dear". He is thoughtful for their comfort, though he does not always consider their convenience. Often he goes back to the office after dinner and expects to find at least one confidential secretary there. One evening he finds the victim, a girl, asleep, worn out. That makes him more considerate. He likes to talk to his women secretaries; they listen with respect, with adoration. He picks their brains too; finds out what features in the newspaper they value or neglect.

With other women, those who go to his house, those whom he meets at other houses, he is seldom on terms warmer than those of politeness. They don't interest him. He cherishes an old-fashioned doubt whether they are really the equals of men, as they declare in these days. He is more at ease, at any rate, in men's society, always excepting, of course, that of his mother and his wife. He has a vague notion that women's interests are different from men's, that they would value a lady-like newspaper: one which dealt with most emphasis upon the gentler, pleasanter aspects of existence; which would give them scraps of French, scraps of poetry, "articles they could understand", nothing sordid, brutal, rough; only light, agreeable topics, handled with a graceful, feminine touch.

Alas! he is driven to conclude, as he says with rueful humour, that "women can't write and don't want to read" —a conclusion not less erroneous than his belief that they would welcome a daily paper which condescended to their special interests, which proclaimed them the inferior sex. He is puzzled, hurt, uneasy. He knows Fleet Street is buzzing with the suggestion that his day is over. The Old Journalists are chuckling. They see their predictions coming to fulfilment. They knew this mushroom prosperity could not last. The brilliant young genius is no genius after all. He made a lucky hit or two. Now he is finished. He will soon be bankrupt. He and his creations will fade out of view.

Even friendly observers ask whether he can stand the

strain of this heavy loss. About that he feels no anxiety. He is already a very rich man. What stings him is the smart of failure, the weakening of his confidence in himself. In a fortnight the circulation of the *Daily Mirror,* which began by being four hundred thousand, is down to forty, and still drops. He is at his wits' end to know what to do.

Now is the moment, he says bitterly, for K.J.'s wonderful experience to make itself useful. K.J. undertook at the outset to supervise the *Mirror's* production. He has lived in the office. He has shaken up every department. His nerves are overwrought, partly by the toil and excitement, partly by the effort he must make not to speak with his usual freedom before this staff of women. "If I could talk to them as I talk to men," he confides to a friend, "I should be all right." He has to mediate between the women, who know nothing whatever about the mechanical side of producing a newspaper, and the printers. He has to search proofs for phrases which convey double meanings unperceived by the women. "What a mind you must have, Mr. Jones", they murmur, blushing; they do not suspect what an uproar of delight and scandal would arise if K.J.'s blue pencil were not doing its nightly work. This was in the early years of women journalists; they are less ingenuous now.

No help can K.J. offer. He shared blindly in "Alf's" delusion. He knows little more of women than does "Alf". He is too tired and irritable to be able to think. He goes on getting the paper out, but makes it clear that he will not continue to do this for long. When he is asked: "What can we do?" he shrugs his shoulders, a disappointed, angry man. "We'd better get a new editor," he snarls, "and get him quick."

"Him" not "her": the women have been tried and found wanting. Now a man must be put in charge. There is agreement about that. But where can a man capable of taking charge be found? Here a weakness in the Northcliffe system reveals itself. In the business are plenty of men who can do what they are told, who can work along lines already laid. Is there one who can stand by himself, who can be left alone to carry on this terrible failure while its proprietors recover from their shock, their weariness, their wounded self-esteem? No, in the business such a one cannot be found.

"Never mind," says Alfred, his buoyancy returning, "I'll get a man." He has been watching during the past year the changes made in an old newspaper by a young editor. Nothing of this kind escapes him. He has had his eye on that young editor. He wants that type of journalist, the type that has plenty of ideas and is not afraid to act upon them. Actually, when he gets this type into his employment, he expects them, as a rule, to act upon his ideas. But now he confronts a new difficulty. For the first time in his life he is obliged to admit that he has no ideas. For the recovery of the *Mirror* his bag of expedients is empty. Perhaps this energetic young editor can hit upon one. He is wasting his time on that old newspaper. Its owners do not appreciate what he has done. "Ask him to come and see me." He sees K.J. as well as Northcliffe. In ten minutes an arrangement is made. (Incidentally, friendships are begun with both men which last throughout their lives.) "You'll take over the *Mirror*—as soon as possible?" "In a week", replies the young editor. The proprietors breathe sighs of relief.

"The first thing you have to do", says Alfred, when the new editor has been installed, "is to get rid of the women." He always leaves unpleasant duties to others. He enjoys engaging people; he never dismisses them, unless he loses command of his temper, which occurs rarely. "Clear 'em all out", he ordains ruthlessly, and stands aside, invisible, while it is done. He is for clearing out men as well as women, for there are a number of men on the staff. He does not even try to save his own brother, engaged as leader-writer and reviewer. "I'm afraid he has not got the popular touch", reports the editor. "He ought to be on *The Times*. So I propose. . . ." "Yes, sack him, sack him", is the cheerfully acquiescent reply.

By this time several more of the family have followed Brother Harold into the business. None take in it a commanding place such as he occupies. That could not be expected. His peculiar talent is exceptional. But they show ability and gradually drift off into enterprises of their own, made possible for them by the generosity which the head of the family shows. Cecil, the one who was wasting his talents on the *Mirror,* goes into politics—with his brother's help, although he is a Liberal; he becomes Under-Secretary of State for Foreign Affairs. Another (Leicester) makes a fortune for himself in business; a third (Hildebrand) tries newspaper owning, not with much success; a fourth (St. John) becomes proprietor of a well and widely advertised table-water.

Of them all St. John is the one for whom Alfred feels the warmest, the most constant affection, especially after the accident which robbed him of the use of his legs. Tall, strong, athletic, good at games, he was being driven home from a lawn tennis party when at a difficult turn of the country road the driver ran into a bank. The car overturned, the young man inside was horribly injured. For weeks he lay in a cottage, on the mattress laid for him when he was carried in unconscious. The only chance of saving his life, said the surgeons, was to keep him lying perfectly still. His life was saved, but he never walked or stood again.

Everything that money could do to make this affliction bearable was done for him by his two eldest brothers. Alfred not only bought him every comfort and the best advice, but looked in to see him every day. However worried he might be, however many the demands on his time, he would show a smiling face to St. John; he would cheer up the sufferer, often depressed, often in pain, with diverting accounts of all that was going on in the business, with anecdotes he had taken trouble to remember, with family gossip. When he travelled, he sent picture post cards every day, with little jesting, affectionate messages scribbled on them. To his nephew Vere (Harold's son), who strangely resembled St. John as a boy, he extended the feeling which St. John inspired. Vere's death in action during the war was a very great sorrow to him, as it was the tragedy of his father's life.

Bringing his brothers into the business naturally provoked humorous comment. One story told how, going up in the elevator, Northcliffe saw someone disappearing round a corner and asked in his quick way, "Who was that?" to which the attendant replied, "That was one of your Lordship's brothers." This was an echo of a much older anecdote about the famous editor of the London *Spectator,* Richard Hutton. He also had a number of young relatives on his staff. A door-keeper, being asked who a certain young person leaving the office was, replied, according to legend, "One of the nephews, I believe, sir."

Northcliffe himself did not exclude his brothers from the range of his exuberant humour. For information about a car that had killed a man and driven on, *The Daily Mail* once offered a reward. The car was identified as belonging to one of the brothers, though at the time of the accident no one was in it but the driver. Some time later it was suggested to Northcliffe that the *Mail* should offer a reward for the capture of a miscreant who had murdered a young woman in a railway carriage. He said, "Yes, yes", then he suddenly asked the date of the crime, went to the telephone, called up the same brother, asked him what he was doing that night, acting the whole thing as if it were serious, not a joke.

This schoolboy sense of fun, arising from his abundant vitality, helped him to recover quickly from the disturbance into which he had been thrown by the catastrophe of the *Mirror*. He is soon jesting about it. He does not see as yet how the defeat can be turned into a victory, but he is sure a means can be found. He will not be in a hurry. "We must be certain of success this journey. Any man may make a mistake once; to make it a second time proves him a fool." This is a favourite maxim of his. Without too sudden a change the editor, left to himself, gradually transforms the paper. It is aimed now at readers of very simple intellect. Everything is to be explained to them in words of one syllable—or as near that as may be.

Alfred is pleased with this. He has maintained always that the language of newspapers should be as clear as possible, that they should contain nothing which even a mean intelligence will not understand. He disliked allusions to people or events which might leave readers wondering who or what they were. He complained once that the phrase, "He has been to Canossa" was used in an article. When he saw it he rang up several people on the staff and asked them what it meant. Not one of them knew (so he said; he was probably romancing). "I do not suppose one per cent. of our readers know anything about it", he added, and was probably correct, for the episode of the Emperor Henry IV's pilgrimage of penance at the bidding of the Pope is unlikely to be contained in elementary historical school-books. Another time he objected to the use of the term "chukka" in reports of polo matches unless it was carefully explained. An article about a politician (Lord Younger) came under his censure because "it does not say who he is". He went on: "I believe him to be Younger of Younger's Brewery, of Edinburgh, whose advertisements have the slogan 'The Beer with a Bite in it'—surely most applicable to this man himself." A touch that would have amused in addition to informing everybody—a touch that illustrated Northcliffe's genius for journalism.

He approves, too, of the effort in the transformed *Mirror* to hit upon topics which will cause the paper to be talked about. "If we could only get a sermon preached, denouncing it!" he snaps out with brisk humour. But no one denounces, no one says anything about it, except that it must soon die. He hears of that rumour, and laughs at it. "They said the same thing about the *Mail*. Said we were losing so heavily that we should have to stop, and all the time money was rolling in!" He sees significant looks exchanged. "Ha, you mean that money isn't rolling in now. That's true, but it soon will be. I'm not worrying about the *Mirror*," he declares (as he will declare many years later that "he is not worrying about the war"). "It will turn out all right."

Destiny, indeed, is now spinning the threads that will, before long, be woven into triumph. In charge of one of his "little papers" is an editor named Sapt. A restless, look-ahead, resourceful fellow. His little paper, printed on a flat-bed machine, not on a rotary, is full of pictures reproduced from photographs by the half-tone process. The *Mirror* has pictures, but they are drawings reproduced on the old "line engraving" plan. No daily paper is illustrated by any other means than this. Quick printing on the rotary press has not yet been reconciled with the use of the half-tone block. A few experiments have been made, with more or less satisfactory results. As a regular method of illustrating a daily the half-tone process does not at this period exist. Sapt says he can make it exist.

He has worked out the problem in theory. Now he is eager to try whether, in practice, it will give the desired result. He does not see why the *Mirror* should not be illustrated in the new way, be turned into an illustrated paper of a new kind. Alfred listens, frowning, which shows that he is thinking hard. He nods. "All right, my boy. Go over and see my new editor. I'll tell him I sent you. See if you can persuade him to let you try."

To the editor he says, "I've sent you over a crazy fellow called Sapt. He thinks he can print half-tones on rotary presses. Have a talk to him. I don't suppose there's anything in it. But you never know." The two men talked. Sapt did not appear to the editor to be crazy. Odd in manner, perhaps, but his ideas seemed to be sound. "I think there's something in it", he reports. "I should like to give him a machine to play with. Let's see what he can do." Alfred agrees at once. Suppose this should be the solution? News in pictures, real "news pictures", not drawings: no doubt about the success of that! Well, Sapt shall have his machine, he can make all the experiments he likes. In the meantime, lots of other things to occupy the Chief's mind. That is what he is called now; addressed as "Chief"; signs his notes "Chief". Many will never think of him, however far away they drift, whatever may be their employment, as anything but the Chief.

So he goes on with his other business, Sapt plays with his machine, the *Mirror* loses more and more money. From the moment when the disappointment declared itself expenses have been cut down to the lowest possible. Nothing is to be spent beyond the bare sum required to bring the paper out. Even that, however, is alarmingly big. There is no thought in the Chief's mind of killing it; that never occurred to him in his gloomiest hour. It is as true of him as it was when he started *Answers* that "the word failure is not in our vocabulary". He will get the ship to port somehow, leaky though she is, damaged her engines, feeble her power to move. He will force Fleet Street to acknowledge his ability more freely than ever it has done. But, for the moment, keep the loss down; spend no more than is necessary. Here one can perceive Brother Harold's prudent economy. It will be time to pour out money again when we know where we are going.

Running off pages of half-tones, Sapt gets presentable results. They are shown daily to the Chief. "Not good enough", he says at first. Then, "Can you be sure of doing as well as that every day?" Then, "How fast are you printing? Don't let's have any hanky-panky over it." Then, "Now take your time. You want alterations in the machines. Don't hurry them." And at last one morning, "I am satisfied it can be done."

Now once more advertisements of the *Mirror* appear. It is to be a halfpenny news-picture paper (it cost a penny in its original "high-class" shape). The money tap is turned on again. This time the Chief is certain that the flow will not be wasted. K.J. is not so sure. He still feels resentment against the *Mirror;* in some moods would not have been sorry to see it killed. He has stood ostentatiously aloof from the conclaves at which the new policy has been discussed. He agrees that this is the best thing to do, but "Alf", he grumbles, is, as usual, over-sanguine. "Alf" nods with tight lips, then opens them to say, "You'll see."

Less than four months after the catastrophic launch of the old *Mirror* the reborn *Mirror* appears. The news-agents believe in it. Their orders are encouraging.

Everything depends on Sapt's pictures. How have they come out? Alas! not well. Some are badly blurred. "Were they all taken in a fog?" asks the Chief savagely. One is simply a black smear. Next day, however, there is vast improvement. The fault has been discovered. Too much ink was put on. Now the picture pages are attractive, the news pages are readable; the editorial page, with a newly discovered cartoonist (W. K. Haselden) and a novel style of leading article, almost a daily sermon, is original. From the start prosperity is assured.

This now becomes once more Alfred's chief pursuit. He holds that when an enterprise is going well it should be energetically pushed. Leave it alone while it goes badly; let it trundle along until you have decided to quicken it up. As soon as it gathers speed apply yourself with all your strength and cleverness to making it go faster and faster still. Every morning he goes over the whole of the paper with the principal members of the staff. There are now, in pursuance of his favourite policy, two editors. His hope is that each will display furious energy in efforts to outvie the other. They are sensible enough to make a compact dividing editorial duties between them. This is almost the last time he follows that method, though it gives more satisfaction when he puts in a second picture editor to run against Sapt, who, after a while, gives up the contest and goes—without the reward which he deserved for laying the foundation of a very valuable property.

Still the Chief's anxiety is to keep the paper up to the standard which he calls "high-class". "Good paper for cabmen this morning" is his frequent greeting, not unkindly spoken, but with comical reproach. "If we give pictures for cabmen, only cabmen will buy us. If we can please the people at the top, everyone will, cabmen and all." That is a lesson of which he never tires. He has discovered that the mass of people, whatever their rank in life, whether they are "at the top", in the middle, or at the bottom, have much the same tastes.

> The colonel's lady and Judy O'Grady
> Are sisters under their skins.

But the colonel's lady with more surface refinement will not enjoy anything which is not on the surface refined, while Judy will be doubly gratified with a paper which is evidently meant for "her betters", yet interests her all through.

That is the line of his thought—a profitable line it proves itself to be. The *Mirror* is very soon as firmly established as the *Mail*. The early losses on it are wiped out; it becomes a marvellous money-maker. It passes in course of time, some years before Northcliffe's death, into the possession of Brother Harold. Northcliffe was tired of it; it had "settled down". But he well knew how valuable it had been to him, not in money alone, not so much in money as in reputation. It put the finishing touch to his fame as a newspaper genius. It made that genius appear even more extraordinary than it would have done if the *Mirror* had succeeded from the start. He had dramatically disappointed all who believed and hoped that his career was broken. He had snatched victory from the jaws of defeat. He was, it seemed, a man who could not be beaten. None now, in 1908, contest the claim of his admirers that he is the most astonishing person Fleet Street has ever known.

CHAPTER VII

THE DEVELOPMENT OF THE STUNT

The founder of The Daily Mail *had something of an artist's love for the productions of his restless genius.*
The Economist, 3. xi. 1928

"IN repose, Northcliffe's features are massive, in conversation they become boyish." So notes a discriminating American journalist, Will Irwin. Never must that be forgotten in judging his character. For close on fifty years he remains a boy. Sometimes it seems that his boyish characteristics are intensified rather than diminished as he grows older.

Boyish in his power of concentration upon the matter of the moment, boyish in his readiness to turn swiftly to a different matter and concentrate on that. Boyish in his irritable humours, boyish in his expansive kindliness; boyish in his occasional impetuous cruelties, boyish in his far more frequent and lavish generosity. Boyish his enjoyment of effort and its recompense. Boyish the limited range of his intellect, which seldom concerns itself with anything but the immediate, the obvious, the popular. Boyish his irresponsibility, his disinclination to take himself, or his publications, seriously; his conviction that whatever benefits them is justifiable and that it is not his business to consider the effect of their contents on the public mind.

There comes a time when he "grows up". He will then impress on his staffs that "publicity such as ours is a terrific responsibility. The power of suggestion by type is enormous. If we keep on suggesting that masculinity in women increases, masculine women will be more numerous and many learned people believe that masculinity in women is interfering with the Birth-rate." "Remember," he will conclude with a final vivid flash of facetiousness, still boylike, "our tons of ink make millions think." He will then, too, set himself with the utmost serious purposes to influence the public mind. He will fix his gaze on the future, ignoring the deceptive appearances of the present. He will at moments risk unpopularity. But this is not to happen yet. All through his middle period he is a Peter Pan; he remains a boy. Impossible to understand, hard even to credit, if we do not keep this in mind steadily, the inconsistencies in his behaviour, the leaps and bounds of his imagination, the working of his mind.

It works with especial vigour in the execution of stunts, to which his method of journalism owes a large part of its success. What is a stunt? It is something which astounds. The word denoted first of all a startling feat, an unexpected performance in athletics. Thence it has come to mean any act that is—or is intended to be—surprising, theatrically effective. Had it been in use when Disraeli purchased the Suez Canal shares, that might have been called a stunt. Newspaper stunts were not invented by Northcliffe, yet he may be called the father of them, for he was the earliest to see what could be done by means of them to make a newspaper known; the first to use them deliberately for that purpose.

Stunts can be worked with success only by those who possess a sense of dramatic value, who in a sense act, who take a boyish pride and pleasure in their acting. The boy, the conscious actor, Will Irwin discovers in Northcliffe when, after letting himself be seen at work, conversing with editors, shooting out instructions, discussing the bad conduct of a machine, "he looked across at me with that peering, searching glance of his and I felt the Celt in him coming to the surface. 'Oh, man, am I no a bonny fighter?' quoth Alan Breck in his moment of triumph to David Balfour.[1] 'My boy, do I not know this business?' Northcliffe seemed to say."

That was how he appeared to one fellow-journalist. Here is a sketch by another, an Englishman this time. "He rises from an easy-chair as if he had been spending hours in reverie over a cigar. He sets his visitor at ease by the exercise of a studied charm of manner. He conveys the impression that the matter under discussion is the day's only interest to him." There again the manner is studied. There is something of the histrionic to be noticed in it. Yes, "the Chief" often acts—his staff know it well; and he always enjoys his own performances. See him walking up and down his room smoking a cigar and dictating an article. Watch him at "conference" seizing the right moment to "drop a brick", as he calls it, or to impart some piece of "startling" information. Listen to his chaff of a slow-witted secretary or his golf professional, the studied extravagance of his talk with a few intimates at dinner. There is a touch of the skilled actor to be noticed frequently.

He likes to startle with an unexpected decision, an arresting phrase. He has a strong sense of dramatic values, though he cares nothing for the drama of the stage. He notices that one of his favourite writers has grown lazy. He sends him a gift of a gold fountain-pen. The hint is taken. He picks up a wayfarer in his automobile, is amused by his conversation. "You shall dine with me tonight", he says; has him scrubbed and barbered, puts him into dress clothes; introduces him at dinner as "Colonel Smith"; sends him off afterwards with a railway ticket

[1] R. L. Stevenson's *Kidnapped*.

and a five-pound note. He inquires of a reporter what his salary is, whether he is satisfied with it. The reporter says, Yes. Northcliffe looks him over.

"I want no one on my staff", he declares, "who is satisfied with a salary like that!"

Is it dramatic instinct, a desire to make the punishment fit the crime, or is it irritation, which makes him discharge an office-boy eating an apple, a reporter who smokes a pipe in his presence, a messenger with a cigarette in his mouth, who, it turns out, is not in his employ? In either case such hasty edicts are most of them revoked. Everyone knows that Alfred is liable at any time to pass from severe displeasure to smiling forgiveness. In one of his early morning telephone onslaughts he taxes an editorial man with some fault, "You know I'm devoted to you, but if you do that again, out you go." Explanation is offered. The fault has been committed in the rush and confusion of acting as substitute for a sick colleague. "All right, my boy, don't worry about it. You did your best." Another example. He rings up the office. A certain Briggs replies, inquires "Who is it?" When he hears a voice say "Lord Northcliffe", he laughs aloud. Then the voice becomes furious. "I have been using the telephone for fifteen years", it says, "and no one has ever laughed at me on it until now. Come and see me at twelve o'clock."

An office conclave is held. The trembling Briggs is provided with an excuse. When Northcliffe accosts him icily, "You are the man who laughed when I gave you my name!" the guilty one answers, "I believed the statement made in your newspapers that you were in France." Northcliffe looks hard at him. "Quite right, quite right. I am in France. Say no more about it." And when an unfortunate mistake is made about his father in one of his own

THE DEVELOPMENT OF THE STUNT

publications, which causes him acute annoyance, he replies to the editor's telegram of apology and regret, "Don't worry, dear Hammerton. I have made worse mistakes myself."

Dramatic, but deeply prudent also, are some of his decisions in the interest of what he calls "our decent readers". In no publication of his appears anything suggestive of indecency, nothing prurient, coarse, or unclean. He is anxious to keep them free, also, of anything that will offend good taste; he does not want his papers to cause offence even to the fastidious. He knows that the big battalions are on the side of God. It is far more profitable, as well as more respectable, for him to be on God's side too. Advertisers say that readers who buy papers for their uncleanness are of no use to them. If they have money to spend, they spend it on liquor and gambling. Advertisers like to feel that the papers they use go into prosperous homes and are read by solid, honest, decent people. No hypocrisy in taking this line, neither deliberate nor unconscious guile. He does genuinely dislike dirt; dislikes anything that is sordid, "unpleasant" in the Victorian sense. So he "kills" at a blow all photographs, secured at heavy cost, of the Jeffries-Johnson Prize-fight at Reno, Nevada. "Women wouldn't like them. Don't print any of them. Don't argue. I won't have them." The staff think that sometimes he carries respectability too far.

Dramatic his prompt action when *The Daily Mail* has published false news of a massacre of British, Americans, and Europeans in Peking. It is the time of the Boxer Rebellion. The plight of the white folk in the Chinese capital, all gathered in the Legations quarter, causes painful anxiety. From a *Daily Mail* correspondent comes a cablegram to say that they have been massacred. Details are given. To the Foreign Office the editor sends it, by the Chief's order. The officials say they have no news themselves, they cannot either confirm or deny the correspondent's statement; but they have only too much reason to fear it must be true. So the cablegram is published, causing grief and indignation. A few days later it is established that the Legations are unharmed. At once Northcliffe decides that a man must start for China by the first steamer available. "Unless our news is trustworthy we may as well shut up shop", he says. "I must know how this terrible thing has happened."

Upon accuracy he has always been insistent. "I want the *Mail* to be as sure of its facts as *The Times*." When King Edward is operated on for appendicitis, he gives orders that one of London's leading surgeons shall be employed, no matter what it costs, to look over everything that is written about the illness and make sure there are no mistakes. He has a lawyer sitting in the office every night, reading all proofs, calling the editor's attention to any statement which seems to need fuller verification, any reference to person or institution which might cause annoyance or give pretext for legal proceedings. One of the delusions prevalent about Northcliffe attributes to him a reckless disregard of truth, a desire to publish anything that will startle, even though it be contradicted within a few hours. He is, in fact, as severe as any Old Journalist could be upon carelessness, loose statement. "We've got to get to the bottom of this", he says about the Peking massacre message. "When is there a boat for China?" One is found to be leaving within a few hours. "Very well, he must catch it. He can buy all that he needs on the way or when he arrives." So off goes a member of the staff in a top-hat and tail-coat, just as he had arrived at the office, on a journey that is to last for some months.

The story he brought back was surprising. He first

satisfied himself that the correspondent received his information, as he declared, from Chinese Government officials. Then he probed for the motive which caused them to give it; he found that too. The rulers of China were nervous about the penalties which might be laid upon them and the Chinese nation for the injuries suffered by Europeans during the Boxer trouble. They argued that if the world were led to suppose that a massacre had happened and were then to learn that the white folks were safe, there would be a revulsion of feeling in China's favour. People would say: "The Chinese are not so bad after all"; they might get off pretty lightly. So they laid the plot to hoax *The Daily Mail,* and did the paper an incalculable harm. They caused it to be mistrusted just when it was struggling hard to prove itself worthy of confidence.

From another shower of abuse—"those showers", Northcliffe used to say, "which helped to make the paper"—it escaped with more credit. A liner named *Aden* was wrecked off the island of Socotra. The nearest *Daily Mail* correspondent sent off a triple-paid cablegram briefly announcing the disaster. At once Northcliffe cabled him instructions to send all he could about it and a large sum of money to pay the cable tolls. The news appeared. The owners of the vessel denied its truth; they had not yet heard of the wreck. The paper was denounced for "lying as usual". Questions were asked in Parliament. Then it had to be admitted that every detail in the *Mail's* cablegrams was accurate. It had beaten every other paper. That was very quickly made clear. Unfortunately the truth about the Chinese matter cannot be so soon discovered. By the public it is never known. The *Mail* suffers severely from the distrust it created. For many years "the Peking massacre" is remembered against it and used as a gibe.

Nothing more damaging to a new paper could be imagined, if the new paper depended on its news alone. But *The Daily Mail* does not. Its appeal is not so much to readers who want exact and complete intelligence of events as to those who ask for "something to read" daily in newspaper form.

For the first time this demand is now satisfied. For the first time a daily newspaper is published that the mass of people find it worth their while to buy. Hitherto they have had to be content with Sunday papers, budgets for the most part of crime, sensationalism, obscenity. Now an offer is made to them of a clean, varied, entertaining mixture every morning; they are not slow to take advantage of it. During the first eight months of its life the *Mail* sells an average of 202,000 copies a day. In 1897 the net sale goes up to nearly 300,000, in 1898 to 439,000, in 1899 to 610,000, in 1900 to nearly a million. Then, partly because the South African War news is not so thrilling, partly by reason of the Peking massacre misfortune, it drops in 1901 to 836,000, and continues to fluctuate in the 700,000's until the war.[1]

[1] The complete figures of average net daily sale 1896–1929 are:

Year	Sales	Year	Sales
1896	202,077	1913	765,446
1897	299,848	1914	945,719
1898	439,499	1915	1,105,214
1899	610,323	1916	1,172,245
1900	989,255	1917	938,211
1901	836,695	1918	973,343
1902	807,638	1919	1,030,641
1903	771,937	1920	1,136,885
1904	809,485	1921	1,394,570
1905	768,177	1922	1,784,313
1906	750,627	1923	1,768,172
1907	720,330	1924	1,745,853
1908	713,321	1925	1,742,772
1909	716,362	1926	1,740,365
1910	764,517	1927	1,802,255
1911	759,212	1928	1,933,293
1912	773,994	1929	1,945,635

At one time Northcliffe plans an invasion of the field occupied by Sunday newspapers; he announces that he will publish *The Daily Mail* seven days a week. America, France, Belgium, these and other countries not less religious than Britain have journals that appear on Sunday as well as during the rest of the week. In Austria and Germany certain journals do not appear on Monday mornings, so that work may be avoided on Sunday night. But the work for Sunday papers is done on Saturday night. Surely no objection can be raised to that? Objection, however, is raised, and raised so forcibly that the project has to be dropped. A certain complication results from the existence of religious papers among the many weeklies and monthlies which the firm publishes, notably the *Sunday Companion,* with its Order of supporters called the Bible Band of Britain, all wearing badges with the lettering B.B.B. upon them. A useful stunt, this, of the editor's, much applauded by the Chief, a great help to circulation. But a nuisance the Bible Band make themselves when the seven-day newspaper is projected. They are really imbued, it seems, with the sabbatarian doctrine which their favourite organ, the *Sunday Companion,* has preached. They cannot swallow "the desecration of the Lord's Day" by *The Daily Mail*. A man of weaker imagination, of lesser capacity, would show obstinacy; would insist on defying illogical opposition. Northcliffe sees that he has struck on a deeply rooted prejudice. He gives up his plan, substituting for it the purchase of an old Sunday journal, which is published without protest.

With this he never fully succeeds as he succeeded with his other newspapers. He does not know the purchasers of a Sunday paper like the *Weekly Dispatch* as he knows those of the *Mirror* and the *Mail*. They are manual workers mostly. K.J. tells him they lie in bed and read till public-houses open. They want their Sunday paper to give them the same kind of titillation which well-to-do people get from novels about divorce, seduction, murder, forgery. "Fill it with crime, not excluding the unmentionable sort, and it will sell like hot cakes." But "Alf" says No; he will not adopt such means. Sport, he agrees, shall bulk largely in the contents, though he takes no interest in it himself and believes that as a pursuit it is degrading. But salaciousness he will not have. He will persuade the manual workers to like other features that he will introduce. K.J. smiles grimly on one side of his face. He does know those manual workers. He can imagine their reception of the chatty little articles, the bright little interviews, the woman's page, the magazine page. But he shrugs his shoulders and says no more. He knows "Alf" is immovable from that resolve.

Of all the stunts, therefore, by which Northcliffe's papers advertise themselves, keep people talking about them, force people to buy them because they are talked about, none appeal to the taste for winking nastiness, none to the appetite for dirt. This is not commercialism, though it pays. It is the reflection of his temperament. Apart from that field the stunts are of the widest variety. The subjects are not deliberately chosen. They are taken, upon impulse, from the happenings of the day. Northcliffe's genius for journalism shows itself in his almost infallible instinct for the topics that are likely to be talked about. He knows how to stimulate that likelihood, how to whip up interest, how to keep it alive for days, weeks, sometimes months.

If we define the stunt as "treatment of news in a manner designed to provide subjects for conversation", we perceive at once the difference between the Old Journalism and that which Northcliffe introduced. It may be illustrated by comparing funds raised by newspapers before his time with that which *The Daily Mail* worked up to £100,000 during the South African War. The Absent-minded Beggar Fund was a stunt. It was enormously profitable to the paper, in addition to benefiting soldiers in the field and building a hospital. Every means of pressing the appeal that ingenuity could suggest was employed. Rudyard Kipling's verses with Sullivan's music were sung in hundreds of theatres and concert-halls every night. They were recited by favourite actresses, ilustrated by favourite artists. They supplied the nation with catchwords. They were dinned into everybody's ears. Day after day the paper recounted what was being done. Its readers felt that they were personally concerned in swelling the Fund. Whereas the Old Journalism invited subscriptions and left it at that, merely printing a list of amounts received, Northcliffe sent out into the highways and hedges and compelled gifts. That was, of course, better for the Fund; it was also better for the paper which was raising the Fund.

Many other large sums of money were collected for the relief of misfortunes which touched public imagination, which touched Northcliffe's imagination. That was the reason of their success. When taxi-cabs came into use, the plight of horse cabmen losing their employment excited general sympathy. The *Mail* started a subscription, taught five hundred of them to drive motors, pensioned off others. When the *Titanic* sank, dependents of the poorer victims owed to a Northcliffe Fund an easing of their misfortune. Is a Club for soldiers and sailors needed in London? The *Mail* in four days can get £16,000 for that purpose. Is there a difficulty about money for sending British athletes to the Olympic Games? By the same agency the sum requisite is quickly forthcoming. No newspaper in any country has had so immediate an influence over so large a number of people. No newspaper has ever been read at the same moment in almost every part of the British Isles. This is made possible, a few years after its establishment, by printing in Manchester as well as in London. Save for small differences in local news, it is the same paper which is produced in both cities. Now from north to south, from east to west, the land is provided with *Daily Mails* at breakfast-time. And later comes a Paris edition, a *Continental Daily Mail,* which extends the Northcliffe power over English travellers abroad, makes it familiar to foreigners even.

A shade sceptical about the extent of that power is Northcliffe himself. "How far does it go?" he asks, not very much caring, it would seem. Clearly it is not at this period a political power. To Joseph Chamberlain proposing Protection for Britain he lends support, stipulating only that food shall not cost more. For the Conservative Party at the election fought on this issue his newspapers vociferously demand votes. With what result? Protection is rolled in the dust, Conservatives are heavily defeated. Northcliffe has taken the unpopular side. This, he reflects, will never do. For the future rule out political stunts. It does a paper no good to be identified with either Party. All very well to beat up passing excitements over an increase of the Navy, an unpopular tax. When the ships are voted, the tax withdrawn, drop the subject! It has served its purpose. Why should he use his newspapers to serve the purposes of politicians? No more of it. Stick to stunts which do not have to be voted upon. Touch only subjects that are of interest in the home.

Eminent among these is the subject of food. No stunt attracts more attention than that which deals with Standard

Bread. It does not succeed in its ostensible aim, which is to induce the nation to eat bread made from stone-milled flour, instead of eating white bread from which steel rollers in flour-mills have separated the most nourishing elements; its real purpose, to make people talk, is accomplished completely. The general opinion is that Northcliffe "must have some interest in stone-milled flour". "He must be doing it to make money." Yes, but not to make money in the way such gossip-mongers imagine. They do not understand that he has no interest, either intellectually or financially, in anything but newspapers. Here are the circumstances in which he starts the Standard Bread stunt.

"A fine old English gentleman, quite in the ancient style", as the song puts it, has been long convinced that whole-wheat bread is vastly more valuable as food than white bread. He dwells on the presumed connexion between the invention, about 1850, of the milling process which made white bread possible and the deterioration of teeth which has been noticeable since that date. He has stone-milled flour used always for the bread of his household. They like it better; it does them, he believes, more good. He is healthy, they are healthy, why should not all be healthy? Down he sits and writes to *The Daily Mail* a letter to this effect, offering at the end to supply to anyone who cares to write for it a loaf of the bread he recommends. The letter is published. A day or two later Northcliffe, arriving at the office, sees what he described as "a mountain of correspondence". He inquires about it, is told that these are the requests for Sir Oswald Mosley's Standard loaf.

"What! You mean to say this mass of letters, which almost prevented my getting into the office, are all from people who want to try this bread? Why, there must be enormous public interest in this. I'm not surprised. Food is more attractive to most people than any other subject. We must run this, make a big thing of it. Start it to-morrow. Keep it going. We can make a lot out of this."

He is himself a standard-bread eater. He is ready with all the arguments in its favour. He becomes an enthusiast. "I want an article in the paper about it every day for a year." People will not eat it, he is told. "Why won't they? Because you aren't telling them enough about it." The staff groan. They are sick and tired of standard bread. They curse when they hear the name of Mosley. "No, you are to blame if it doesn't catch on. You are not making half enough of it. Don't you know there are fifteen million people in England who have never heard of Pears' Soap?" That is a favourite maxim of his. Pears' Soap has been very widely advertised for many years, yet not enough. He calls the *Mail* his "modest violet", sometimes, as in this case, reproaching it for not "coming more out into the open", sometimes in jesting allusion to its pushing, unblushing determination to be always in the public eye. Of his *Evening News* he says that "it is the best paper for those who live on fish and chips", the *Mirror* is "the cabmen's little favourite". Of *Answers,* though, he never speaks lightly, has no nickname for it, keeps its bound volumes in that discreetly magnificent room of his, with heads of philosophers and historians above the bookcases and in gilded lettering the names of Socrates, Xenophon, Cicero, Homer, Virgil, Tacitus. There are sentimental streaks in his nature: this is one of them.

The Standard Bread stunt he always speaks of as the cheapest; the most expensive is the Soap stunt. It served its purpose; it made people talk. But the publicity it provided was not worth over a quarter of a million sterling:

that was what it cost. It begins as an exposure of plans to form a Soap Trust, the Leverhulme plans. There it is on firm ground. But in their anxiety to please the Chief, known to be the instigator of the attack, the staff blunder into bogs, led by will-o'-the-wisps suggesting that some of the Soap Kings do not give just weight. Their pound packets do not contain a full pound; they not only mean to cozen the public by raising prices when they get their Trust, they are cheating their customers now. So runs the accusation. The pebble makes a mighty splash, the surface of the pond heaves. "The *Mail* must be right. They could never. . . ." Alas, they have! The law is set in motion. In the end there is a settlement. The accusation has to be withdrawn. More than £250,000 are paid in compensation and in costs. A gloomy day this. The boyish humour damped, the boyish irresponsibility unable for the moment to triumph cheerfully over unpleasant circumstances.

Anything that will make people talk, anything that will show the influence of his newspapers, anything that will convince advertisers of their pulling power, is fit material for a stunt. No one has ever discovered materials so cleverly as Northcliffe did, no one ever worked stunts with an energy or with results so great. The schoolboy in him leapt to the fun, the excitement of it. A stunt to be successful must be worked with enjoyment, with conviction. Coldly conceived, carried out as a part of the daily routine, it falls flat, dies of inanition. Northcliffe put into his stunts all the vigour of his luxuriant vitality. His imagination teemed with devices for stirring the slow public mind. He was often misjudged, misrepresented. When he found that Max Reinhard's *Miracle* was being played to a more than half-empty Olympia, he asked a writer on his staff to go and see it and, if he thought it deserving, to contribute an article about it every day for a fortnight. At the end of a week money was being turned away at every performance. "Of course he had money in the show", declared the Know-alls; he had none, nor even did he care about its fate. His object was to prove what the *Mail* could do. When he made people talk about a *Daily Mail* rose and about his sweet-pea exhibitions, when he campaigned for pure milk and more convenient small houses, he used for his purpose things by which he knew numberless people would be attracted. When he made a stunt of saving the Crystal Palace, a huge glass building that housed the first international exhibition in Hyde Park (1851) and was then moved to Sydenham, a suburb of London, someone said to him: "Why do you want to save that awful place? It ought to be blown up." He retorted with his schoolboy smile of mischief, "I'd just as soon raise a subscription to blow it up."

That is the true spirit of the stunt artist and it was by stunts that the New Journalism captured its readers. But it had to keep them by sound journalism, by trustworthy news. He never forgot this. The stunt had immense publicity value. Newspapers, he was well aware, needed a value other than that. Because his newspapers were clean and did aim at giving this other value there was little adverse comment when he was created in 1904 a baronet and in 1906 a peer of the realm with a seat in the House of Lords. His title he took from the sea-coast close to his beloved Elmwood. "It will be a relief", he said, "to have a name without an h in it. I was so tired of being called 'Mr. 'Armsworth' by one of my most capable secretaries that I felt it quite a relief when he had to call me 'Sir H'Alfred'. Now I'm glad to be rid of that too." A delightfully boyish peer!

CHAPTER VIII

THE STRUGGLE FOR *THE TIMES*

The Times *owes Northcliffe a debt of gratitude, for he rescued it from decline and did much to vitalize it.*

WICKHAM STEED
in *Through Thirty Years*

HAD Northcliffe been attracted by any other pursuit than journalism, now was the time for him to use his overflowing vitality in wider fields. At the age of forty-two he had won a more spectacular success than any man of his period. That he had made himself very rich was the least of his achievements. His fortune was merely a by-product of his prodigious activity. He was famous, not in his own country alone, but far beyond it. He had built up out of nothing an organization, including three daily newspapers with the largest sales in Britain, two Sunday newspapers, a host of periodicals flooding over the land by millions every week. So far as he chose he could exert over public opinion a power that had never been approached, though, as we have seen, there were still solid barriers beyond which it could not effectively be employed. The Government had recognized his unusual capacity and influence by allowing him to become, within two years of being made a baronet, a peer of the realm.

Had he been inclined for public life (like Lord Burnham, of the *Daily Telegraph*), had he been devoted to any sport (as Sir Thomas Lipton was to yachting, Sir Edward Hulton to the Turf), had he cared for a career of philanthropy, it would have been easy to gratify his ambition. The ball was at his feet; he could kick it in any direction he chose. Being the man he was, he wished for no triumph beyond that of owning and controlling newspapers, he paid little attention to anything outside the province of journalism. In that field he sighed for new conquests. It was inevitable that he should cast his eye upon *The Times*.

No newspaper in any country has ever held a position quite like that which *The Times* created for itself during the middle part of the nineteenth century. In existence since 1789, it had not during its first forty years taken the lead of its rivals. It was one among several London newspapers equal in public esteem. By the energy and enterprise of the second John Walter, son of the original proprietor, aided by his two editors, Barnes and Delane, it was pushed to the front; it gained a world-wide reputation for early and trustworthy news. More valuable than that, it was mistakenly given credit for knowing at all times the mind of British Governments and of being employed by them to make announcements to the world. This lent to it a character of its own, an authority surpassing that of all other newspapers. Also it made *The Times* profitable to its owners—so long as it was competently edited and managed.

After the death of Delane its vigour declined, it sank gradually into stagnation. The editorial side was in the hands of men who had no knowledge of journalism outside *The Times* office. The management looked more carefully after the interests of the Walter family than after those of the paper. For the Walter family were not merely predominant partners in *The Times,* they were its printers. They owned the buildings in Printing-house Square and Playhouse Yard, near Blackfriars Bridge, which contained office and works. They owned the printing-plant; they had a perpetual contract to carry out the mechanical production and could charge what they pleased. The head of the Walter family by hereditary right stood at the head of the proprietors; he was not likely to quarrel with himself over the bills he presented to himself for the printing of the paper. This farcically unbusinesslike arrangement had the result which might have been anticipated. The shareholders in *The Times,* some three hundred in number, saw their dividends dwindle and then almost cease, while they also saw the Walters still making so much money by their printing business that they could overlook the loss of income on their shares. They became uneasy. An application for accounts since 1900 was made to the Court of Chancery in 1907. The Walters agreed to furnish accounts. When the shareholders saw them they were indignant. The Court was now asked to dissolve the partnership and to order that its property should be disposed of. *The Times* was for sale.

Northcliffe had watched very carefully the moves in the game. He had resolved to take a hand in it when the right moment came. What he did not foresee was that the Walters would be imprudent enough to close hastily with an offer from another newspaper owner of inferior capacity and with notoriously smaller resources. For twenty years Arthur Pearson had been copying Northcliffe. He set up a rival to *Answers,* he set up a rival to the *Mail.* Failing to make his *Daily Express* pay, he took over and ruined an old newspaper called the *Standard,* which he then proposed to merge in *The Times,* with himself as managing director of a new *Times* company. To this wild scheme, without asking advice either from manager or editor, the Walters agreed. Then, stupid as their assent had been, they made a mistake still stupider. Without consulting or informing anyone on the staff they published an announcement of what they had done. The public gasped when it learned that Northcliffe's unsuccessful imitator was to have control of *The Times*.

Northcliffe did not gasp. He smiled. He saw that the moment had come for him to enter the game. The Walters had no power to sell the paper: that power lay with the Court of Chancery. They could propose a scheme, but before the judges would sanction it they had to be convinced that the shareholders were satisfied and that their interests were reasonably secure. The Court would also require proof that a prospective purchaser could produce the purchase price. It would be easy, Northcliffe believed, to induce shareholders to object to the Pearson plan; it would not be difficult to persuade the Court that an offer with cash behind it was better than one which proposed to present the shareholders with nothing but shares in a new company. Fairly sure now felt Northcliffe that he could become proprietor of *The Times*. Had he known what was passing in the mind of the manager of *The Times* he might have felt quite sure.

The name of the manager was Moberly Bell. Engaged in business in Alexandria (Egypt), he had acted as *The Times* correspondent there. In spite of his total ignorance of newspaper production he had been asked by Arthur Walter to remove to London, and at a crisis in the history of the paper to take over the commercial management of it. He was a man of vivid personality, impulsive temperament, uncertain temper. At one period he was hated as fiercely by *The Times* staff, who derisively called him "The Assyrian", as was K.J. by that of the *Mail*. He was despised, too, for his ludicrous lack of acquaintance with matters which to them were familiar. He never to the end of his life thoroughly grasped the principles of newspaper business; to its details he had remained up to this period a complete stranger. Hard and loyally as he worked for his employers, he learned very little about newspapers, so his labour was in vain. He did his best to learn, but he did not know how to go about it. One of his efforts was to send a circular to all regular subscribers asking for criticism and advice. He received 17,000 replies, from which he learned nothing.

In one thing, however, Moberly Bell achieved striking success. He had not been able to save *The Times* for the Walters, but he saved it from them. As soon as he had read their statement about the result of negotiations carried on behind his back and clearly meant as his dismissal, Pearson having no use for him, he determined that he would bring their plan to naught. "I am going to smash it", he confided to an intimate, and poured into the task all the intensity, not alone of a man with a grievance, a man who had been badly used, but of a man who felt himself responsible for preserving the high character and independence of *The Times*. What he might have done if Northcliffe had not approached him it is hard to imagine. He had a vague notion of inducing financial houses in the City of London to buy the paper. Schemes in the raw, grandiose, unpractical, simmered in his imagination. It is unlikely that any one of them could have ripened. He must himself have had an inkling of this, for when a meeting with Northcliffe was proposed he at once assented, and from that meeting he came away a Northcliffe man.

On this occasion, as on many another, the charm of Northcliffe's manner, the fascination of his eyes and smile, his grave kindliness shot with playful humour, completely overcame unpleasant expectations. It was Bell's first meeting with him. He admitted afterwards that he had imagined the proprietor of *Mail* and *Mirror* to be a cocksure vulgarian. To his relief he found instead a man attractive, simple, sincere, a man who came quietly but directly to his reason for requesting the interview.

"Mr. Bell," he said, "I am going to buy *The Times*. With your help, if you will give it; in spite of you, if you do not."

Bell replied, "I will help you." They sat down at once to draw up a plan of campaign.

Or would it be more correct to say that Northcliffe proposed a plan drawn up beforehand and that Bell accepted it? This was the plan which formed the basis of the arrangement by which Northcliffe became chief and controlling proprietor of *The Times*. There is no doubt that it was drawn, and all other financial-legal details arranged, by Brother Harold. Their skilful simplicity and the smallness of actual expenditure called for bear the unmistakable impress of his ingenious mind. Equally characteristic of Alfred are his wise precautions to secure secrecy and the boyish delight he takes in being a conspirator. He leaves England, has his departure for the South announced, stays under an assumed name at an hotel (the Chrystol et Bristol, of which the title always amused him) in Boulogne-sur-Mer. Hence he watches the smouldering of the fuse he has laid, talks to Bell daily on the telephone. Here, as he motors every afternoon through the pleasant winter landscape, he chuckles over the discomfiture of Pearson, the surprise he has in store for even his close friends, the attainment of his long-cherished ambition.

In London the plan so cleverly conceived moves unhasting towards its purpose. Moberly Bell does not mention the name of Northcliffe in his office or in his house. One day (this was before the departure to France) Northcliffe rings up his home, gives Mrs. Bell a message. Mrs. Bell passes it on to her husband at the office in Arabic, a language they had used in their Egyptian years. Thus few are aware of what is passing. Bell ignores the Walters, ignores the Pearson scheme, of which nothing more is heard. He makes arrangements with shareholders, presents a scheme to the Court (Brother Harold's scheme), gets it sanctioned. The purchase is made in his name. The name of Northcliffe is not spoken. Not more than a score of people know who is behind Bell with the money. Even the head of the Walter family is kept in ignorance (this is Bell's revenge) until a month after the contract of sale has been signed. Then he is told, upon a sudden impulse which arises from Northcliffe's dislike of double-dealing. Curious that there should be linked together within the same bodily frame the schoolboy who enjoys mysterious plotting and a man whose sense of honour is so scrupulous that he cannot allow Mr. Walter to be deceived by an assurance from a common acquaintance that *The Times* has not been sold to him. Curious, but beyond doubt. This was far from being an isolated instance of such delicacy of feeling.

Another may be noted at once; it falls naturally into place here. When the time came for the purchase-money to be provided, Northcliffe's lawyer suggested that, as a matter of discretion, it should be deposited with a bank in the joint names of Moberly Bell and of someone representing Northcliffe. "No," replied the new proprietor of *The Times,* "I won't do that. I should like to please old Bell and show that I believe in him. He has made all sorts of conditions for the staff and about the conduct of the paper, but he hasn't asked anything for himself. I have decided to make him managing director and to hand over the purchase-money to him." It was a generous, kindly act. "A splendid fellow", Bell said, in a glow of grateful enthusiasm.

So *The Times* passed from the control of the Walters, who had guarded it jealously for more than a hundred years. "Their decadence", Northcliffe said, "shows the weakness of the hereditary system." The third John Walter had every one of the so-called advantages which his supremely competent father lacked. He had been sent to a very famous school, and to one of the ancient and exclusive Universities. He was bred for the occupation which awaited him, yet he proved grotesquely unequal to his task. He was not only a dull man, he was conceited. He was both morose and shy. In the office corridors he would pass those who worked for him without any sign of recognition, without seeming to know they were there. Whether his eldest son would have brought the dynasty into better repute no one can say. He was drowned just as he reached manhood. When John Walter the Third died there was no John the Fourth to succeed him. His second son, Arthur, reigned in his stead.

Certainly he was an improvement on his father. His bearing was courteous, he suffered neither from stupidity nor from conceit. But he suffered, as Northcliffe put it, from heredity. Softly reared, schooled without serious intention, put into the family business at the top instead of the bottom, he knew precisely nothing about it. Also his health was poor. He was little inclined either to industry or to resistance when disastrous expedients were pressed upon him by one or both of the two men in whose hands he left the management of the paper. Bell was one of these, his brother, Godfrey, the second. In appearance resembling his father, John the Second, Godfrey Walter was unfairly credited with being like him in character. He was shy, indeed, and gave, as many shy persons do, the impression of being supercilious. He was, in truth, kind-hearted, anxious to be on friendly terms with all. But he too was without any understanding of the newspaper business, apart from the printing of *The Times,* which had been placed under his special care.

He and his brother had, for example, been beguiled by Moberly Bell into the strange adventure of the *Encyclopædia Britannica*. The ninth edition (1875–89) of this massive work in many volumes was bought from the British publishers (who supposed it to be no longer saleable) by two ingenious Americans named Hooper and Jackson. The publishers thought they had been lucky to sell it; they had no idea that the purchasers would make out of it far more than they had made when it was a new work; would, by skilful advertising, induce the public to find room in their homes for many times the number of sets which had been taken up before the work became "out of date". The two Americans gave the British People a useful lesson in salesmanship; they owed their success largely to the adroit arrangement they made to sell the *Encyclopædia* in the name of *The Times*. This arrangement was accepted by Bell enthusiastically, by the Walters with misgiving, for the peculiar reason that they did not believe the paper could be made self-supporting, let alone earn dividends to keep its shareholders quiet. Bell, in his total ignorance of newspaper management, said it must be "subsidized". It was "too good" to be a paying proposition. The better it became, the smaller grew the number of those who bought it. It must therefore be supported by the proceeds of some ancillary enterprise, such as book-selling on the American plan.

That was Bell's line of fantastic argument, only to be understood if we recollect that he knew nothing about journalism and had a queer twist in his capricious, impetuous mind. He was an adept at discovering odd reasons for his acts or his supineness. When, for example, the Governor of the Bank of England urged him to reform the chaotic manner in which the contents of *The Times* were flung together and to print each day the same matter in the same place, he replied with a meaningless comparison between the variations of news and those in the value of money. If, he said, the Bank would make its rate of interest invariable and the price of Government stock invariable, he would try to make the arrangement of *The Times* invariable! It was not surprising that he lacked acquaintance with newspaper production when he became manager; the strange thing was that he gained scarcely any in the course of eighteen years. However, his arrangement with Hooper and Jackson served its purpose for awhile. *The Times* made money out of the old *Encyclopædia,* set about preparing a new one, sold other works on the instalment plan, still drew handsome profits. Then he risked a more speculative venture and got his fingers badly burned.

This time he managed to outwit his American associates at their own game, which proved that a long familiarity with Oriental methods of business had taught him how to drive an adroit bargain. The idea came from the busy imagination of Hooper. "Start a *Times* Book Club", he proposed, "to which all who take the paper regularly shall belong. They will have the advantage of a lending library and of being able to buy new books cheap the moment the library has done with them." Northcliffe laughed when he heard of the new scheme. He saw in an instant its two fatal weaknesses. "Quite a good notion", he said, "to sell off books at about half-price directly they cease to be asked for by borrowers—if the publishers would allow it, which of course they won't. Quite a good plan, too, to attract new subscribers for the paper by offering them the Book Club—if you didn't have to let all the old subscribers belong to it as well." He saw what delusive hope was leading Bell on—the hope of securing so many new subscribers that the circulation of the paper would be doubled, which would justify the doubling of advertisement rates. His forecast came true. The Book Club became a liability instead of an asset. The publishers, after much public correspondence with an enraged and furiously sarcastic Bell, declined to supply the Book Club with books; they also took away their advertising. The public smiled at Bell's discomfiture, at this farcical climax to his attempts at "subsidizing" *The Times*. The last state of that unhappy organ was worse than the first, and it was clear that under such incompetent controllers there could be no improvement. The prospect grew steadily darker.

When the shareholders started their revolt and revealed the fact that *"The Times* did not pay", advertisements fell off, its character as a national organ for the interchange of views was injured. No effort was made to ward off these disasters. The ship drifted nearer and nearer to the rocks. What no one in authority saw, though many of their subordinates saw it plainly, was that changes in the paper were required. While they planned contrivances for propping it up from outside, they strangely overlooked the obvious need for internal reforms, long overdue. Northcliffe had seen, several years before he bought it, what was necessary. Mr. Walter had asked his advice: should he reduce the price?—then threepence. "No," replied Northcliffe, "I shouldn't do that. I should make the paper worth threepence." This is what he now sets to work to do.

Not yet is it generally known he has become chief proprietor (at surprisingly small cost, thanks to Brother Harold's cleverness). He has promised in all sincerity to keep up the old traditions; it was with this purpose that he came forward to rescue it. He has appointed as directors men who have long been connected with the paper. He does not intend to interfere, if they can carry on without him. He equips the printing-office with new machines. He makes suggestions but gives no orders. He declares that so long as they spend money with wisdom he will not stint the supply. Few noticeable alterations, therefore, at first. A fixed make-up is introduced gradually. ("I think it took four years", Northcliffe said once, "to get *The Times* into the habit of printing the letters in the same place every day.") A system of news-gathering is set up; gone now the old plan of taking what was sent in and loftily disregarding what was not. K.J., who is a large shareholder, offers advice in his mildest tone. He is as anxious as "Alf", he avers, to keep up the dignity of the paper and at the same time to make it the best in the world. "All we have to do is to give the best of everything." When someone rudely asks, "Who will tell you what is best?" he does not answer that he is experienced journalist enough to tell without guidance. He is anxious not to disturb the harmony which prevails for some months after the purchase; he does not answer at all.

For some months, yes, harmony. After the purchase *The Times* office is "a happy home for the old staff", so one of them admits ingenuously. Northcliffe is waiting to see whether the directors will of their own initiative do what is required in the way of reforms. K.J. urges him not to be impatient. "We can't understand these people," he says, "they don't talk the same language as we do, they don't think in the same way. Leave them alone for a bit. Don't scare them. Don't get their backs up. They may do all right if they are not hurried." So Northcliffe does not hurry them—and they do not hurry themselves. When he alters his attitude he is goaded more by his hatred of incompetence ("I hate, like sin, all bad workmanship," he might quote from Goethe) than by the money loss. He discovers that neither directors nor, with a few exceptions, heads of departments know their business. Either they do nothing or they make what he considers to be mistakes, and even lower that dignity which he had been implored to respect.

He objects, for instance, to a page advertisement of brandy, a page covered with barrels. "It is a disgrace," he declares, and when the excuse is made that the money is badly needed he retorts sharply, "Your excuse is that of a burglar or embezzler. Never take an advertisement because you want money." He refuses equally to accept a full-page from Mr. Selfridge on the day when his store opens. He learns now, he says, that the high tone of *The Times* was the result of apathy, of laziness. "As soon as they bestir themselves they forget about it; they are willing to let the paper down to any depths for money." The staff cannot understand him, any more than he understands them. He tries this man and that, seeking someone who will grasp his ideas and act upon them. Thus he excites jealousies, thus he arouses hopes never to be realized, thus he creates discord in the office—without seeing many improvements. Then he determines that he must make these himself.

New men are appointed, old ones are "invited to retire". Not for some while is there a change in the editorship, not until Moberly Bell has died at his desk after three harassed years, years in which his sharpest pang was caused, not by being superseded, pushed to one side, sent up to the top floor of the office building as useless, but by realizing how inadequate he had been in the days of his power. Northcliffe sorrowed for him, did everything that could be done to show it, paid public and private tributes to his memory. He had outlived the bitter feelings stirred up against him by his rash judgment and savage letter-writing (it was typical of his incapacity for management that he wrote all letters with his own hand). He had softened, been tamed by adversity. The best in his character came out as his life drew to its end. K.J., who had for him a certain fondness, though very often he had been irritated by him, pronounces a cynical epitaph. "Poor old Bell, he always meant to do the right thing, but he couldn't count beyond five." On which "Alf" frowns disapproval. He had joined in laughing at "poor old Bell" for his sudden enthusiasms, his impossible schemes, the penny memorandum book in which he kept *The Times* accounts and daily circulation. But he recollects Bell's "I will help you" and the loyalty with which that promise was kept.

Yet there have been moments when he has cursed Bell, there will arrive others when he will think of him in not so kindly a way as he does now. For the liquidation of the difficulties in which *The Times* had been involved is still a heavy task. Getting clear of the Book Club liability is both disagreeable and costly. Sloughing off the subsidy-maker and turning to the proper business of a newspaper entails hard work and anxious hours. What especially puzzles and occasionally infuriates Northcliffe is the calmness of everyone at Printing-house Square, the slowness to grasp the fact that the outlook is still cloudy and the future uncertain. He used to relate this story of a meeting he had with an old member of the staff, who told him there was general regret at a certain highly placed man's resignation.

" 'Not more regret than I feel,' I replied.
" 'Is there anything behind it?' he asked.

" 'Only the fact that we have not got the money to pay him,' I answered.

"The man looked fairly startled.

" 'Do you mean it?' he inquired.

" 'Of course I mean it,' was my reply."

He would describe, too, the odd people and circumstances he discovered when he went all round inquiring what each employee received and did. "One old fellow said he was 'night petty cash man'. He had to be there every evening prepared to pay out money for expenses to any correspondent or reporter who might be sent off suddenly to a distance. 'Does this happen frequently?' I asked him. 'Oh, no,' he said. 'Oh, no.' 'When was the last time you had a call made on you?' 'Some years ago, I think; yes, some years ago.'" He makes kindly provision for the old fellow and he always admits that nothing discovered in *The Times* office equalled the strange story of Beer Tickets which came to light when Pearson bought the *Standard*. "It was the custom to give to any person who delivered a letter or parcel at the *Standard* office a ticket which could be exchanged for beer at a saloon close by. This was so valuable to the saloon-keeper that he made no end of a fuss when he heard the tickets were to be done away with, and he had to be compensated by Pearson, pretty heavily, too!"

So, enjoying humour wherever he finds it, easing the strain of constant effort by treating the whole thing every now and then as a joke, Northcliffe takes up this fresh burden. Now he makes his 6 a.m. notes on *The Times* as well as his other papers. Soon he will spend much of his day in his room at Printing-house Square. In the struggle for its possession he was easily victor. The struggle to rebuild its fortunes, to put it on a secure foundation, is going to be more severe and protracted. He will succeed here also, but not until his life nears its close.

CHAPTER IX

NEWFOUNDLAND AND THE CONQUEST OF THE AIR

λέγειν τι καὶ ἀκούειν καινότερον.
(*To tell and to hear of some new thing.*)

ACTS OF THE APOSTLES, XVII. 21

SHOULD the memory of his other doings fade, Northcliffe will be recollected as the man who did much to develop the British Dominion of Newfoundland and who hastened, by princely encouragement, the conquest of the air. No record of the earliest efforts to fly can ignore him. His prizes gave a vigorous impetus to the designing and building of aeroplanes. World interest in flying was strongly stimulated by the enterprise of his newspapers in following its infant hops. Equally sure is it that no history of the oldest British colony will ever omit the creation of the Anglo-Newfoundland Development Company. This may not grow to the size and importance once imagined by Lord Rothermere. Yet its territory now includes, within twenty-five years of its purchase as virgin country, a town second only to St. John's, the capital. It has a port of its own with trade steadily growing. Among its possessions are two railways, a line of steamships, some of the largest pulp- and paper-making machinery in the world.

To trace its origin we must go back to 1902. Brother Harold in that year speaks much about the disaster that may crush their firm if there should be a shortage of paper. Paper is the raw material of their factories. They buy paper cheaply; print various matters upon it; sell it then at prices which yield large profits after all expenses have been paid. Their prosperity depends on their raw material being plentiful and cheap. Their purchases are larger than those of any other publishers. Upon the foundations laid by *Answers* fifty periodicals now issue weekly, fortnightly, monthly, from the Amalgamated Press. Their newspapers must be fed night and day, week-days and Sundays. Can they afford, asks Brother Harold with habitual gloomy emphasis, to risk paper being "cornered" against them, to risk diminution of supply from other causes? Asked what he proposes, he shrugs his shoulders. "We ought to have a supply of our own", he declares. Just the idea to fire Alfred's imagination.

"Why not? We'll buy forests, cut down trees for pulp, put up the finest paper-making plant you can think of. The question is, Where?"

He goes forward so fast that Brother Harold draws back a little. It is settled, however, that an emissary shall be sent forth to search the globe for suitable forest land. Northcliffe considers himself now committed to this vast enterprise. The resolve to take in hand so momentous a scheme, entirely unlike any other of his enterprises, marks him infallibly down a Great Adventurer. The swift realization and success of it prove his possession of very rare constructive ability.

The emissary travels, travels, travels. He visits Norway, Sweden, Russia, Finland. Canada he searches through and through. He tries Newfoundland; there discovers what he is looking for. Fir and spruce in abundance, a mighty river down which the logs can float, falls that can be harnessed, made to provide power for the machines. It is an act of faith to discern in these untrodden wilds factories, mills, power-stations, means of transport, population. The commonplace mind would boggle at it. Northcliffe's is aglow with enthusiasm. Brother Harold makes calculations, goes to Newfoundland himself, finally agrees that the right spot has been chosen. In 1904 they receive a Government lease for 198 years over 2,300 square miles, a territory about as large as the State of Massachusetts, larger than the English counties of Sussex, Surrey, and Kent. At once they begin work on it; very soon Northcliffe must go over to see how the surveys, the clearing, the lumbering, the saw-milling, the farming, the railroad-making, the dam-constructing get on. How difficult the task of colonizing so far from home his journey shows. Having arrived at the eastern end of Canada, he has to wait there at North Sydney until the boat for Port-aux-Basques comes over. Its running is irregular, especially when ice is coming down the Saint Lawrence River, across the mouth of which it runs. After two days' wait comes an old whaler, steel-shod, and ten miles out her stout sides are being tested by the masses of ice that crash continually against them. All night she steams dead slow, grinding through the floes, buffeting the hummocks, some of them twenty feet thick.

He finds it a grand sight: ice on every side as far as eye can see, so continuous that it looks like a solid mass, under a sullen, cold sky. He enjoys the evening meal of fresh cod and asks whether this can be the same fish as the tasteless, stringy stuff that is known as cod elsewhere. Some of the party play bridge in a snug little deck-house. He plays no card games, goes to bed early, to be half-awakened now and then by noises louder than usual when the ship drives a huge chunk of ice before it or goes astern to find clearer water where the drift is not too thick and dangerous to be fought outright. The passage should be made in eight hours; it lengthens to nineteen. Only at breakfast-time, in a bitter wind, can the snowy shores of Newfoundland be seen, and this the month of May!

At Port-aux-Basques—a small rocky harbour with a few huts perched here and there above, a few fishing schooners sheltering under the cliffs—waits the train which runs across the island. It has sleeping- and dining-cars, it offers warmth and comfort, yet he never forgets the disagreeable sensations of his first journey in Newfoundland. The train sways and heaves and jolts and rolls. No ease is possible. Impossible even to sit still. He is told that passengers are often sick; does not feel too sure about his own stomach. That uncertainty is not allowed, however, to dull his interest in all that is passed on the way.

Not that there is much to be seen. No towns, only scattered villages, where the wooden dwellings are of simplest, plainest construction. The people strike him as being still half frozen. They look as if their energies had been exhausted by the effort of keeping warm through their long winter. They have, he comments, a stiff, awkward air which suggests that they are but partly thawed (it is really due, he learns, to the many layers of under-clothing they wear!). Their faces seem to him pleasant and childlike under mops of yellow hair. They look immensely strong. They are friendly when he talks to them in his lively, bantering way. He likes them, indeed, better than the scenery. From the car windows Newfoundland appears desolate, dreary. The sparks from the locomotives have burnt all the trees within sight. Trunks of pine and fir stand up white and corpse-like, the soil is littered with branches, charred and bleached. It resembles some ancient battle-field strewn with the bones of long-forgotten combatants. Towards evening the sun breaks through, puts a sparkle on lake and river, gives the hills a golden background, which flushes deeply red as dark comes on and throws over the magnificent Bay of Islands a tender glow.

Soon after four in the morning he leaves the train with relief. He has arrived at Grand Falls, the town that is to be, site of the pulp- and paper-mills. Only two years ago this was virgin forest. Already there are numbers of houses going up to replace the shacks in which the working-parties have lived so far. Not houses of the kind seen from the train, but pleasant, picturesque houses with red or brown or green wood-shingle roofs and well-proportioned gables and eaves. There are offices with busy clerks and cashiers. There will soon be a school, there will soon be a shop. He walks about delighted with everything, asks shrewd questions, wants this and that explained.

He makes many suggestions for the convenience and comfort of the settlers. Newfoundland no longer seems the barren, useless country which it looked from the train, habitable only on the coasts where fishermen live. Its possibilities have been revealed. If such a change can be wrought in so short a time here at Grand Falls, why not elsewhere? He tastes the joy of colonizing, of winning from Nature land for the service of Man. This, he reflects, is the best kind of work there is. These people are making things, solid, lasting things. They are up against realities. In an old country like England the chief occupations are spinning cobwebs, worrying over problems which don't really matter, devoting strength and skill to petty ends for the sake of immediate gain. In a new country, above all in a new settlement won from the bush, great bases for eternity are being laid. The gifts of vigour and ingenuity are turned to their finest use.

From the windows of the Log House where he stays he can look down upon the great wooden dam-construction towers. There are the Falls, there is the water swirling, foaming, thundering over the red sandstone, around green fir-covered islands of grey volcanic rock, hurling itself at last with immeasurable force over a ledge with a drop of 120 feet. "White coal", he says gleefully; "never at any time of year less than forty thousand horses." And there are the workers on the dam preparing the harness for them.

All around is primeval forest, broken only by a few paths which Indians and trappers made. Under his eyes is a busy ant-hill of human activities. The earth is made to yield her increase, food for man and beast. The plough turns up land that has never been trodden save by feet of forest animals—fox, caribou, bear. Roads are forming. The engines puff to and fro with self-important snortings. The saw-mill stack sends out its white smoke all day long; inside the mill big trees are being converted with uncanny swiftness and dexterity into smooth planks. Every now and again there is a shrill whistle of warning, then a bang and a shower of rock fragments—another obstacle to the taming of the Falls has been blasted out of the way. At regular intervals a hooter, calling the workers together or setting them free, fills the "streets" with hurrying footsteps. At night the hillside is thick with homely lights. Never, he declares, has he felt before the power which money confers, never has he known the joy of creation as he learns it here.

At dinner with the heads of departments (two of them Scots, canny and cheerful; one a man from Maine, humorous, lean, lithe) he is in the highest good humour. They are struck with respectful admiration by his quick grasp of the nature of their tasks; by his habit of listening quietly, then going to the heart of a matter without hesitation. They are not less delighted by his fun and friendliness, by his total freedom from the airs of the "great man". On all he leaves the same impression. His presence has a bracing, tonic effect. "I could live happily here all the rest of my life, if it weren't for the midges", he avers. But he does not stay long. Other interests call him. He is restless, his moods are incalculable. He absorbs so rapidly, he is so soon ready to turn his mind to fresh combinations. Yet he speaks candidly when he says that no enterprise has given him the same wide satisfaction, the same sense of mastery, the same certainty of value. When he gets home, he talks about nothing else. He wants to send all the principal members of his staff out to see Grand Falls. To one or two it seems a pity that he should immerse himself again in the affairs of newspapers, magazines; should fall to discussing stunts, appraising the merits of a serial story, criticizing the pictures in *Comic Cuts*. His spirit for the moment has been finely touched to a fine issue.[1]

He will never lose the glow of satisfaction that this great adventure in a new field has given him. He is a bigger man for it; his mind has been widened, his grasp enlarged. Yet he takes up again with content the daily round of his old preoccupations. He does not to the full appreciate, as Brother Harold can, the magnitude of their new undertaking, how it towers above *The Daily Mail, Answers,* the *Sunday Companion, Home Chat*.[2]

Yet he perceives more clearly than any of his associates, more clearly than any of his editors, the far-reaching possibilities of the flying-machine, as well as its value to an enterprising newspaper man. He is the only newspaper

---

[1] "Spirits are not finely touched but to fine issues."—*Measure for Measure,* Shakespeare.

[2] The supply of paper from Grand Falls began in 1910. Sixty thousand tons are manufactured every year. Twenty-five thousand tons of pulp are made and shipped for use in England. A million and a half trees are felled yearly, and all the time planting goes on, so the forests renew themselves. In every way the Development Company has been a triumphant success.

man in England who has these perceptions. Like all who think ahead of their time, he is laughed at, sneered at. He pays no heed, though, for he understands both the power of the petrol-engine and the eagerness of the public for something fresh to talk about, some new thing to stir its imagination. His own is joyously stimulated by the efforts of the earliest aeroplane pilots. From the moment in 1906 when he watches the Brazilian, Santos-Dumont, leave the ground on a November day near Paris and remain in the air long enough to cover seventy yards, he says boldly that the conquest of the air is at hand. He offers then and there a prize of £10,000 to the man who first flies in an aeroplane from London to Manchester. Ridicule fills the air. Hardly anyone thinks he is serious. As usual, he is charged with merely seeking to attract attention to his business. He pays no heed to sneers or sarcasm. He nods his head calmly. He knows that he is right about flying, as he was right about the automobile.

When in 1896 he founded *The Daily Mail,* the English mind was as sceptical about the gasolene motor and the revolution in road traffic which that was to effect as it is sceptical now in 1906 about the aeroplane. In the first number of the *Mail* he urged the repeal of the law which "made England lag far behind Continental countries in the latest development of road traffic". This law ordained that no mechanically propelled vehicle should travel on the roads at a speed of more than three miles an hour. Further, it forbade any such vehicle to travel at all unless a man with a red flag walked in front of it. It is hard now to believe that it was the work of years to induce the rulers of Britain to abolish these restrictions, intended to apply to steam-rollers and traction-engines. Those who, like Northcliffe, demanded their abolition were obliged to do it warily.

Thus the article in the first number of the *Mail* assured lovers of the horse that "they need not be jealous of the homely little petroleum-engine which disputes the road with their favourite. The motor-carriage will never displace the smart-trotting pony or the high-stepping team." Northcliffe knew that there were enough influential people in the country to delay the change in the law if they thought that "the smart-trotting pony and the high-stepping team" were to be displaced by automobiles. He did not want them to think that, so he dissembled his certainty of its happening and defended the gasolene-driven carriage by a plea which could not fail to move horse-lovers. "It will end", he wrote, "the cruel labours of the poor equine drudges that strain before omnibus and dray, and save the broken-down favourite of the Turf from the bondage of the nocturnal cab."

This wily tactic broke down opposition. In a short time he was able to take over to England the Panhard-Levassor car which he had bought in Paris and kept there. With its six horse-power it could do twenty-five miles an hour. Most of his friends smiled at it, and at him, but his faith in the new invention never flagged from the time when he mounted one of the first motor-bicycles and felt the exhilaration of making it go. "It is true", he would say, smiling, "that, having made it go, I could not get it to stop. I was trying it on a race-course. Somehow I ran through the fence at the side and found myself in the middle of a meadow. I was lucky to get off without harm. A Frenchman who tried it next day had a spill. The thing caught fire and he was killed." That did not in the least discourage Northcliffe. His early attachment to bicycles and road-touring disposed him to see in the gasolene-driven vehicle a natural development of the pneumatic-tired "safety". He wrote one of the earliest books on motoring (*Motors and Motor-driving,* Badminton Library, 1902). He gave great help to the motor trade, always had the latest thing in cars, helped his country to make up the ground lost at the beginning by its slowness to admit change. Now, in 1906, he is determined that Britain shall not, if he can help it, be left behind in the conquest of the air.

It requires courage to tell people that they must take these "aviators" seriously. For every one person who admits that flying in heavier-than-air machines may be possible there are a thousand ready to demonstrate with figures and diagrams that it can never be done. His prize of £10,000 is treated either as advertisement or joke. Anyone who predicts that in a few years' time the prize will be won is regarded as a fool. Next year, however, come strange reports from a place on the coast of America, where two brothers named Wright are said to be making experiments with a machine which really does fly. This is 1907. The year after that these brothers are acknowledged to have solved the problem. When they go to Europe to show what they can do, Northcliffe, you may be sure, is one of the earliest to welcome them. He makes the acquaintance of Orville and Wilbur Wright and their sister at Pau. Wilbur amuses him immensely. Men with the most resounding names in the world are flocking to this impromptu flying-ground. Kings, princes, and governors; statesmen, financiers, captains of industry—all want to see the miracle, all want to shake hands with the first men to fly. Orville bears his honours prettily. Wilbur hates the whole thing. One day it is announced that King Edward VII of England is to be among the visitors. "Of course, Wilbur, you must wear gloves", says the sister, anxious that her brother shall do the right thing (so Northcliffe delighted to tell the story). When gloves are bought and have been with many protests put on, Wilbur is the most uncomfortable man in France. The gloves seem to paralyse him. Not until Majesty has taken its departure and his hands are free once more is Wilbur himself again.

Northcliffe likes the brothers, admires them, gives them full credit for their patience and ingenuity. But he sees they have a weakness which will prevent their going much farther. They believe that their machine is the last as well as the first word in flying. They maintain that their cumbersome arrangement for starting—a platform, a weight, a pulley, a chain—must always be used. "Absurd!" says Northcliffe. "That will be done away before twelve months are over." And so it is. "The French are the people who will go ahead in this flying competition", he prophesies. He knows the French well. He is fond of France. He respects their quickness of intellect, their skill with machines. His prophecy comes true. In the summer of 1909 it is a Frenchman, Blériot, who wins the £1,000 prize which Northcliffe has promised for the first crossing of the English Channel. Another Frenchman, Hubert Latham, is his rival; he flies in a graceful monoplane, an Antoinette designed by one Levavasseur. He camps on the top of the cliff not far from Calais, the cliff under which the Channel Tunnel works once were. Blériot, with his monoplane, not so fair to look on, rather a home-made contraption, is at a village on the flat nearer to the town. To Dover is but twenty-one miles, yet there must be still air, no breath of wind stirring, before they will attempt it. Newspaper men from many lands rush to and fro between the camps. The world watches eagerly. Which of the two will make the earlier start?

On a Sunday morning—it is high summer—there is every prospect of a windless dawn. Blériot has given the word late at night that he is ready. Latham goes to bed, trusting Levavasseur to rouse him if the chances look good. A while before sunrise Levavasseur rolls out of bed, looks out of window at the sea. He is sleepy. The air is cool, even chilly. "Not to-day", he says to himself; goes back to bed. An hour later Latham wakes, hears the noise of a propeller, runs to the window, sees Blériot's machine disappearing into the light haze. The professional has beaten the amateur. Afresh is vindicated the wisdom of the saying: "Never trust anybody to do for you what you ought to be doing for yourself."

Latham is a young man of leisure. He has sought adventure by hunting in desert and jungle. He has taken up flying as a sport. Blériot is a hard worker, always has been. He has done well out of the lamp he invented for automobiles. He has gone into aeroplane building as a business. He trusts nobody to decide for him when he shall set forth. On the shore lies his monoplane. He has been hoisted into it, for he has an injured foot. He is waiting for the moment at which the sun is timed in the almanacs to rise (the crossing must be made between sun-up and sun-down). Just before he is given the sign by the correspondent of *The Daily Mail,* he leans down and asks his great friend Leblanc, "Tell me, whereabouts is Dover?" ("Où est Douvres?") There is a gasp of surprise from the newspaper men standing round. Leblanc waves his hand. "C'est là-bas", he answers. ("It's over there.") The mechanics swing the propeller and the machine runs. Runs, rises, drops, rises again, lifts into the air. In twenty-five minutes Blériot is nosing along the cliffs of England, trying to find Dover. He has struck the coast ten miles too far eastward. Such a casual affair was flying in those experimental days!

The instant Northcliffe hears of the winning of his **prize,** he hits upon the surest means of securing publicity for his paper. He says, "Send out invitations for a lunch at which Blériot will be my guest of honour. Send them to all the important people in the country." How soon? he is asked. There must be time to get the replies. Should it be the middle or the end of the week? "Middle or end?" he repeats, as if the words were unfamiliar to him. Then snaps out, "To-morrow!" (*There is no such word as impossible in our vocabulary.*) The next day the lunch takes place. Large numbers of important people attend, also many of *The Daily Mail's* most faithful advertisers. "Must have them", he said. "They'll be impressed no end." The office chuckles over this Alfredian touch.

A few weeks later he goes to Rheims for the world's first aviation contests. The French have taken the lead, as he predicted they would. He hires a house in the Champagne city, makes friends with the aviators, is hailed as the man who alone among the great ones of the earth believed in and assisted the Conquest of the Air. Within less than a year he is presenting his cheque for £10,000 to the Frenchman Paulhan, who has flown from London to Manchester. There is an unkind saying about news in *The Daily Mail:* "To-day it's a fact, to-morrow it'll be a rumour." Here, says Northcliffe, with his expansive smile, is a *Daily Mail* rumour, one which has been derided and condemned, turned into fact!

Not less dramatic than the Blériot-Latham rivalry is the competition between Grahame-White and Paulhan for the honour and profit of being first to make this two-hundred-mile flight. The Frenchman generously promised that he would not attempt it until the younger antagonist had tried his luck. One morning at dawn Grahame-White leaves London and gets as far as Lichfield in Staffordshire before the wind compels him to descend. He leaves his machine to be looked after by his mechanics. That evening and the next morning are unfavourable, but in the afternoon the weather grows so much calmer that a fresh start is resolved on. Grahame-White drives out to the field where he came down. Just before he gets there he is met by his mechanic, whose glum face warns him of bad news. The machine was not securely pegged down. A gust of wind has tilted it and broken a wing. The same lesson that Latham had to learn so painfully has been taught to the Englishman. Ten thousand pounds is the cost of it to him.

Paulhan now makes ready for his effort. He is at Hendon Aerodrome, to the north of London. Grahame-White, eager for another attempt, is at Wormwood Scrubs, to the west. They are watching one another, waiting for the wind to drop. One evening Grahame-White decides to lock up his machine and go home. But before he has got far he is stopped by the news that Paulhan is in the air. Back he goes, catches the mechanics, has his biplane dragged out, hastily starts in pursuit. Dusk finds him at a village in Northamptonshire, where he saw a suitable field for landing. Soon the village is invaded by newspaper men who have followed in automobiles. They discover him at the doctor's house. All are made welcome. The airman's mother and sister arrive. Everyone is fed; Grahame-White sleeps. He has determined to be off again before it is light. That, he reckons, is his only chance of passing Paulhan. The Frenchman is some seventy miles farther on; by starting at dawn he can be fairly sure of completing his journey. The one hope left to the Englishman is in making his start during the night. It is a desperate resolve. No one has yet flown in the dark. Fortunately he has the lights of the railway track to guide him when he rises into the air. After that he must trust to being able to follow the glint of the rails in the dim moonlight. There is an awed silence when he gives the word to let the machine go. Then his mother's voice says, "God keep you, my boy", and all the villagers, all the newspaper men, cheer. He disappears in the night.

When he comes to the spot where his rival had rested, he descends to make some small repair. There he hears that Paulhan has reached Manchester. Follows another luncheon, with the same important people, the same advertisers. Yet another Frenchman wins the 1911 prize of £10,000 in a Circuit of Britain Race. But when the third £10,000, offered in 1913 for the crossing of the Atlantic, is claimed in 1919, two Britons are the successful competitors (Alcock and Brown). Northcliffe's education of his countrymen had done its work. The British supremacy in the air during the war proved that in construction, in airmanship, in enterprise, England had little to learn and a great deal to teach. Now, urged Northcliffe, let it gain the same supremacy in peace. The accomplishment by two Britons of the first air voyage from America to Britain was one of the last unclouded satisfactions of his life.

CHAPTER X

THE YEARS BEFORE THE WAR

The greatest transforming force that has appeared in British journalism.

THE REV. DR. W. ROBERTSON NICOLL

MIDWAY between forty and fifty, then, Northcliffe has established himself with a reputation spreading wider than that of any Englishman of the age. He has achieved a world fame something akin to that of Edison. At home his newspapers are read both by the ruling, comfortable few and by the toiling many. His name is familiar to Americans. Into all parts of the continent of Europe he pushes his Paris edition. He is popular in France. In Germany he is feared and disliked. Already he has begun that campaign of warning and denunciation which is to prepare the public mind for war.

He is not a war-monger as are those who eagerly anticipate a clash between Britain and Germany. In one of his satires, issued soon after the clash had come, the humorist, E. V. Lucas, wrote as an entry in a journal:

August 4, 1914.—War declared. Lord Northcliffe has his teeth sharpened.

That was a view which many shared. He was supposed to exult in the fulfilment of his prophecies. But in truth he had no more personal feeling about this than he had about other public matters. Indeed, when the war came close, he believed it might still be prevented. One who saw him in mid-July 1914 said to him: "There will be war." Northcliffe replied, "Do you think so? We shall try to keep the peace; we, let us trust, shall keep the peace."[1]

At this time he appeared to the same unfriendly observer to be "restless, resolute, devoid of calm, with clear but unpiercing eyes, and hair that gave the impression of a scratch-wig". But if he seemed externally "devoid of calm", he was inwardly quite other than that. By this time his temperament has steadied, solidified. He dwells in a calm which is like the calm of natural, unconscious things—a tree, a stream, a field. He does not exult when his predictions are fulfilled; he does not complain when his plans go awry. His mental temperature varies little. He is seldom downcast, seldom uplifted. His confidence in his own judgment, or, to put it another way, his belief in his star, is so complete that he impresses it on others. No vanity makes this belief laughable, no aggressiveness in it stirs hostility. He speaks as an oracle with the quiet certainty that he is always right, yet without a trace of bombast or conceit. He claims no credit; he but speaks what is revealed to him. Thus he predicts war because he has a conviction that it must come. He has not reasoned this out, will not argue his position (he never does argue). He is a fatalist. Certain things appear to him to be bound to happen. This is one of them. Useless to try to prevent it from happening. The only thing he can do is to stir up a sense of the inevitable and urge Britain not to be taken unawares.

This illustrated the curiously static nature of his intellect. In action he is dynamic, always on the move. There is no corresponding restlessness in his thought. His mind is like a placid sea, broken into waves only where it reaches the shore. Upon the business, the plans, the adventures of to-day and to-morrow it hurls itself in breakers of

[1] *Mr. Walter Sichel's Reminiscences.*

irresistible energy. Beyond these stretches a flat, undisturbed surface. So far as may be he puts away from him all matters that cannot be settled on the spot by swift resolve, or after brief consideration, with vigorous action to follow. He takes no interest in thinking which is not practical, which is not to have immediate result. Having decided that war is unavoidable, he spends no time on reflecting whether it can be avoided. He does not concern himself with what the Government may be doing. It does not seem to him to matter what any Government or any individual might do. The thunder-cloud is there, the storm will burst over us. His business to urge that his countrymen provide themselves with protection against it. So he follows Lord Rosebery (with whom he has much intercourse) in warning the nation not to be misled by "the calm before the storm".[1] So he backs up Lord Roberts's futile plea for Universal Service; publishes a warlike pamphlet by the one-time Socialist idol, Robert Blatchford; keeps the peril to the front—without, however, letting it detract attention from horse-racing, flying, football, cricket, and other diversions.

It is not easy to get up excitement about the German Peril. Now and then a stunt is worked to arouse interest in some or other aspect of it. For example, a book is published on the subject and falls flat. When Northcliffe hears of this, he says, "The book shall sell." He draws up an outline of an article about it. He calls it "the book that will not sell". Agony of author and publisher! Why advertise the reluctance of the public to buy it? This will destroy any chance it might have had to win favour. Northcliffe nods his head. He knows what he is doing.

The article tells of a writer ideally qualified for his

[1] "This calm before the storm is terrifying" (Lord Rosebery, July 9, 1909).

task. It tells of a publisher certain that the book would make a sensation. Yet it has attracted scarcely any notice. It is written in attractive style, it is concerned with a danger which at any moment may fall upon the country, on every man, woman, and child in it. Why won't people buy it? Famous folks have read it and praised it. There is every reason why it should sell, but it will not. What is the explanation? Send your idea on a post card to the editor and you may win a hundred pounds. That is the prize offered for the solution which seems most probably correct. There is an immediate demand for the book: it is widely talked about, its popularity is assured. Northcliffe smiles, he knew it would be. "The public", he says, "can be made to take an interest in failure as easily as in success. All depends on how it is done." Did he not, after the disaster of the *Mirror's* false start, tell in its pages, "How I lost £100,000", meaning the money he spent before the paper appeared? So he scores hits on two targets with the same shot, proves how the *Mail* can sell a book and directs attention to the German menace.

While he thus waters seeds of distrust in one direction, he is doing all he can to encourage growth in the plant of friendship between the British and American Peoples. He has the advantage of knowing the United States and their inhabitants as few Englishmen know them. Since 1894, when he paid them his first visit, he has crossed the Atlantic many times, made troops of American friends. He has never committed the error of talking and writing as if the two nations were connected by a close blood-relationship. "Cousins," he says one day testily, "no more cousins than Chinese and Japanese! Our cousins are the Germans. That's why we can't get on with 'em." With Americans he has always got on very well indeed. The total absence of pomposity or awkwardness from his manner won their liking. His quick perceptions and the freshness of his ideas delighted them. Interviewers who approached him were not sent empty away. He had a fellow-feeling for them. He had been in their position himself. Also he knew the uses of publicity. Thus it happened that the American newspapers featured him prominently and the American People came to regard him with friendly interest.

In 1901 his name went all over the Continent as editor for one day of the New York *World*. On the first morning of the Twentieth Century he was to have the opportunity to show what was his conception of a Twentieth Century newspaper. The staff of the *World* were inclined to look upon the experiment as a joke. Most of them appeared in evening dress. He treated the occasion seriously. He told them he intended to alter the size of the paper, to make it much smaller, more convenient to hold and easier for quick reading. The size he chose was that which he adopted three years later for the *Daily Mirror*. The style which he asked the staff to follow was that of what he called "tabloid journalism". No piece of news was to be given at greater length than 250 words. No pictures were admitted, which showed that for once his instinct was faulty: he did not foresee that tabloid treatment of newspaper topics would cause a desire to grow for "something to look at" in place of "something to read".

The *World* which he produced had points which readers praised, but his demonstration of belief in the "portable, pocketable, logically arranged" newspaper did not win converts among American publishers. There already the newspaper had become first and chiefly an advertising sheet, which requires reading matter in order to carry its advertisements—that is to say, to induce people to buy it

—but is not issued for the sake of the reading matter, as newspapers once were. This system leads to the size of newspapers being increased so that they may accommodate more and more advertisements. It reached England in due course. Northcliffe, being a journalist, struggled against it—in vain. During these years before the war he protests frequently against the "swamping" of the *Mail* by the progressive enlargement of the space given up to advertisements. He cannot reconcile himself—he never does—to the new view of the newspaper as a purely commercial proposition. He had to retreat before it because it was immeasurably more profitable than the old way; he did so with misgiving. He made advertisement managers more important than editors, paid them more money, secured for them more consideration. In his position he could do no other. But his interest was in newspapers as newspapers, not as advertising sheets. His attachment was to journalism as a profession, not to journal-producing as a trade.

That was why American publishers smiled at his tabloid New York *World;* it would not suit them at all. But the incident fixed him in the American imagination. Henceforward he was listened to with even more attention in the United States than in his own country. When he took his mother there in 1908, they were invited to the White House by President Roosevelt. The legend went forth that the two men formed an instant friendship, which is supposed to have lasted throughout their lives. They were in truth too much alike to enjoy one another's society. Both superficial in most of their judgments, both impatient of contradiction, both gifted with the dramatic temperament, they clashed instead of flowing together. Both were fascinating to everybody else; on each other they jarred. Yet they shared many opinions about the American people

—opinions which Roosevelt was glad to see uttered by Northcliffe, since he himself was barred from expressing them.

Northcliffe did not hesitate, for example, to call Americans "white Chinese". He deplored the "standardization of personality" which he noticed as a feature of their national development. Outwardly and inwardly, he saw them becoming, from end to end of the Continent, more and more alike. "They cut their hair in the same way, eat exactly the same breakfasts, tie up the small girls' curls with precisely the same kind of ribbon fashioned into bows exactly similar. In every way they all try to look and act as much like each other as they can." He was fond of the story told to him by one of his special correspondents as an illustration of this. This man arrived in Washington about the middle of September. The weather was brilliant, hot. He wore his lightest suit and a straw hat. Going down town with an American friend he heard some hooting as they passed a crowd waiting outside a newspaper office for baseball results. "Have they got some result they don't like?" he inquired. "Is that why they're hooting?" "No," his friend replied, "they are hooting you. You see, no one wears a straw hat here after"—he mentioned some date in September—"and you're wearing one to-day."

Northcliffe did not hesitate to tell Americans that he considered this desire for uniformity deplorable. "I believe in individuality", he said. "I do not believe in standardizing human beings. I believe that one of the reasons why so small a country as Great Britain maintains so vast a place in the world is that we produce individualities. Scotland has never had a population of more than five millions, yet the highly individualized Scotsmen are to be found at the top in all parts of the world."

Another apprehension of Northcliffe's which Roosevelt shared was caused by the dominance of Jewish business men in American commerce and finance. Neither had any prejudice against the race. Both liked and trusted individual Jews. But they feared for the traditions which inspired early settlers; they doubted whether America could Americanize Orientals before they managed to Orientalize her. On this subject Northcliffe made no public remark; in private he did not conceal his opinion that Jewish communities, keeping up their old habits of life, their old exclusiveness, were against the interest of modern States. He enjoyed joking about Jews as much as he enjoyed joking about Scotsmen. He professed to be able to discover traces of Jewish descent in many public men who did not acknowledge it. Some people believed this amounted to an obsession with him. They did not understand that it was more than half due to his playfully mischievous schoolboy humour. His satire was especially sharp against those who attempted to disguise their race, usually by pretending to be Scotch. He said to someone whose name was, let us say, Stewart Hamilton, "I'm sure you must be a Jew; you've got such a Scotch name." But he had many Jews in his employment and thought highly of them, to some became warmly attached. Charles Benham was one of these. He has related how Northcliffe at Sutton Place one day pointed to another of them and said, "That is the noblest Jew I ever had in my employment."

He had himself no religion in the ordinary sense of the term. He went to no place of worship. He had neither curiosity nor anxiety about a future life. Yet he had a simple, genuine respect for any belief that was sincerely held. Nothing was more obnoxious to him than making fun of things sacred to others, even if these others might be feeble folk and few. He admired, too, any man who devoted himself without reward to working for kindly purposes. When he was parliamentary candidate at Portsmouth he fell in with an Anglican priest, Father Dolling, who was adored by his slum parishioners. "You can come or send to me whenever you want money for any of your charities", he said, and was as good as his word. When the priest took over a very poor district in the London Dock area, he was invited to bring a band of youngsters to camp on the cliffs near Elmwood. That camp became a yearly event. Northcliffe used to say that he enjoyed it fully as much as any of the slum children.

In the years before the war he is living partly at Sutton Place, that beautiful ancient house of Elizabeth's time, near Guildford in Surrey. It is one of the show houses of England. There he entertains, plays golf, fishes, builds himself on the top of a hill a hut to sleep in, while his wife makes the gardens exquisite, puts on the house the stamp of personality. In London he has left Berkeley Square for Saint James's Place, which is no less fashionable and quieter. But he still likes to be at Elmwood better than anywhere else. He can work there uninterrupted in the work-room built during the early days of his success. He can take his big setter, Sport, down to the beach for a swim, though he does not care for one himself. He plays lawn tennis sometimes, has golf within easy reach; but he regards games as duty rather than pleasure. If he has for partner or opponent anyone connected with his business, he will often betray, by sudden remark or unexpected question, that his mind is on his "dear work". His whole existence is organized for it.

He has fallen into ways which were unknown in his boyhood's home. He has adopted the habits of the rich, not in the least because he cares about proclaiming himself

Your Egyptian work was perfect

VILLA STE BAUME,
VALESCURE.
ST RAPHAËL.
VAR-FRANCE.

I have slowly seen Tyke, but I am told surely. But about you? I have asked again & again & no answer. When I read your delightful work I feel that you must be all right again, but then I know your unselfish efforts for the papers. That gull of dear people never spares himself else. How are you? Most secretly I go toward

Holt Ritz Paris

A LETTER WRITTEN BY LORD NORTHCLIFFE

for an electrical treatment on my 15th—if you should be (where everyone ought to be) in France or out come to see me I shall be very hurt. My lady goes to Sutton tomorrow. I am weary of the roses & the nightingales of Descanso & long for Fleet St or Abbd-Senter. But they are not for me.

My compliments to your lady & please remember that I am

always yours attached

N

DURING AN ILLNESS HE HAD IN 1911.

one of them, but because it is easier for him to get through his daily round of work if servants can relieve him from the necessity of thinking about anything else. He could do without a valet if he were not rich: as he is, he may as well have his clothes looked after and get the process of dressing speeded up. He has now picked up the custom of "changing for dinner". He regularly puts on evening dress, sometimes after a short sleep, and thus "makes a fresh start". He says this recovers him from fatigue, pushes aside all the cares and problems of the day. After dinner, marked by that simplicity which costs more than any display, no work, only preparation for sleep. This may be quiet talk, never on any topic likely to cause disagreement; or it may be gramophone music of a variety which musical ears find distressingly mixed. At nine o'clock or soon after, bed, and, as a rule, slumber unbroken until 6 a.m., the hour at which the reading of papers must begin. One evening a week he goes to bed before dinner and has himself read to sleep.

By this regular mode of life which he has worked out for himself, combined with the moderation that is natural to him in meat and drink, he keeps his energy at the full. Specialists, qualified and unqualified, have made much money out of him. The strain he put upon his strength by excessive toil of mind he expiated by maladies of stomach and sight. At last he seems to have these overcome, thanks rather to his own mastery of their causes than to any advice he has bought. He has tried in different periods of discomfort all sorts of diets, all varieties of treatment. One doctor has ordered him wine and no whisky, another changes the regimen to whisky and no wine, a third allows neither. He decides for himself now. He eats what he likes, but never a great deal of anything. His dinner drink is champagne.

The improvement in health caused by exercise, which is now taken diligently as part of a cure, has smoothed and sweetened his manner. The tendency to abruptness wears off. He does not lose his temper—unless he loses it deliberately. Generous always in his impulses, he grows more thoughtful for others. He writes to one of his staff: "I did not think you looked well yesterday. You have been doing too much work, all very good work. Please take a holiday. If you are seen or heard of near the office during the next month, I shall take desperate measures. Ask for whatever money you require." To another correspondent, who has protested against certain articles being overlooked and others maltreated, he replies: "I entirely sympathize with you. None of my own efforts are ever printed—perhaps deservedly so! I have, however, taken steps which I think will prevent further machine sub-editing of the kind you complain of. The next time anything of the sort occurs, go straight to my secretary, Mr. Butes, and I will apply the pointed end of the coke hammer instead of the flat end, which apparently has no effect on the editorial skull."

Mr. Butes has come to him from Mr. Pulitzer of the New York *World*. "The best secretary God ever made", Northcliffe calls him. "I know I'm not an easy person to work for", he adds in a burst of candour. Yet he is a great deal easier than he was. Gone the devastating fierceness of his earlier energy, gone the irritability due to bad digestion. There has come in their place a large benignity of manner, a purposeful vigour shorn of violence; less flashing and more tolerant are the blue eyes. The slim figure has filled out into a man of heavy build, and as movements of body have become more deliberate, so the spirit is less subject to sudden motions of annoyance, impatience, **rage**.

Not that the energy of earlier days is abated. It is, indeed, more abundant than it was in youth. He tires out almost all who work or travel with him. In 1909 he carries Moberly Bell off to Canada and the United States. This is what Bell writes when the trip is ending:

I have enjoyed it very much, but I have a feeling that I want more rest than I did when I started. . . . He has every day some new project that must be written about and telegraphed about, and next day it is something else.

An hour ago he said to me: "Now I am going to have three days of absolute peace, nothing to read, no one to abuse, I'm going to store my batteries." Ten minutes ago he hammered at my door. "Just look at this!" showing a local paper with some figures about immigration. "We're not taking this nearly seriously enough. Wire to Cook, write to Buckle, leave letters for Grigg, try to get hold of Amery", etc.

I was rather tired of living in portmanteaux and, as we had all our baggage brought up, I spread my things about in the numerous drawers and wardrobes and meant to enjoy three days' rest. But I calculated without my host. We were all enthusiastic about the hotel, the view, the comfort, and he more than anyone else, but someone told him that the Emerald Lake was even more beautiful than this, so off we went again.

I shall be thoroughly glad to get back to my "humble home" again. I am rather satiated with new experiences, and feel as if I had eaten a very large meal rather too quickly and want to digest it.[1]

Had Moberly Bell known him better, he would not have felt so battered and worn out. He could be a delightful companion—to those who accepted his peculiarities as part of himself and were not disturbed by them. When his sudden instructions were received calmly and with appreciation of their importance (at the moment), he straightaway passed to other matters. If he saw that they caused flurry and surprise, his placidity broke up: the atmosphere

[1] *Life and Letters of C. F. Moberly Bell.*

became charged with irritation, sometimes expressed openly, sometimes suppressed—and worse when suppressed.

Into Society he still goes very little. It does not amuse him to study character, nor to exchange gossip, nor to flirt with pretty women. For social purposes "a mind at leisure from itself" is necessary. His mind knows not that degree of relaxation. If he is not energetically using it, he is deliberately slacking, giving it repose, preparing it for further activity. He finds, too, that those who would like to see him at their parties and among their guests for weekends are not above trying to get something out of him. It may not be for personal advantage, it may be to benefit some charitable cause, or to further some political aim. He dislikes this intensely.

Sometimes he is amused by the naïve efforts of humble folk to secure his help. When "an elderly Portuguese chauffeur" in Honolulu "acquainted him with a grievance against the British Government which my newspapers might take up", he thought it a good joke. But it annoys him that politicians, charity organizers, and society climbers should seek his society in the hope of getting themselves or their pet schemes puffed in the Press. As for the ordinary round of Society's occupations—the race-course, the opera, the polo match, and the like—he shudders at the thought of so boring an existence. He stands apart from it all. He is not mentioned in the "fashionable intelligence". His newspapers have an order to say nothing about him or any member of his family. Publicity of that sort he abhors.

And, as he keeps aloof from the social, so he avoids the political arena. He is content that his support should be given generally to the Conservative Party, but he is not going to be tied to any chariot-wheel. Sometimes he shows his independence in disturbing fashion, in order partly that the public may not take his opinions for granted, in order to "throw his pebble into the pool". Once he is genuinely moved about a political question, which he sees not from the political but from the national view-point. In 1911 an effort to define the rights of countries at war and of neutrals, embodied in a document known as the Declaration of London, has to come before Parliament for ratification. Naval opinion is divided. One section believes it would serve British interests. Another denounces the limitation of the right of search in neutral ships and similar restrictions as damaging. Northcliffe, siding with the latter, calls upon the directors of *The Times* to oppose the changes. They are all believers in the value of the Declaration. For the first time there is a direct clash of opinion between the chief proprietor and those to whom he has handed over the control of the paper. He has been busy on the management side. Having at the start given the staff a free hand in spending money, in the belief that they would spend it wisely, he has been disappointed with the poor result of this policy, he has set himself to the task of winning back prosperity. He has "sent almost daily telegrams to Moberly Bell, criticizing the make-up of the paper, which he had spent a couple of hours in studying before he got up, commenting on the merits or demerits of each issue, demanding endless statistics". But until the controversy over naval rights he has not come into conflict with the editorial side. Now the battle is engaged. With a flash of the spirit that will show when war comes he declares that he will be no party to ruining his country. There are solemn protests, there is talk of resignations, but he gets his way. *The Times* does not oppose the Declaration, does not support it. It keeps silence. Northcliffe is appeased.

There the one real passion of his nature, love of country, was engaged. Here is an example of his freakish delight in giving the public surprises. When the nation is discussing Lloyd George's proposals to tax the rich more severely, Northcliffe drops in one hot Sunday afternoon at the *Mail's* editorial conference. This is one of the practices he has introduced to British journalism, borrowing it from America. It is a gathering of all the editors—these are now so numerous that one of the old school, beholding them, murmurs, parodying Shelley, "Ye are many, I was one." There is the News Editor, the Foreign Editor, the Sporting Editor, the Magazine Page Editor, the Literary Editor, the Woman Editor, the Picture Editor, as well as the Editor in Chief. They meet every afternoon to display their wares, to decide how these shall be arranged in next morning's paper. Another innovation, also American by origin, is "the splash", a large heading across two columns which announces the most exciting news of the day.

From this particular Sunday conference the editor is absent. The regular leader-writer is absent. "What about subjects for leaders?" the Chief inquires. One or two are mooted, then the man who is to write them says: "Haven't we denounced the Budget too much? It is popular with the man in the street."

"Is it?" asks Northcliffe, lying back in his deep chair and studying the walls of the room.

Continues his lieutenant, "I'm sure that the objectors are few compared with the masses who think it a sound thing."

"Well," the Chief commanded, sitting up, "say so, say so."

The acting leader-writer looked at the acting editor, who nodded approval. So with due precautions the leader was written, telling the truth about the general view that there was much in favour of Lloyd George's proposals, which had until then been utterly condemned by the paper. No change of policy was foreshadowed. The article merely urged that the popularity of the Budget should be taken into account. But the effect on Conservative headquarters next morning was devastating. Was Northcliffe changing sides? How could a supporter of the Opposition admit anything in favour of a Government measure? Panic seized on the Tadpoles and Tapers. The fat in the fire sputtered and boiled. Back came the editor to take charge. The decision having come from the highest quarter, he could administer no rebukes. But the thought of what the Chief might do made him shiver. The Chief in the background smiled benignly. People that day were talking about the *Mail* more than ever.

An impulse of the same kind, springing partly from genuine desire for the truth, partly from the desire to surprise, to startle, led to a sudden outburst of sympathy with the protest against Congo atrocities. The frightful punishments inflicted by the agents of King Leopold of Belgium on natives who failed to collect rubber had been exposed by E. D. Morel. On the eve of publishing his book, *Red Rubber,* he calls at the *Mail* office. The Chief receives him, listens attentively to his story, then for half an hour questions him. "Who is behind you? Who is engineering this? What are you doing it for? Whose axe is being ground?" Morel, amused though bewildered, continues to assure him that he has no motive but those of pity and indignation. So far from gaining anything by the campaign, he has lost his employment in a shipping firm. "Very well," says Northcliffe at last, "I will review your book myself, and you shall write a leading article." *Red Rubber* is to be the talking-point of next day's *Mail*. Before they part he says to Morel, "My papers are open to you whenever you want them." But nothing more about the Red Rubber campaign appeared in any of them. Morel thinks Northcliffe has been "got at", does not understand that he was found useful on that one occasion, but is not useful any more.

Northcliffe's interest in Ireland is of a more continuous character, yet he takes no strong line about it; he doubts whether the English care much one way or the other. His own policy would be to disregard politics, to apply economic remedies. "There would be no Irish Question", he declares, "if there were prosperity in Ireland." To that he returns again and again. "Let them harness their rivers", he says, "and create white coal, as we are doing in Newfoundland. Let them encourage the building up of industries. No one but a few politicians will be any better off for the political independence of Ireland, though of course that will come. Everyone in the country will be better off when there is more employment, when more money circulates, when wages rise as the opportunities for work increase."

He can understand Protestant Ulster's unwillingness to be linked with Catholic Southern Ireland, yet his sympathy is more with the South, though often it seems as if his attitude were "a plague on both your houses". He laughs at the reluctance which he finds in all parts to let bygones be bygones. "In Ulster they talk about the Battle of the Boyne as if it happened last week, and in County Cork they will speak of Oliver Cromwell as if he had massacred their own parents or their own children." His large, practical mind, free from sentimental prejudice, free from religious rancour, detects the strong and the weak points in the pleas of both sides. He sees that the disease from which Ireland suffers is poverty. "Attack that", he urges, "and you will see a wonderful change." Unfortunately no one pays heed to his words; his papers do not drum them into the public ear. Things go from bad to worse.

Ulster raises an army. There is drilling and route-marching—what Dickens (Northcliffe remembers) called "allong-ing and marshong-ing". There are manœuvres and reviews. Carson seems to treat it all very seriously, but in an unguarded moment wonders, as he watches a parade of citizen soldiers, "what they will do when it's all over". Ulster is a frequent talking-point. Northcliffe must run over and see for himself this preparing of civil war, this open threat of rebellion against the Crown. He goes into all parts of the province, talks to everyone at the head of the insurrectionary movement, says little, might be thought to have crossed the Irish Channel more for the sake of trying famous golf courses than as an observer of events. That is his way. When he appears to be taking no notice he is seeing most. He has no doubt about the gravity of a situation which many deride as "comic opera". "Asquith ought to have nipped it in the bud", he says. "It was criminal to neglect it. The South will arm next. There will be two armies in Ireland." Before the end of the summer there are.

Yet all through these first seven months of 1914 his newspapers are making people talk far more about social and sporting events than about any affairs of State. "No problems", say the advertising managers. "Don't give readers the idea that there is anything dangerous afoot. If they are alarmed, they won't spend money. The frame of mind we want to encourage is one of faith in the future, contentment with the present, readiness to spend freely. Keep everyone cheerful. Then we can get all the advertising we require." So reports of Parliament shrink, political news is cut down, attention is focused on the agreeably trivial; tea-table topics oust subjects for serious discussion.

Northcliffe the fatalist does not think this matters. "What will be, will be." That is his belief. "Newspapers in the middle of the nineteenth century were filled with serious discussions. They contained little else. Yet we had the appalling disaster of the American Civil War, we had the tragic absurdity of the Crimean War. Certain things will happen, whatever we do."

One pleasant result of the revolution which has changed newspapers from organs of opinion earning small profits into organs of entertainment and publicity earning very large ones is, thanks mainly to Northcliffe in its early stages, an improvement in pay and conditions for most Press workers. He distributes shares to those who hold prominent positions in his business—shares which make them rich men and women. He pays his principal private secretary, his confidential assistant, a woman, not in hundreds but in thousands of pounds a year. He pays higher wages to editorial staffs and to workers on the mechanical side as well. When on his fiftieth birthday (July 15, 1915) he is handed an address signed by nearly eight thousand men and women employed by his companies, it spoke of him as "their beloved Chief", and Claud Burton wrote in his verses of congratulation

The unseen bonds that bind us all are strong

This was not flattery, there was truth in it. He had many tussles with the Printing and Kindred Trades Federation, but when the proposal for a Northcliffe Memorial was made in 1929 that organization sent out a letter recalling his "strong, practical sympathies with the benevolent and industrial aspirations of the printing trade", while the National Union of Journalists set to work to raise money with equal readiness.

This recognition of what he is doing for the material advantage of those whom he calls his "fellow-workers" in the days before the war has not yet come. That makes no difference. It is not recognition he covets. He wants everybody he employs to be comfortable. He is a benevolent despot. He will be absolute master, but all who do his will shall be well off. He pays higher wages than any other publisher, his rate for contributions is on a scale hitherto unknown. Also he introduces wherever he can a five-day week. He says that a worker, whether man or woman, will be fresher, more energetic, more nimble-minded, for a long week-end devoted to pursuits unconnected with his work. He is strong on the value of hobbies, though he still has none himself. Nor has he yet known any absorbing interest outside that which his business draws from him. The moment is now at hand for his entry into a wider field.

CHAPTER XI

THE FULLNESS OF HIS STATURE

Lord Northcliffe makes history without knowing it.
THE HON. BERTRAND RUSSELL

ALL who had more than a passing acquaintance with Northcliffe felt the power of his personality. Not all felt its charm. He could at times (it did not happen frequently) be repellent instead of fascinating. But men and women who had insight into character were impressed, whether they liked him or not, by some quality in him, difficult to define, which set him apart, which suggested that he might show greatness if occasion called for it.

So far no such occasion has presented itself. He has founded innumerable publications; he has made a large fortune, been created a peer; he has given generous aid to great enterprises. But nothing has yet stirred the deeper chords of his nature. He has been bold, magnificently bold, but always in his own interest, never for the truth's sake, never in an impersonal cause. Now there occurs an event which changes for a time the course of his career, seems likely to change it permanently. He breathes suddenly a purer atmosphere. He who had become famous and rich by pleasing the multitudes dares now to make himself unpopular. Personal interests are swallowed up by a greater interest—that of the nation.

The war liberates in Northcliffe the potential great man. It supplies him with what he has never yet experienced—

a disinterested motive. It stirs enthusiasm, hitherto expended upon material triumphs, for something that transcends the material. It awakens emotions and instincts which till now lay hid. It develops sides of his nature which hitherto had been dormant.

Up to this time he has laughed at everything, including himself. Now he has found something at which he does not want to laugh. Scarcely ever before has anything appeared serious to him. The war he sees as an affair of immense seriousness. He has predicted it, but that does not weigh with him. He gets rid in an instant, as it were, of individual pride, ambition, desire. For the first time in his life he sinks himself in the common peril, the common cause.

It may be said that all his interventions were in material issues, that he did nothing to lift minds above the poisonous fog of lies and artificial hatred, that he could not see beyond the aim of "winning the war". That is true; but who among the prominent men of the age in any country showed a more spiritual perception than he did? Woodrow Wilson had his hours of vision. No other front-rank politician or newspaper man saw the crisis otherwise than as Northcliffe saw it—or dared to own that he did.

Where the greatness in Northcliffe became evident was not in vision but in action. It has been explained that his mind concerned itself scarcely at all with matters outside the scope of speedy accomplishment. That was both its strength and its weakness. It made him able to do what he did, to be what he was. But it also set limitations to his achievement and his power. The exclusion from his thoughts of everything not concrete and practical was deliberate. Certainly the trend of his temperament pointed that way, but his absorption in the present and the immediate future was conscious, intentional. It seemed to him that was the right line for a journalist to follow.

Once he complained that he could not get through a novel because "it led nowhere". That was his feeling about fiction generally. He liked books that were informing. Fact was useful, speculation was to him waste of time. In an article about a new Atlantic liner he picked out a passage in which the writer, looking down upon the steerage passengers, wondered what destinies awaited them in America. He read it aloud scornfully. The public did not want that sort of stuff, he said; it wanted facts, it wanted to know what the ship was like. "Have you mentioned that there is a Grill Room as well as the dining-saloon?" he inquired. "No? Ah, I thought not!" The writer of the article did not defend himself. He said he would rewrite it. Instantly Northcliffe threw off the attitude of severe critic, became the affectionate friend. "Yes, my boy," he assented. "Take it away and put it right. I am sure you can."

That was his frame of mind all through the war. He wanted facts, all the facts, nothing but the facts. Useless to cover up blunders, to shield commanders who had made them. Foolish to be afraid of giving the enemy information. The enemy knew. Futile to consider what should be done when victory came. Concentrate on making victory certain. "You talk about the Peace Conference and the repatriation of the Belgians," he wrote in May 1915, to one who had urged consideration of future policy. "England's present business is to defend Calais." The threat to the Channel ports was a fact. There were plenty of other facts not less disquieting. Stick to facts! From that position no sentiment, no argument, could make him budge.

He did not rush headlong into the belief that it was, as

he called it, "our war". He weighed the reasons for and against British intervention as soon as Germany decided to fight. At *The Times* office a conference was held on that fateful Saturday the 1st of August; Northcliffe announced to the editors of *The Times* and *The Daily Mail* that according to his information the British Government was disinclined to stand by France and Russia. Powerful influences, financial for the most part, were being used to keep Britain neutral. If the Government yielded to those influences, what should his newspapers do? Wickham Steed, then Foreign Editor, later on Editor of *The Times,* said at once, "We must pull off our wigs and go bald-headed against the Government." The editor of *The Daily Mail* was of a different opinion. "Attack the Government in a moment of national crisis? Impossible! The country would never forgive us." Northcliffe nodded several times, a trick habitual with him. "There is much to be said in support of each view", he murmured. "But we ought not to be in a hurry. I think we should adjourn until to-morrow afternoon." By Sunday afternoon it was known that the Germans were on the point of invading Belgium. Now Northcliffe felt that he had a fact to go upon.

He saw, as a fact, the clash of German and British interests, the conflict of ambitions which he believed could be decided only by war. "We had to fight Spain in Elizabeth's time", he would say, "to prevent the Spaniards from dominating Europe. We had to prevent Louis XIV and Napoleon from doing the same thing. Now the Kaiser is trying it on. We have got to stop him." Those who up to the last moment hoped that "Britain might be able to keep out of it", who derided the notion of going to war "in defence of Serbia", seemed to him to be criminally ignorant. "It is ourselves we have got to defend", he maintained. "We are fighting a battle for our existence as a nation", he told Asquith in a letter written during November 1914. His aim in writing it was to urge that more pains should be taken by Ministers to make the nation understand this.

"I have been asked by the head of the Recruiting Department of the War Office", he said, "to use my many newspapers as an aid to recruiting. I think it my duty, however, to tell you that, having for some time been engaged in careful inquiries throughout England and Germany, I find that whereas there is in Germany immense enthusiasm for the war, there exist in many parts of this country apathy, ignorance, or ridiculous optimism, more especially in the provinces."

"The chief hindrance to recruiting", he went on to say, "is that whereas the German public are supplied with the work of photographers, artists, cinematograph operators, and war correspondents, our people have nothing but the casualty lists and the mutilated scraps with which it is quite impossible to arouse interest or follow the war intelligently.

"The public *cannot* be aroused by present methods, and I believe that unless the matter is taken in hand speedily you will be rapidly forced to a measure of conscription that might possibly bring about a split in the national ranks."

"A real service to the national cause", was Asquith's comment many years afterwards when he printed this letter in his *Memories and Reflections*. At the time he took rather a different view of it. He saw that it was intended to reproach him with apathy. He had not yet altogether recovered from Northcliffe's insistence on the appointment of Kitchener as War Minister when the war began.

It appeared to Northcliffe to be of cardinal importance that war should be regarded as the business of soldiers and should be left to them. A soldier, he considered, ought to be installed as War Minister. Asquith, who had taken temporary charge of the War Office, wished to put Lord Haldane back there. No doubt Lord Haldane had done well; he had let the soldiers prepare their plan for sending troops to France as soon as war broke out. The plan was all ready to be acted upon. Let Lord Haldane have credit for that. But to leave the War Office in charge of a civilian, "one who had not had even a business education", would, he contended, be insane.

So he quotes a rebuke by Napoleon to his brother Joseph, who had been interfering with the generals in Spain: "It is the greatest of all immoralities to engage in a profession of which one is ignorant." So he calls upon the Government to appoint Lord Kitchener, declares that he will agitate for the appointment if it is not made. That is not necessary. On August 4, Kitchener had received a vague note from Asquith saying the Government would be glad of his advice. On August 5 he is asked to take the post of War Minister and accepts. No one dreams that ten months later Northcliffe will be attacking him as vigorously as he has now urged his nomination.

Whatever his shortcomings as an organizer, Kitchener was right in the view that he took of the war from its start. It would be a long war, he insisted. It would be won by the last million that Britain could put into the field. Northcliffe had formed the same opinion. "You are talking nonsense", he says quietly to a member of his staff who talked about the British troops being back at home by Christmas. "We shall have two or three war Christmases, perhaps more." Quiet he is now in all that he says, in all his doing. He seems to carry a burden that has not rested on his shoulders before. That burden he is never to throw off. The schoolboy in him shrinks. A man conscious of power, and the responsibility of power, stands forth in the schoolboy's place. He has predicted this fearful event, he has helped to bring it about. He feels that the obligation lies on him to use his power so that it may turn out well.

He has no faith in politicians. He has faith in soldiers, and this, in spite of disappointments, he keeps until he is forced by "facts" to let it go. "Trust the soldiers", he told those whom he left in charge of his newspapers when he went to America. When he returned he saw reason not to trust commanders who were throwing away lives. "We don't mind being killed, but we do mind being butchered", his nephew, Lord Rothermere's eldest son, said to him before he died of wounds received at the Battle of Cambrai. Northcliffe went to the Front after that costly fiasco and was shocked by what he saw and heard. He never thenceforward had much belief in Haig. He tried in vain, however, to find any general to whom he could transfer his confidence and who could be "run" as Haig's successor. It was naturally with the men of action that his sympathies lay. He was pathetically anxious to believe each general a superman. He was unhappy when forced to let the belief go. In turn he set up as idols Kitchener, Joffre, Cadorna, Haig. Though he did not demolish them all, as he demolished the first, he was compelled to admit their feet of clay.

In one direction he is at loggerheads with the generals from the beginning. They do not allow any correspondents to be with the forces. They talk about "the fog of war". They issue statements by officer "eye-witnesses" which nobody believes or wants. Northcliffe reasons, cajoles, abuses. No result. He has correspondents in the field, of course. They are unrecognized, but they send dispatches. One day Kitchener announces in the House of Lords that they have all been cleared out. Not any remain. Two days later *The Daily Mail* publishes a message from one of its men taking up nearly a page, describing the arrival of the first British wounded at Rouen. Upon which Kitchener threatens to have the man shot if he is caught, and Northcliffe begins to wonder if Kitchener is really as big as most people suppose.

On one memorable Sunday, Northcliffe brings out a special issue of *The Times* with a mutilated dispatch giving the earliest news of the British rout at Mons. It has been mutilated by the Press Censor, F. E. Smith, afterwards Lord Birkenhead. He has, by striking out sentences here and there and leaving blanks, made it much more alarming than it was in its uncensored state. It gives England a shock. Next day in the House of Commons, Asquith solemnly denounces its publication as calculated to spread terror and confusion. Few were then aware that the Press Censor had urged its publication, saying that the message would have a good effect by making people realize the war was serious. The Prime Minister said nothing about that, nor did the future Lord Birkenhead come forward to accept responsibility. Northcliffe kept silence, but he did not forget.

Not for many months is he able to persuade the generals that correspondents at the Front would be a help to them, not a hindrance as they imagine. He goes himself to Belgium and visits the front-line as an assistant to the Chief Scout of the Belgian Army! For a few days the schoolboy is in the ascendant once more. He escapes drowning by a few inches as he is being driven from Calais to Dunkerque; the driver, having no lamps lit and the night being dark, nearly runs off a plank bridge over a dyke full of water. He is among falling shells at Pervyse. He watches an air-raid and says: "We shall have those fellows dropping bombs on London before long."

He is intensely interested by everything. He bears the jolting over rough roads with cheerfulness surprising in a man of his size and weight. He enjoys the scratch meals and the rough lodging. "There is so much happening every day", he says, "which could be told to the public and which would help to keep up its spirit." He renews more vigorously his effort to force correspondents on the unwilling generals. "If the Government wishes to avoid strikes and enlist in the country the services of the whole people, they should", he writes to Lord Riddell in 1915, "strain every nerve to make clear that the war is a matter of life and death to the nation."

Even when consent has been wrung from these unwilling soldiers, aloof from the life of the nation, strangers to the world outside their mess-rooms and their offices, they display a strange, barbaric ignorance of what war correspondents are to do. When the first batch arrives in France, Haig addresses them, telling them he knows what they want, "something for Mary Jane to read in the kitchen". However, they are there, and before long even generals are thanking Northcliffe for his persistence, admitting to him that it would have been better if his advice had been taken at the start and correspondents sent out with the troops from the first.

Even when he is working all day, and half the night sometimes (though he tries to keep up the "no work after dinner" rule), even in the midst of his most wearing campaigns for efficiency, he can make time to keep touch with his correspondent in far-off Russia. Here is a letter written in May 1915, while shells weigh heavily upon him and are just about to burst:

My dear ——,

I love to get letters from you. They always tell me something.

I am sorry to hear that the Russians are impatient with us. I do not think they can grumble at lack of recognition on the part of the British Press. Owing to the censorship, which I have now succeeded in lifting, we have heard more of actual Russian fighting than of British fighting. The superb heroism of the Russians is recognized by everyone.

If your dispatches are sometimes cut down, you should realize the difficulties of our task. Frequently, as late as one in the morning, the Press Bureau flings in six or seven columns of, let us say, Dardanelles news. The best editors in the world cannot deal with that situation satisfactorily.

The Russian *communiqués* themselves arrive ridiculously late, and I took upon myself to wire to the Russian Minister of War, urging that they be expedited. The Germans get out their *communiqués* with extraordinary speed. Their battles usually begin at daylight, and in the afternoon we always know the result, and on the whole fairly accurately—that is to say, so far as the German Main Headquarters Staff is concerned. The Russian *communiqués* are not so accurate.

The Russians are quite wrong in mistrusting Joffre. The French Army is to-day the finest fighting machine in the world. The French are very well off for officers. We are not. We did not have too many to start with, and have fewer now. I do not take a gloomy view of things, despite the bad news that is about. This is a war of character, and eventually character will win.

The war, in my opinion, has not yet begun. That is, I believe, the opinion of the Germans, about whom I hear by a very secret means practically every week.

If you read *The Times* and *The Daily Mail* leading articles, you will see very plainly what my views are. I write most of *The Daily Mail* articles myself, and have a good deal to do with the concoction of those in *The Times*.

I think we are in for a series of air-raids, and I believe that our people are under-estimating them, just as they under-estimated the intention of the Germans to torpedo the *Lusitania*.

You say you have not seen a green leaf, and I do not want to harrow your feelings by telling you how very lovely England is just now. It is, however, a tragic spring, and my wife, who is living at Sutton Place, now a hospital, says she cannot bear to look at the flowers.

I hope you will be careful of your health in the treacherous days of the early Russian spring and that you will always remember that you have very warm friends at Sutton Place and Carmelite House.

Your much attached
Chief

A few months later he writes again to the same correspondent to reassure and encourage him:

Sometimes your letters seem to indicate that you think I am dissatisfied. I hope, my dear ———, you know me well enough to know that if I am dissatisfied, I say so. Some people say I am too vigorous in saying so!

Every article that is received from you is submitted to me, but the censor "kills" an immense amount of matter. The articles from you that are "killed" I put before important members of the Cabinet, either verbally or in your writing, so that nothing is wasted.

Having been myself at the other end of a cable, I thoroughly understand the feelings that arise in a man's mind when he is away from the home office. But in your case, my dear ———, you should also realize that at the head of affairs here is one who is warmly devoted to you personally, quite apart from business relations. You also stand high in the esteem of your colleagues.

Yours affectionately,
N.

These letters serve to illustrate, not alone the close attention which he gives to all sides of his newspaper business, but his genius for getting the best work out of those whom he employs and the devotion he inspires in them.

His expressions of regard are entirely sincere. His nature has large seams of affection in it. He is thoughtful for the mental as well as the material comfort of those whom he is accustomed to speak of as colleagues. He sends frequent cables or telegrams of congratulation on good work done. If he is emphatic in his dissatisfaction, he is not less emphatic when he is pleased. "I can give you great opportunities", he says to those whom he judges worthy of trust. He is thinking, when he says this, not so much of the value their work may be to him, as of their future and of their rewards.

It is true that "out of sight" is very often with him "out of mind"—or perhaps it would be more accurate to say that though he does not forget people he will allow long periods to pass without his giving signs of recollection unless they are brought in some way to his notice. That is partly due to the absorbing character of his occupations; partly also to the predominance over his attention of the actual, the immediate, the seen.

He will pass days, weeks, it may be months, with a friend. Then by a change of circumstances they are carried, one in this direction, the other in that. It may be weeks or months before the friend hears anything from him. Not because his feeling has changed: when they come together again he will be exactly as he was before. The reason is, as one of these intermittent intimates expresses it, "when you're there, he makes you think he couldn't do without you; when you aren't there, he does without you quite well".

Yet the slightest reminder, the faintest indication that a word of friendship would be welcome, is responded to with genuine warmth. Even at times when he is grappling with most difficult decisions he can detach himself from his problem to write letters such as those which have been quoted. The earlier of the two was sent in the week before he determined to make public the truth about high-explosive shells.

The crisis caused by the lack of this kind of ammunition has been variously represented. Mr. Lloyd George has been accused of exaggerating the shortage in order to force upon Lord Kitchener his plans for munition-making on a vast scale. Lord French (then British Commander in France) has been accused of exaggerating it in order to place on shoulders other than his own the blame for an unsuccessful action (Neuve Chapelle). It has been said that the supply of high explosive was already assured when the agitation began. It has been denied that operations were ever hampered by scarcity of it. The truth is simple. There would have been no shell crisis if Kitchener's management at the War Office had been irreproachable in other directions. The indignation aroused by the deficiency of high explosive was the result of dismay at his lack of method and at the muddle created by it. What would have been in other circumstances merely a regrettable episode brought to a head all the criticism, all the irritation, all the alarm caused by his reluctance to delegate authority, by his attempt to work all strings with his own fingers.

The campaigns against the Khalifa in the Sudan which had made him famous he had organized himself entirely, from first to last. But these were campaigns against untrained troops armed with obsolete weapons and led by a religious maniac. In South Africa he had not added to his reputation save by his wise, masterly handling of the negotiations for peace. He had not, after that, the opportunity to learn that there was any mode of organization other than that which he had practised.

"Lord Kitchener was not himself an organizer," wrote a distinguished British general (Sir George MacMunn, K.C.B.), "and was in many ways profoundly ignorant of the principles on which the business of a great machine like an army must be conducted." The delay in supplying British troops in France with the shells for want of which they suffered severely was not, in the opinion of those who knew what went on at the War Office, an isolated shortcoming; it was symptomatic of Kitchener's administration.

His appointment was not regretted. He had been very useful in steadying the public nerve at the outset of the war. His name had made recruiting for the New Armies far easier than it would have been without that aid. But, while as a figurehead he had proved of great value, his continued supremacy at the War Office was held by nearly everyone acquainted with the facts to be inadvisable, even dangerous.

Kitchener, in the phrase of Lord Grey, believed the management of the war to be a one-man job. He "did not realize that the whole industries of the country must be organized for war and that this could not be done inside the War Office". Nor did Lord Grey realize it at that period, or he would have told the Prime Minister (Asquith) plainly that there must be change. Two men realized it and between them they got the change made. Those two men were Northcliffe and Lloyd George.

It was characteristic of the new Northcliffe, the Northcliffe who had come to his full stature, that he readily agreed to risk the consequences of an attack on Kitchener. Lloyd George ran no risk. It was not necessary for him to do so. He could not, as a member of the Cabinet, openly denounce another member. It was left to Northcliffe to come into the open, to draw the fire of Kitchener's admirers, to expose himself to the insults and the obloquy which were certain, he knew, to be the result for a time.

He might well have hesitated. He had himself urged Kitchener's appointment. He must now confess that his judgment of the man was wrong. He might have excused himself from damaging newspapers which were not entirely his own. Yet he raised no objection whatever to performing what he knew to be, what Lloyd George assured him to be, a public duty—and a dangerous one.

In smaller ways several times during the war he attacked men whom he had forced into office. Lord Devonport, for example, said ruefully one day to an acquaintance: "Northcliffe is a strange person. He moved heaven and earth to get me into the Cabinet" (as Food Controller) "and now he is moving heaven and earth to get me out." Northcliffe smiled when this was reported to him. "Devonport", he said, "seemed to lose all his business sense the moment he got into the Cabinet." Competence was Northcliffe's only test. "It is the last thing", he said, "that politicians seem to care about."

As happened later, when it was necessary to supersede Admiral Jellicoe, Northcliffe had to do the politicians' work for them. "You kill him, I'll bury him", Lloyd George said of Jellicoe. Northcliffe was now obliged to "kill" Kitchener. Not merely was it necessary to remedy the shell shortage; it was even more essential, he considered, to reveal Kitchener's incapacity. Orders had been given for high explosive; there would be a larger supply of it soon. If that had been the sole issue, Northcliffe would not have thought it right to disturb the public mind. But the much larger question lying behind was: Can the nation allow its effort to be weakened by Kitchener's retention of the supreme authority which Asquith had given him? So long as he had that authority Asquith would take shelter behind him. He was used "as an umbrella", said Northcliffe, "against criticism". The public belief in him must be shattered. His authority must be curbed.

Kitchener went to the War Office fully conscious of its

shortcomings. He had often talked openly about reforms needed there. A friend of his writing in 1912 (*Blackwood's Magazine*) said that his opinions were calculated to produce "a very considerable fluttering in Pall Mall dovecotes and among the old women of both sexes when Big Ben chimed out his hour of office and responsibility". That hour had chimed in 1914, but, instead of making things better, Kitchener had made them worse. Especially dangerous was his opposition to creating a Ministry of Munitions, for without a Ministry of Munitions Northcliffe foresaw endless disasters. All that he could do by bringing influence to bear on the Cabinet privately had been done. Lloyd George urged him, Lord French urged him, other soldiers in high positions urged him, to put the facts before the public. How else could the adequate manufacture of munitions be ensured? How else was it possible to prevent Kitchener from treating the war as a one-man job?

On the night when *The Daily Mail* printed it, Northcliffe sat in the editor's room at *The Times* office "with an expression more grim than I had ever seen on his face or ever saw again". So Wickham Steed (then Foreign Editor and later Editor of *The Times*) described his Chief's mood. There was cause for grimness. The exposure was certain to be savagely resented—by the people who did not know the facts. He had made up his mind, however; he would face the consequences. "I don't care", he said, "whether the circulation of *The Times* drops to one copy and that of *The Daily Mail* to two." He took counsel with only one person, his mother. She was convinced that his duty was plain. She agreed that he must speak out. "God helping you, my boy, you can do no other." The war, he knew, had "become too big for Kitchener. The public belief in him which was indispensable at the outset was now an obstacle to military progress. Therefore I did my best to shake things up." (Wickham Steed. *Through Thirty Years,* vol. ii, chap. 12.)

In the middle of the tenth month of the war (May 1915) the shortage of high explosive and its consequences —failure of British efforts, long British casualty lists— were made known. At once followed what Northcliffe had foreseen, a wave of fierce anger against him. The nation had been taught to believe in Kitchener. His name and fame had been of evident value in securing the men for the New Army without conscription. The shock of being told that he had failed in one very important direction aroused bitter resentment.

If there had been time to make the disclosure little by little, to let people get gradually accustomed to a new view of their idol, there would have been no burnings of *The Daily Mail* on the London Stock Exchange and in other places, the sale of the paper would not have dropped so dismally, Northcliffe would not have been abused and insulted. But time for that was not available. What Northcliffe felt, and said with his usual emphasis, was that lives were being lost which ought not to be lost and men maimed for life every day who need not have suffered; he did not care what happened if he could help to put an end to that.

Many people, of course, knew the facts before they were made public. Northcliffe had told to all who might be able to put pressure on Asquith what Lord French and others had told him. Thus it happened that the beginning of his open attack coincided with a change in the Government, caused mainly by the shell crisis. Attempts have been made to show that it was the resignation of Admiral Lord Fisher and not shells which forced Asquith to form a Coalition Ministry by getting rid of some Liberals and putting Conservatives in their stead. Facts do not bear this out. The Conservatives had declared their intention of demanding a parliamentary debate on the shell shortage before Lord Fisher flung out of the Admiralty in a semi-lunatic state. Asquith's own private secretary, in setting out the reasons which made a Coalition unavoidable, gave "the shell shortage disclosure" first place and the resignation of Lord Fisher second place. As Mr. J. L. Garvin has testified, "the explosion at the Admiralty would not have occurred as and when it did but for the general feeling about 'shells'".

For that general feeling Northcliffe was more responsible than anyone else. Neither soldiers nor politicians could talk about the mismanagement of the war with the freedom which he used. Lord Beaverbrook's view (in *Politicians and the War*) is that Northcliffe "did not bring the Government down—what he did was to make certain of the creation of a Ministry of Munitions with adequate powers". It was, however, the reluctance of Kitchener and Asquith to create such a Ministry which brought the Government down. Its transformation from Liberal to Coalition was in large part, therefore, Northcliffe's doing.

Far more important than that was his preponderant share in getting the whole of the industries of the country organized for munition-making. This was a change which can now be looked back on as one of the turning-points in the war. He saw the urgent need for it and, being a man of affairs, not a politician, he saw how it could be done. With his steam-hammer energy he drove the idea into the heads of all whom he could reach. When he opened the campaign in his newspapers he knew that by his exertions behind the scenes the victory was already almost won. Publicity might not have been required to make it complete if the Conservatives admitted to the

Cabinet could have been trusted to back up Lloyd George against Kitchener. But Northcliffe had as little confidence in them as he had in Asquith. His judgment was proved to be just when they refused to supersede Kitchener or transfer him to another post, which had been even in the mind of the Liberal Cabinet.

The only way to limit Kitchener's power of obstruction, to confine him to the doing of the things which he understood and did well, was to reveal to the world what had been happening. Northcliffe's resolve to do this and to take the consequences gave proof of a courage which few had suspected him of possessing. When he called his staffs together a short while after he had done it he explained without any bombast, any defiance of the public opinion he had challenged, why it had been necessary. Everyone who heard the speech he made then was impressed by the change which war had wrought upon him.

"I had never before thought Alfred capable of being serious about anything", said a man who had been with him for a very long time, as the gathering broke up. "There is no mistaking his seriousness now. He is like a man with a mission."

He was a man with a mission. His mission was the winning of the war.

CHAPTER XII

"MOST POWERFUL MAN IN THE COUNTRY"

Lord Northcliffe occupied a position apart. He not only prepared and co-operated; his was often the directing will.
                                               PRINCE MAX OF BADEN

Northcliffe did great things during the war. It must never be forgotten what he did for munitions when their supply was impeded by the menace of drunkenness among munition workers. Without him the Board of Control might not have been able to carry the necessary measures.
                                               LORD D'ABERNON,
                                   Memoirs of an Ambassador of Peace

"THE most powerful man in the country." That is how he begins to be spoken of in the year 1916. To the unpopularity which followed the attack on Kitchener has succeeded an uncomfortable, rather grudging respect. Even people who still do not like him have to admit that their judgment of him erred. In the matter of the shells he is now known to have acted from the most disinterested motive and to have acted for the best. The Asquith Government helped to rehabilitate him by their rash, vindictive prosecution of *The Times* for "publishing information which might be directly useful to the enemy". A letter had been published urging that British man-power should be used as that of France was being used. "The last of the French reserves are out," it said, "and at the present moment young raw recruits are being called up." When the case was heard by a police magistrate it was easily proved that this information had long been possessed by the enemy; had appeared in German newspapers; had been mentioned in the French Parliament and reported in the French Press. The case was dismissed; the public verdict was that it ought never to have been heard of.

Yet, although a Ministry of Munitions was now in existence and doing very valuable work, although the changes aimed at had in fact been made, Kitchener was retained at the War Office, was given the Order of the Garter (the highest honour a British Government can bestow), appeared to those who saw only the surface of things to have been affected not at all by Northcliffe's onslaught. But all who saw beneath the surface knew that much of his authority had been taken from him. He was not allowed, after the public exposure, to treat the war as a "one-man show", to stand in the way of necessary changes. His stock fell lower and lower, until, a year having passed since Northcliffe assailed him, he was asked to go to Russia on a mission as a means of getting him out of the War Office in a manner that would avoid both humiliation and reproach. He perished on the way, fortunate in the hour of his death, for by that time his shortcomings at the War Office were common knowledge.

Northcliffe, acquitted of the crimes alleged against him, now stands out as one who has refused to be a respecter of persons, who has spoken boldly on a matter of the most urgent importance, who has deserved well of his country. The view that whatever he said must be wrong gives place to the belief that anything he advocates must be right. His newspapers have an influence upon opinion so great that many deem it to be dangerous. He is credited, and credited correctly, with playing a very big part in the war drama behind the scenes. If he comes into conflict with the politicians, the mass of the nation is now on his side.

To say that Northcliffe was ever popular in England, as he was in America, would be untrue. He never entirely conquered in his own country the prejudice stirred up against him in his early days by disparagers of the New Journalism. In the United States he was better understood and therefore better liked. He was cast in a mould with which Americans are familiar. His personality was made known to them by their newspapers. His pithy sayings and amusing comments were printed from end to end of the Continent. He thus became a prominent public character, which he never was in England, not even during the war.

For this the reason was that he did not seek prominence. He was always something of a mystery. He came of a stock, the British middle class, which shrinks from publicity; he never entirely got over that shrinking himself. He was sensitive also to intellectual and moral atmosphere. If he were sure of being among people who understood and admired him, as Americans did, he became sure of himself, he expanded. Ireland had the same effect upon him, the North as well as the South, though not in quite the same degree. The English nature seemed to have the opposite effect; it chilled and slightly depressed him. Thus he remained always "the man behind the newspaper". He made no public appearances, save in connection with newspapers. His name was scarcely ever mentioned in his own Press until a late period in his life. The rest of the Press excluded it as far as possible. He was not known by sight to more than a few.

Often he would go into newsagents' shops and ask questions about the sale of this or that publication; he was very seldom recognized when he did this. Often he would pick up wayfarers in his automobile, caring little how they were dressed, giving lifts to tramps as readily as to neatly shawled and bonneted old ladies or to men going home from their work on long country roads. They rarely knew who he was. They had probably never seen a photograph or a caricature of him. He drove very frequently between London and his favourite Elmwood. Yet he could go unrecognized into inns and small hotels along that road and indulge all kinds of Haroun-al-Raschid impulses. One day he sat on a bench outside an alehouse with an old farm labourer and asked him about his life. It had not been varied or exciting. He had never been to London, although the city was but forty miles from his village. "Well, now," said Northcliffe, "if you could have anything you liked in the world, and could have it this minute, what would you choose?"

The old man looked at him shrewdly.

"Well," he replied, "I reckon I've most of what I want. My grandchildren take care of me. Still, there are times when my bacca runs short and times I'd like to have a little money in my pocket. I'd choose two pounds of bacca and some clay pipes to smoke it in, and a sovereign."

Those were the years when gold coins were still in use in England. Northcliffe produced a sovereign and gave it to him, then he sent for the pipes and tobacco. While the old fellow was trying to thank him, a woman came along, and, hearing that money had been given away, began to beg for "something to buy a meal with".

"What do you do for a living?" Northcliffe inquired in a friendly tone.

"I'm a gipsy, your honour", said the woman. "I get my living mostly on the race-courses. I sell newspapers, and sometimes I tell fortunes."

"No", said Northcliffe, when she offered to tell his. "I don't believe in fortune-telling. I'm not superstitious in any way. I've never had my fortune told."

"Nor you don't need to", she retorted. "You've always got everything you wanted. That's plain enough."

Northcliffe looked at her sharply and nodded.

"You bet, I suppose, when you are at the races?" he asked. "Of course you do. Now, tell me which of the papers gives the best tips."

She named one which did not belong to him.

"I thought *The Daily Mail* was the best", he told her.

"Was once," she replied, "but the other beats it now."

"You've told me something I wanted to know", he said, and put some silver coins into her hand. The Sports Department soon heard that story.

Another he often told was of an experience in the remote Hebrides of Scotland. He went into a tiny village store and saw children come in with eggs in their hands, which they exchanged for tea, salt, sugar or matches. The storekeeper told him that eggs were in use as currency because coin was scarce. Everyone had eggs, he said. But at that instant a little girl came in without one. She spoke to the man in Gaelic. He turned to his visitor with a grin.

"Her mother wants me to trust her with a pinch of tea", he interpreted. "The hen has no laid the morn."

It was not surprising that in the Hebrides he should be unknown, but it seemed strange that a man whose name was familiar to everybody should pass almost everywhere unrecognized. No doubt it was partly this cloak of invisibility which made his power seem so irresistible and all-pervading. That he was something of a mystery enhanced his reputation for being right so often when others were wrong. The solid basis of this reputation was the bold line he took in the Munitions crisis. Within a few weeks of the gust of rage against him the debates on the Bill to create a new Ministry for the organization of military supplies proved beyond dispute that his boldness had been necessary. It was admitted that the management of this branch of the war by the War Office had been inadequate. What he had printed was now repeated and emphasized by members of both Houses of Parliament. Lloyd George, the new Minister, did not try to hide the inadequacy. The revulsion of feeling throughout the country in Northcliffe's favour was rapid and sweeping.

He was as little elated by the nation's new mood as he had been depressed by the other. He had more important matters to occupy his mind. Now that factories were being taken over or built for the production of equipment sorely needed by the armies; now that hundreds of thousands of men and women, boys and girls were being set to work; now that the best scientific and business brains were being called upon to aid, he felt that he could turn his attention to the supply of men. On this both the Government and Kitchener were, he complained, flabby. His dislike of politicians was intensified by Asquith's shrinking from any decided step. He was sardonically amused when the Prime Minister related to the House of Commons that he had formed the Coalition as a patriotic duty, the truth being that the Conservatives, instigated by Northcliffe, had refused to support him any longer unless they were admitted to a share of Cabinet offices. But he was angry and scornful as he watched Ministers run away from the idea of conscripting labour, if that should be necessary, for the making of munitions, and shiver at the thought of compulsory service for all men of military age. From the beginning he had favoured treating all in the same way. The highly placed "shirkers" got no sympathy from him. Bluntly he told men in his own employment, men who could not easily be replaced, that they ought to be ashamed to "wait until they were fetched". He applauded the reproach uttered in the House of Lords by Lord St. Davids: "There are men here in this Chamber who have never done a day's work in their lives. There are a few even of your sons who are hanging about the theatres and music-halls and will not face the dangers of war."

Northcliffe was not content with reproaches, however. "Action, not words", was his demand, repeated day after day. He urged Conscription as a matter of common fairness as well as an urgent necessity. "Call up every man who can be useful in any capacity. Except no one for social reasons. Treat all alike." He has declared all along his certainty that this would have to be done in the end. In the end it is done, and the doing of it is attributed to his persistent agitation.

Here is the second of his campaigns for more energetic conduct of the war. He has to hammer away at this door for a much longer time than was required to get the Ministry of Munitions created. As long as possible the politicians lean their weight against it. They do all they can to discredit him. The charge is made against *The Times*. Later an attack is led by Sir John Simon in the House of Commons; it begins and ends with words. Its only result is to raise Northcliffe in the public esteem, since members who reply to the attack recall his great service in leading the Munitions agitation, in securing sufficient supplies for the British armies and those of Britain's Allies. Day after day his newspapers urge that Conscription must come and that the sooner it comes the more effect it will have in shortening the war. Day by day this view gains converts, and when it prevails at last, after many futile expedients have been tried, people say to one another: "It is Northcliffe's doing. He has been urging it all along. He has got his way now. He is the most powerful man in the country." His opponents say this as well as those who think he is right. Both point to other matters which have been dealt with as he advised.

There is the matter of the Blockade of Germany. He has pointed out continually the folly of doing things by halves. He has shown where and how Britain is allowing Germany to import large quantities of food and raw materials. At length the blockade is tightened.

There is the matter of the internment of enemy aliens who have remained in the country either from choice or because they could not get away. His demand that they be not left at liberty has met with general public agreement. He admits that hardship may be caused, he is sorry for it. But war is war. "We cannot afford to run any risks." Enemy aliens are in course of time interned.

When a strong movement is on foot for War-time Prohibition, he brushes aside the plea for the abolition of alcohol as "not the real question". The real question is: How can we speed up munitions and clear up the muddle at the War Office? The Prohibition movement fades away.

There is the question, too, of the unwieldy size of the Cabinet. How, asks Northcliffe, can twenty-three men carry on a war? No wonder that activity evaporates in talk. No wonder that it is hard to get decisions, hard to fix responsibility. Let three men, or four at most, be given control. To this also Asquith is obliged to consent. He announces that a small inner Cabinet will be formed. True, it consists of six or seven. But the nation murmurs that Northcliffe has enforced his will again.

It is not, of course, quite so simple as that. The mass of people, if they take notice of public affairs at all, see them in a dramatic light. They like to believe that an idea for improvement springs from a single brain. They imagine conflict. They must have a hero and a villain. In this drama Asquith impresses the public estimation as the senile, blundering pantaloon and Northcliffe as the brisk, resourceful clown who tells him what to do. There is this much of truth in it: Asquith is by temperament unfitted to carry on a war; Northcliffe by temperament is at his best when action, ingenuity and initiative are called for. He is the spear-head of those who want more energy, more enterprise, thrown into the conduct of the struggle. Ideas are brought to him. He has the means of bringing them to public notice. He can be counted upon to listen, to give an opinion, either to say "No good" or to promise that he will render all the help he can. In the main the measures he supports make immediate appeal to the popular imagination. Even the suspension of sport, not racing only, but football and cricket, is accepted as a necessity when he points to the trenches and tells what he has seen of the men in them and how they are waiting anxiously for the engines of warfare and asking whether people at home know there is a war on.

By this time (1916) he has made many visits to the war zone, has described in articles what he saw, sold in large numbers a book containing these descriptions. It is called *At the War,* and sells for the benefit of the Red Cross. Certainly this helps to spread the belief in his power. It is in the popular view just the kind of book a powerful man would write. No words are wasted. There is no fine writing. His sentences are short and pithy. He gives the facts. And in his thought as well as in his phrases he reflects the common sentiment, the common opinion. Therefore the book wins for him a great many admirers, who say they did not know Northcliffe was that sort of man. The sort of man who speaks of the troops as "our dear soldier-boys", who calls the war "this grim, grim war", who admits that he does not like to have shells falling around him, but does not shirk going where they fall if there is an advanced dressing-station to be visited or a ruined village to be seen and described so that his readers may know what "the front" is like. He shares the belief of nine-tenths of his countrymen that "the Germans are naturally extremely cruel". He says: "The faces of our soldiers, unlike those of the Germans, are full of individuality." He finds the bulk of the German prisoners "miserable creatures".

Furthermore, he shares the contempt for politicians which the most of his readers feel—or at any rate profess. He calls the House of Commons "the Upas Tree of Westminster". And he throws out hints very welcome to the mass of people that their conditions will never be again what they were before the war.

"The meeting of Scotsman and Southerner, Londoner and Provincial, Irishman and Englishman, is bringing about an interchange of thought that will materially alter British politics as soon as the boys return home."

In the "dim and distant days known as 'After the War' no self-respecting male will again be seen matching ribbons behind counters, typewriting, standing behind aldermanic chairs, or playing the piano at kinema theatres. The men who have been bomb-throwing will have no appetite for the hundred-and-one gentle and essentially feminine pursuits by which they have hitherto earned their living."

What will they do? Listen to a conversation of wounded men on board ship bound for home. He hears them discussing a newspaper article which outlines a project for settling soldiers on land in the British Dominions. "Many will go to Canada, some to Australia, I dare say," says one man, "but I am one of those who mean to have a little bit of Blighty (England) for myself. We see enough in France to know that a man and his family can manage a bit of land for themselves and live well on it." A similar conversation Northcliffe remembers near Ypres, when a young sergeant who had been a gamekeeper at home and a working-man Conservative observed: "The men in the dug-outs talk of a good many subjects, but there is one on which they are all agreed. That is the land question. They are not going back as labourers or as tenants, but as owners." All of which creates a warm, comfortable feeling and strengthens the belief that Northcliffe is on the side of the People and will see that justice is done to them.

All of it sincere on his part. He is convinced that nothing can be too good for the men who are winning the war. If they want land, they ought to have it; they must have it. But it is a grateful, generous impulse; nothing more. He has not thought it, or anything, out to a reasoned, logical conclusion. He accuses himself of "sentimental nonsense" because "the first time I saw a cannon fired in war, I did so with reluctance, not wishing to participate even by observation in the sending forth of that which would destroy life or wound. But the spectacle of smashed towns and babies' graves in France and Belgium" removed that reluctance. "Quite right, too", approved the Populace. It does not understand, not yet, that those anticipations of after-the-war reforms and benefits are "sentimental nonsense" also, and that when "after the war" comes he will have forgotten all about them. In the meantime, they help to build up his reputation as the country's most powerful man.

So the war years number already two; the third wears on; still the issue is in doubt. When the *Lusitania* was sunk, he waited for an outburst of anger in America which should sweep that country into the conflict. He was disappointed when this did not happen, though in public he said he did not wish it to happen. When the use of poison gas began, he denounced it with genuine horror (though the French were known to have been experimenting with this weapon), and with equally genuine anxiety that his side shall suffer no disadvantage said that of course the British Army must use it too. So uneasy does he now feel about the conduct of the war in the air that he makes a speech in the House of Lords, and wins general approval for his suggestion that the Air Ministry should set up a Board of Inventions to examine at once any suggestion for the improvement of aircraft or aeroplane tactics. Things, he feels, and says, are not going well. A greater effort is required. A man more active-minded than Asquith should be at the helm.

He says this so often and so loudly that another attack is made on him in the House of Commons. The Liberals do their best to discredit him. He is accused of belittling the value of the Russian armies, of stating that the Tsar has actually in the field less than half the number of effective men whom Britain has sent to France. The attack languishes for lack of ammunition. The attackers have only vague rumour of what was said to go upon. He is vigorously defended. No harm is done to him. "Northcliffe knows more than the politicians", is the popular verdict. Yet there are politicians whom both the populace and Northcliffe value. Of such is Mr. Hughes of Australia. When he arrives, although he is Prime Minister of the Commonwealth, there is a slight disposition to shrug shoulders at him. He is a fluent, frothy orator. Strange that Northcliffe should at once hail him as the type of statesman the British Empire needs in this crisis. He is well advertised in the Northcliffe Press. There is even some idea of giving him high office in the Cabinet. Possibly, meditates Northcliffe, he might be the man to take Asquith's place.

For all this time the conviction that Asquith cannot win the war has been gaining upon him. He complains that leadership is lacking. Here is the nation prepared for any sacrifice, yet Asquith shrinks from telling it plainly what is required. Party politicians have failed to rise to the greatness of the occasion. They cannot distinguish between tactics permissible in peace-time and the resolute handling of affairs which the conduct of a war demands. They have been too timid to organize the nation so that everyone may contribute to the supreme effort called for. They have been too heavy-witted to mobilize the men of science, to set inventors to work, to secure by this means new methods of production, new engines of warfare, new sources of food supply. Asquith, he declares, would make a very good chairman of a debating society. Neither his mind nor his habits fit him for the task of directing the nation's energies in war-time.

The reply to this made by many political notabilities, even by members of Asquith's Cabinet, is that "no one could take Asquith's place". To which Northcliffe retorts "Rubbish!" The Hughes notion, is however, abandoned. No support is lent to it. The man most capable of energizing the British effort seems to him now to be Lloyd George. He tells everybody that Asquith cannot last much longer. The Government is unpopular. It has failed in boldness, it has recoiled from decisions that would have ensured greater vigour in carrying on the war. It has not aroused the spirit of the nation or drawn out its full productive capacity. He prints these charges in *The Times*. He engages in a whirlwind campaign for the replacement of Asquith by Lloyd George.

The main obstacle is Lloyd George himself. He does not wish to supplant his chief. He doubts whether he could make sure of a following. He betrays the politician's dread of not having the majority with him. "I should perhaps stand alone", he says. To which Northcliffe scornfully replies that strong men always stand alone, and to close friends he describes with impatient humour the "pushing and shoving" of Lloyd George towards the Premiership, the holding up of his reluctant hands.

Asquith complained later of "a well-organized, carefully engineered conspiracy" to turn him out. That the fall of the Ministry was due to intrigue Northcliffe never admitted. "There was no conspiracy, no intriguing", he declared. "None was necessary. Asquith's Government died a natural death. All that I helped to do was to arrange for the succession. We had to have a man ready to take office immediately. There was no time to waste in casting around for one." Yet actually it is a leading article in *The Times* which puts the match to the powder and blows Asquith up, finally extinguishing his career.

Towards the end of 1916 Lloyd George has proposed that a Cabinet Committee of three shall decide all questions connected with the war, "subject to the supreme control of the Prime Minister". Asquith has after some quibbling agreed to this. Northcliffe is by no means satisfied, but he is willing to try any change that will take the direction of the war out of Asquith's hands. He publishes in *The Times* an article which in effect says as much as this. Asquith angrily repudiates the agreement he has given to Lloyd George's scheme, makes an attempt to get rid of him. In the result he himself is got rid of. Northcliffe's purpose is achieved. Now at last, he says, we shall put away our antiquated peace methods. "We have got a Prime Minister who understands, after having it well drummed into him, that a Cabinet of twenty or more is totally unsuitable in war-time, however well it may do when we are at peace. Lloyd George is alive to the necessities of the hour. I am more hopeful about the course of the war than I have been since it began."

Very unfairly Asquith's friends throw on Lloyd George the obloquy of turning Asquith out. They are sincere in this, for they cannot, being in politics themselves, realize that such things are ever done over the heads of politicians. But the nation sees more clearly what has happened. It attributes to Northcliffe the casting-down of Asquith, as it attributed to him the forcing upon Asquith of a Coalition Ministry eighteen months before. Those who have styled him "the most powerful man in the country" point to this fresh evidence of his dominating will. How he appears to American eyes may be seen in the statement by one of America's most widely read newspaper men (Isaac Marcosson) that "he is the liveliest and most vital entity in England, a man alternately praised and damned, who by the changes he has wrought must be regarded as the Warwick of the war. If he lived in America he would be a President-maker." What the German Government thinks of him is shown by the daily denouncement of him in the German Press, by the bombing of the district of Kent in which his house Elmwood lies. This is how he stands at the close of the year 1916.

CHAPTER XIII

THE MISSION TO AMERICA

Northcliffe is doing good work and is getting along well with everyone. . . . I think his success is due to his force more than to anything else. He is a dominating man with boundless energy. . . . He does what he promises and he rings true.

COLONEL HOUSE,
Diary and Letters

IN the early summer of 1917 a New York newspaper announced that "Lord Northcliffe had arrived at an American port and had gone at once to the Hotel Gotham". The Hotel Gotham being one of the best-known New York establishments, this proved that the absurdities of Censorship were not confined to any one country. Up to that moment, when there was no longer need for secrecy, nothing had been published about his voyage. Very few people knew that he had left England. The purpose of his leaving was to create and direct an agency in the United States for the buying of supplies needed by Britain.

The British War Mission this agency was called. It employed as many as 10,000 people in America and Canada. It spent something like ten million dollars a day. Upon its smooth and punctual working depended the success of Britain's effort in the war. It was represented to Northcliffe, when Lloyd George asked him to undertake this difficult task, that it was more important than the duties of any Cabinet Minister outside the group of three or four responsible for the management of the war. He replied that this did not interest him, but that if his services were thought to be necessary, he would go at once. Within less than forty-eight hours he had started. He undertook to remain in America for three months. He was actually there for five. During that time he paid no attention whatever to his newspapers or any other private business. He gave himself up entirely to the heavy labour and still heavier responsibilities of his post.

Lloyd George, when he became Premier, had been urged by many to make use of Northcliffe's energy and organizing genius in the national cause. Wisely, he waited until the opportunity came for using them to the best advantage. A British War Mission in the United States required for its head one who knew the country and its people well, one whose name was known to them. Much would hang on the personality of the man chosen. Not only must he be familiar with the handling of business on a vast scale, know how to pick his assistants and get the best out of them, be ready to make important decisions and secure their being carried out: he must be "a good mixer", he must make the leaders in finance, industry, politics feel that he met them on equal terms. The Earl of Balfour (still Mr. Balfour then) had visited the United States two months earlier. His task was to explain to the American People, just entering the war, British methods and British aims. He accomplished it with success, but it was a success of curiosity so far as concerned the mass of the population. He was a type quite unfamiliar to them; unfamiliar, indeed, to most of those who had personal contact with him. It would have been very hard, perhaps impossible, for any man of his type (and nearly all British public men at that period conformed to it) to make a success of the British War Mission. The qualities required were combined in Northcliffe to a very fortunate degree. He saw at once that this was so.

No man of his prominence could have been less vain, less disposed to plume himself on his achievements. It was part of the fatalism which has been mentioned as a strong element in his nature that he took little credit to himself for what he had done. Sometimes he would boast in a joking way about victories he had won over rival newspaper owners or plots he had defeated. It was difficult to be sure whether he meant such boastings to be taken seriously or not. For instance, he would relate how the German Emperor, hiding behind a syndicate, tried to buy *The Times,* and how he himself first suspected and then unmasked the conspiracy. Or he would chuckle over the ingenuity which enabled him to snatch a valuable secretary from Mr. Pulitzer, of the New York *World.* One felt that he was enjoying inventions of his own humour rather than offering the stories as authentic. As for any real boasting, any self-glorification or conceit, these were entirely foreign to his character. He knew what he had done, but he believed that he was foreordained to do it. He knew likewise what his powers and abilities were, but he regarded them as gifts, not as results of his own endeavour. Therefore when he dispassionately considered himself as head of the British War Mission, he saw that he was peculiarly well fitted for the post, and, little as he liked the prospect of official duties and formalism, he accepted it without hesitation.

To leave his home did not trouble him. He had sold Sutton Place by this time. He had moved from the house in St. James's to one very much smaller in a quarter near Buckingham Palace, which was then being transformed from dinginess to smartness, from lodging-house status to that of fashion. He said that he did not feel the need of a home as most men do. He was content to live in hotels. He did not fancy "settling down" anywhere for long at a time. Yet he had not been long in America before he made up his mind that he did prefer a home to a hotel. He rented a delightful house a hundred years old on the shores of Long Island Sound. The name, Bolton Priory, attracted him; its appearance, situation, gardens, quietness impelled him to take it. He was happy there with a small circle of assistants whom he made happy also. He often recalled in later years the pleasant memories of his stay. In Egypt, in 1922, he saw a house "covered with wonderful bignonia such as I had at Bolton Priory in 1917."

He took out, or had sent after him, his personal secretaries and stenographers. For their comfort he was as careful as for his own. He gave the girls grants of money to buy suitable clothes for the hot weather in New York. He took trouble to find out how they were boarded and lodged. He arranged little jaunts and excursions for them. One of them said to him, "You are like a fairy uncle to us, Lord Northcliffe." He beamed and answered: "Well, my dear, I've brought you a long way from your home. The least I can do is to see that you get a little enjoyment."

The most active member of his staff, one to whom he will owe a large part of the success of his stay in America, he engages on the spot. While he is sleeping in the Gotham Hotel on that first night of his in New York, a young man, who is henceforward to play a prominent part in his life, sleeps in the train from Washington to New York. They have met in London, where Northcliffe formed a high estimate of the young man's ability. But nothing was less in his mind when he left England or when he landed in the United States than that the favourable issue of his Mission should be in great measure due to Lieutenant-Colonel Campbell Stuart of Montreal.

He has entertained Stuart in London, praised him to his guests as an energetic young Canadian who, having raised in Canada a regiment of Irish-born—Catholic and Protestant enlisting side by side—took this regiment to Ireland, marching and camping all over the country amid scenes of rapturous welcome. "He did", said Northcliffe, "what John Redmond could not do. He came to London to see the War Office about his regiment and read of the debate in the House of Commons about the failure of the plan for sending over the Liverpool Regiment to Ireland. He at once conceived the idea of taking the Canadian-Irish there. Redmond gave him encouragement and assistance. But all the credit of the idea and its execution is due to the young man himself."

By others, as well as by Northcliffe, Stuart had been marked as a figure of unusual promise, and when a medical board forbids him to go to the Front, Sir Robert Borden, then Canada's Prime Minister, suggests that he shall be attached to the British Embassy in Washington. He takes ship, therefore, and on arrival reports for duty as Assistant Military Attaché to Sir Cecil Spring-Rice, the Ambassador. The title is a blind. Sir Robert Borden's notion had been that Stuart should look after Canadian interests and at the same time interpret to the American People Britain's effort in the war with rather more vigour than the regular Embassy staff possessed. Seeing, however, that he is an Army officer, not a diplomat, it is judged more fitting that he should be given a military post. After he has been three weeks at the Embassy he sees the announcement that Northcliffe has reached New York. He takes the midnight train and knocks at the door of Northcliffe's suite before the chief of the British War Mission is out of his bed. "Let him come in", commands Northcliffe, and, seeing him, asks in astonishment, "What are you doing here?" Stuart tells him. Northcliffe makes up his mind at once.

"How would you like to help me in this job I have undertaken?"

"I should like it very much."

Before they part a cable is on its way to Lloyd George, asking for Stuart's transference from Embassy to Mission. The Ambassador, bitterly resenting Northcliffe's appointment, tries to prevent this, but it goes through. "I never", said Northcliffe long after, "did a better day's work in my life." The Ambassador (Sir Cecil Spring-Rice) changed his mind very soon about the appointment. Northcliffe, he wrote, "got on very well with the United States authorities. I was much struck by the friendliness of his reception." Later he noted "the extremely favourable impression" made by the head of the British War Mission on the Washington Press Club when the members entertained him. His relations with Northcliffe, he recorded, were "very pleasant and friendly". He decided to forget the transference from Embassy to War Mission Headquarters of Campbell Stuart.

It is hard for anyone who saw from inside (as I did) the activities of this ingenious and capable young man to imagine what the Mission would have been like if he had not joined it. No doubt its business would have been carried on effectively. With that, indeed, Stuart had little to do. But in all the wider activities which the office imposed on Northcliffe he was of the greatest value. Northcliffe leaned on him as he had never leaned on any subordinate before. Never until now had he been able to endure for any length of time a personal assistant whom he had to treat as his equal socially. He preferred to have about him while he was at work persons of a social standing lower than his own. Several times he had, as the re-

LORD NORTHCLIFFE IN THE EARLY DAYS OF HIS SUCCESS

sult of taking a fancy to some clever and pleasant young fellow, tried to break with this preference. The attempts had all failed. Now at last one succeeded, and for this reason:

Hitherto he had always known far more than anybody else about the work he was doing. He did not care to trust anybody very far without supervision. He was liable to interfere at any moment and say, "That is being done all wrong." His temper was not always under control. He had so firm a grasp of what was necessary, his acquaintance with the newspaper business was so intimate and thorough, that he found it hard to make allowances for others not so well equipped. Now he sailed seas strange to him. He did not know what course to set. He was not quite sure what might be expected of him. To find a second-in-command so unassumingly self-confident, so ready with suggestions, so full of useful knowledge, was, he admitted, a piece of great luck.

Stuart attracted him from the first. He had exactly the manner Northcliffe liked. He fixed his whole attention on his work, but at any moment humour might break through. Soon there sprang up a real affection between them. "If I had had a son . . ." Northcliffe murmured to a friend one day as he watched Stuart striding out of a room. He did not finish the sentence; he had shown what was in his mind. From this time until the end of his life they worked together in close harmony. This was something entirely new.

In all that concerned the work of the Mission Northcliffe departed from what had up to now been his usual method. He found men the ablest for the work that had to be done and he left them free to do it in their own way. He made no attempt to master the intricacies of the many markets in which he was buying. "It would be absurd", he said, "for me to make a study of the Grain trade or of Oil or of Copper or of packed Meat. There is no need for that. I have heads of departments under me who are experts in these things, and in all the other things that Britain wants. My job is to keep the people who are buying for her from tumbling over one another and getting in each other's way. It is also my job to get any difficulties removed by going at once to the biggest men in the industry affected. For the rest, so long as all my departments work smoothly, I shall leave them alone. They will only hear from me when they are not delivering the goods."

He called the task which had been placed upon his shoulders "stupendous".

"I am a sort of buffer", he wrote to Wickham Steed, "between the United States Government and our own. The entire ignorance at home of American personalities and American ways causes us here great anxiety. . . .

"Make no mistake about it, this country is beginning to make war on a gigantic scale. It is muddling a good deal, but men are being enrolled with great rapidity, and they are fine men, too. The change since I arrived is immense.

"I do my best behind the scenes—urging expedition. I hope I am not flattering myself too much when I say I know I have helped. . . .

"This exile is a great sacrifice and the work is infinitely irksome and anxious. It begins at half-past six in the morning and goes on until bedtime. I have not read a book or visited a place of amusement since I arrived. My consolation is that I am doing my bit, and I assure you that some consolation is required during the heat-wave."

Of the "biggest men" in industry he speaks in terms of gratitude as well as admiration. At one moment there is a hitch in the deliveries of oil. An enormous quantity is on order for the British Admiralty. It happens that the

American Navy needs at that moment an enormous quantity too. Northcliffe's intervention is necessary. In his quiet way he lays the matter before the heads of the oil business. He is grave, yet they can see he has a sense of humour. They recognize immediately a man with whom they can deal as if he were one of themselves. He makes himself sufficiently acquainted with the elements of the problem he means to solve. For a few days he thinks, speaks, writes of nothing else. "We swam in oil", he says afterwards, discussing it. "We breathed oil. The whole place seemed to reek of it." The British Admiralty got its order fulfilled.

Before his arrival there has been competition between British agents, competition between British Departments of State, competition between buyers for Britain and buyers for Russia and France. When the United States joined in the war, American buyers for the Government joined in the competition for war material. This is altered by the coming of the British War Mission and by the appointment of the Exports Administrative Board. No more are fortunes made by adventurers who rush round getting options on metals, rifles, chemicals, grain, and sell at a high profit to the countries fighting in Europe. No more are there sensational rises in the shares of companies producing what these countries will purchase at almost any price. No longer is it possible for the British Ministry of Munitions to discover that the cost of a certain commodity has soared because the British Admiralty is bidding for it too!

The huge profits made at the expense of the taxpayers in his own and other countries both disgust and divert Northcliffe. He would have war profiteers harshly dealt with, yet he cannot help being amused by the open, shameless fashion in which "the poor public" is fleeced. To this particular line of fleecing, however, he puts an end very soon. He does not exalt his office. There is no mystery about it. He explains exactly what it is. He could have been Ambassador at Washington had he chosen. He prefers to confine himself to the one task which above any other so badly needed to be undertaken. "I was sent here," he says in a modest tone, "not only because I have been here twenty times before, but because I am accustomed to directing large organizations, and it was felt by the British Government that someone should supervise the huge disbursements which are passing into American pockets every week. Until my coming all the great purchasing departments in the United States were without a head. Now the business is working smoothly and efficiently."

Smooth and efficient the manner in which he orders his life in New York. The rule of early rising is kept up, or rather, early waking, for he does not rise until he has looked through the newspapers and anything else that calls for attention. Not his own newspapers. He has put them out of his thoughts. That may seem too strong an expression. It is literally true. He has a strange faculty for switching his mind off what he has decided not to think about, just as he has an unusual power of concentrating it on anything that occupies him. He concentrates now on the work he has undertaken to do in America. He permits no leakage of mental energy towards the work he has left behind him in England. Nor does he fritter away any of that energy on speculation as to the prospects of the war or on talking about the course it has taken so far. "I am not worrying about the war", he replies, if he is asked for his opinion on its past, present, or future. He will seldom say more than that. He holds that when a man is not engaged on something practical, material, on some directly urgent problem, he should let his intellect rest. To weary it with fruitless labour seems to him wasteful. Thus he appears sometimes to those who meet him in his hours of leisure to have little to say and that little most of the chaffing or trivial kind.

In the motor, for example, on the way to New York from Pelham Manor, the suburb that is so fortunate as to possess Bolton Priory, he does not frequently speak or think about the business of the day. His aim is to bring a mind as fresh as possible to bear upon it when he reaches his office. Once there, he plunges right into it without any of the preliminaries or small delays in which most men indulge before they make a start. While he is at work nothing but work interests him. As soon as he puts work aside he gives no more thought to it.

The mornings he usually spends at the central office of the Mission on Fifth Avenue. His inclination would be to lunch with one or two friends, but very often he has to entertain large parties. That is a side of his duty which he did not like to think about when he accepted it. But he does not find the obligation so irksome as he feared it might be. At these functions he lets others do most of the talking. Theodore Roosevelt is a guest at one of them and talks for two hours without stopping once, finishing two bottles of Rhine wine during the performance. Work again in the afternoon, a visit, perhaps, to the office of J. P. Morgan & Company, who are his financial advisers, or a conference with those who keep his enormous accounts, chief among them his able newspaper manager, Andrew Caird. "One of the Scotsmen I employ in London to prevent me from spending too much money", he says with a smile when he introduces Caird. Then in the late afternoon the drive back to Pelham, cheerful and talkative because work is done for the day. He never fails to look out of the window in the negro quarter, Harlem, where it is said a wealthy coloured business man has a Swedish butler. He tells that to everybody. "Doesn't it make you think?" he inquires. He likes the laughing faces of the coloured people, their good temper, their contentment. "But what a mistake it was to bring them from their native Africa!" he reflects. "A mistake which a future generation in America may have to expiate."

He keeps Bolton Priory as free of guests as he can. His own taste is for dining quietly in a dinner-jacket with his personal staff and sitting after dinner in the garden with a gramophone turned on, enjoying the cool air from the sea, the silence that is all the more soothing by contrast with New York's din, the heavy scents of flower and herb in the warm darkness. Here he enjoys a kind of happiness that he has not known before. No concerns of his own to think about, no plans revolving in his mind for the launching of new publications or the strengthening of old ones. Far greater the interests which he is handling now than any individual interest could be, yet the responsibility weighs little upon him. He carries it with a confident ease. He has the sensation of being in his right place, of having found the task that he is supremely fitted for.

Even if he were not sure that all goes well, he would not be anxious or perturbed. This business is too big to be worried over. If it were to go awry, the crash occasioned would be so far-reaching, so tremendous: "one does not worry over the possibility of earthquake or tidal wave". When he has done his day's work he can take his leisure with his mind free. Never before since the telephone came into use has he been secure from calls put through by his offices, from requests for decisions, from suggestions to approve or turn down; never been able to refrain from calling up his assistants to inquire how they are dealing with this or that event, or to pass on information he has had brought to him. Never until now has he gone to bed without the knowledge that next day will bring an infinity of matters small in themselves on which he must decide. Now, though he has a private wire to Washington, he is very seldom disturbed after he has got home. Now the very largeness of the matters he is handling has a soothing effect.

Their dramatic side does not escape him. He likes to tell how on a certain morning Britain was within ten minutes of bankruptcy. If a certain document had not been signed on that morning before noon the British Government would have been a defaulter! When the clock hands were at ten minutes to twelve he signed it, thankful that the financial corner had been turned and enjoying the thrill. Thrills, however, are infrequent. For the most part his task is unexciting—ceaseless watchful attention to the large issues under his care, immediate intervention if there is clogging or friction in the machinery, application of the necessary lubricant. A self-important, fussy man could have done infinite harm in such a post. A man who got himself entangled in detail would have endangered the regularity of the shipments on which Britain relied. The largeness of Northcliffe's nature, his genius for dealing with men, his complete freedom from any feverish desire to assert his importance, are of the greatest value. Between him and President Wilson there is little cordiality. They meet seldom, neither seeking the other's society. But with Colonel House he makes friends very soon. They show mutual liking and appreciation. Northcliffe pays a visit to "the Gold Coast", as a strip of seaboard in Massachusetts is called by reason of the many rich people who have summer homes there. He is lavishly entertained. He speaks with gratitude of his millionaire hosts' hospitality. But what he treasures most in memory are his talks with Colonel House, the quiet time he had passed at the unpretentious cottage to which the President's adviser and confidant retires to think and read.

Northcliffe is glad himself of retirement every now and then. He has added gradually to his duties as Chief Purchasing Agent for his country those of an Envoy from the one People to the other. This is mainly Campbell Stuart's doing. He makes arrangements for speeches, tours, conferences, visits to this or that magnate, to a city here or there. As a public speaker, Northcliffe wins no success. In the Madison Square Garden, New York, he fails lamentably to reach with his voice more than a few of the ten thousand people assembled to hear him. After that he addresses no more big gatherings. But on small conclaves he makes an excellent impression. At Kansas City several hundred editors of Middle Western newspapers assemble to hear him and go away chanting his praise. He talks to them as one journalist to another. He is colloquial, confidential. His manner charms them. As for the matter of his discourse, though it be not profound, they receive it reverentially. Is this not the most important man in England? He warns them not to believe the war will soon be over. He tells them that a great effort is needed yet, that America and Britain must make it.

In Chicago, small parties of the leading citizens carry away the conviction, making no secret of it, that if Britain entrusted its destinies to this man, they would be safe in his hands. In St. Louis the same view prevails after he has spoken. Ottawa and Toronto are visited. They are more restrained in their enthusiasm, but they, too, fall under the spell. At Rochester he is made an Honorary Doctor of Laws (the sole University degree conferred on him in any country). At Dayton he renews acquaintance with Orville Wright. At Detroit he makes friends with Henry

Ford. The papers are filled with his comings and goings, his opinions, his humorous comment, his forceful personality.

All this has a twofold effect. First, it wearies him in body. "I know, my dear boy," he says to Campbell Stuart, "that you make everything as easy for me as possible, but it is a strain to be continually on view, to be always affable, to make all these speeches—and to listen to all these replies!" He finds that he needs some stimulant to help him through ceremonial lunches and dinners and to sip now and then while he speaks. What is to be done? He will not be seen to break the law: that would be unbecoming. Yet something he must have. He recollects that Disraeli was once in similar plight. He also required stimulant while speaking. In 1867, during a debate in the House of Commons, he felt faint and ill. He asked someone to fetch him a glass of brandy and water, "mixed strong". His request was interpreted too generously. Towards the close of his speech, when he had drunk most of his refreshment, his voice became husky, his final sentences could scarcely be heard. The comments provoked by this mishap made him anxious to avoid drinking anything which looked alcoholic at a great meeting he was to address in Manchester. He asked his private secretary (Montagu Corry, whom he made Lord Rowton) to get him a bottle of "white brandy". Seeing a puzzled look on his face, the statesman added hastily, "There is such a thing, and you must get me a bottle of it." Corry went all over Manchester. Neither wine-merchants nor saloons had any such liquid. At last he was told where he might buy some brandy almost white. He rushed off, secured a bottle, mixed brandy and water, filled a glass and put it in front of his chief. Everyone else thought it was water. The speech was a complete success.

Northcliffe's solution of the same difficulty was—gin. It had the appearance of water and it gave him just the "kick" he needed. His need of it was a symptom of his bodily fatigue and ought to have warned him. Even more tiring than the tours were the frequent stays he had to make in Washington. The summer climate there he found exhausting, and in hot weather he did not husband his strength as would have been prudent. During the journey from New York he would invite into his airless "drawing-room" anyone prominent in business or politics who happened to be on the train. He would talk all the time, raising his voice above the rattle of the wheels. While other men sat in the cooler Chair Car, reading or sleeping, making no effort, his journey would be one long effort lasting five hours. Sometimes he travelled by night—and called the train "The Flying Oven"! He would arrive in the enervating atmosphere of the capital with only a quarter of his usual energy. He had a pleasant apartment to go to, but he missed the Bolton Priory garden and the quiet and the breeze from the sea.

There was more formality, too, about work in Washington. He seldom felt bound to wear in New York anything but his customary flannel or tweed suit, with soft hat, silk shirt, and the red-spotted tie from which he never varied save on ceremonial occasions. In Washington these occasions were more frequent. He grumbled about having to put on black coat and tall hat. He detested by this time that emblem of respectability to which he had been attached in his youth. Yet he was punctilious in this as in every other duty that his official position required of him.

"American officials", he said, "are quick to notice and resent anything that looks like a departure from British habits of doing business with departments of State. If I wore my ordinary comfortable clothes, they might say to each other, 'He wouldn't do that in London.' You know what psycho-analysts mean by the Inferiority Complex. They suffer from it still. It's far better to dress too much than too little."

There he showed his understanding of the United States —and Canada, he said, was just the same. He would never have made the mistake into which Mr. Baldwin fell when, during his visit to the Dominion as British Premier, he sat at a public luncheon in his shirt-sleeves and appeared on a balcony to acknowledge cheers of welcome with a pipe in his hand. In such small matters as well as in the larger and weightier, Northcliffe adapted himself to the obligations of this new phase in his career. They sapped his vigour more perilously than he or anyone else at the time realized. Yet, as summer gave place to the glorious weather of the fall, with its crisp mornings and evenings and its brilliant sunshiny days, he threw off his weariness. The presence of Lord Reading, who took over at his request the financial side of the work of the War Mission, lightened his burden. He began to enjoy life again. Was the seed sown then which developed into fatal malady? Who can say?

What can be said with certainty is that, whether or not he was stricken in body, his mind was influenced by the constant flow of compliment and flattery, of eulogy and panegyric to which he was compelled to listen. Here is the other consequence of those triumphal progresses in America, those luncheons and dinners and meetings at which speakers proclaim him everywhere the most powerful man in Britain. He begins to believe this himself.

CHAPTER XIV

REJECTION OF CABINET OFFICE

> *Northcliffe has been splendid. The Prime Minister has repeatedly offered him a seat in the Cabinet, which he has refused. He did not propose to relinquish the right to criticize when he thought it necessary.*
>
> COLONEL HOUSE
> To President Wilson, Nov. 16, 1917

BACK to England, then, in November 1917 goes a Northcliffe different from the man who had left there in June. When he had been spoken of at home as "the most powerful man in the country" he had not heard what people were saying. It was a whisper that went round, it never got into print. No one on any public occasion had even hinted at any such thing. In America it was shouted at him wherever he went. He was told how he had forced Asquith to form a Coalition and then driven him from office to put Lloyd George in his place. He was greeted as the saviour of the British Army from the ineptitude of bureaucrats and politicians. All the measures which he had favoured were ascribed to him alone. Day after day this tale was told in his presence. He could not, without displeasing those who told it and disappointing those who heard, deny its truth.

Besides, was it not so largely true as to be difficult of denial? He had not seen himself in this light before. He had until the war smiled at the belief in newspaper power. That attitude had been modified during the last three years, but he did not until this visit to America lose entirely his schoolboy way of regarding the whole of life as a great game, did not cease to think of himself as a player in this game, with no aim but that of getting out of it as much fun and as many prizes as possible. Now he takes it and himself very seriously indeed. He has become acutely conscious of his public self. He feels that he has vast power and vast responsibility. What if this which he has heard so often should be true? What if he be truly the most powerful of all Britain's public men?

In that case, ought he not to be taking part in the government of the country, in the management of the war? He asks himself that question; others ask it. There are men in the Cabinet—some of its prominent members—who think he ought to be there. There is talk of his being asked to take the highest office of all. But would he take it? Would he take any post? And if he did, would he make good? These are queries bandied about and discussed just after he has returned to England from the United States.

Futile now, but yet of interest, to consider for a moment whether as head of a Government he would have been a success. Before his Mission to America everyone who knew him would have said, No. But his complete change of method in changed circumstances and the completely admirable results which that change gave proved him to be one man in private business and a totally different man in public affairs. All doubts as to his capacity for handling transactions of the utmost consequence and of the largest size were then dissipated. He rose at once to the level of the task entrusted to him. He won golden opinions from all sorts of people. He showed that he possessed just the qualities which the head of a Government requires. His assistants were left to do each his own work without interference so long as the work was well done. His own activities were confined to general supervision and the clearing up of obstacles to progress. He did not try to do other men's work for them, yet the atmosphere which he created stimulated them to do their best and to desire his approbation. At the same time he was able to keep touch with the public, as the head of a Government must, making a favourable impression, producing the belief that public affairs were secure in his hands.

But this is not the final balance of the account. It has to be remembered that as head of the Mission he worked alone, he had no immediate colleagues whom it was necessary to consult before anything important was done. He was independent; he was, if the word may be used without derogatory meaning, despotic. Would he have been able to work with a Cabinet? Would he have consented to submit his decisions to the judgment of fellow-Ministers? Could he have taken place as member of a team or had he been too long firmly convinced of the value of "a committee of one"?

Again, we must recollect that as head of the Mission he had no criticism to endure, no attacks from opponents to repel. How would he have acquitted himself in the cut and thrust of political controversy? Could he have defended a policy in Parliament or justified some momentarily unpopular act to a public meeting? Unless colleagues and crowd were ready to accept his "I tell you it is so", and to give their entire confidence, he might have found it difficult to convince them. He never argued a case. He did not move step by step in reaching his conclusions. He took flying leaps. Having taken one and thus reached a conclusion, he could not explain what had led him to it, for he did not know. His mental process was neither induction nor deduction; it was pure intuition. The reason of his success in almost everything he attempted was that his intuitions were almost always right. Would the nation have put faith in them and dispensed with explanations? Would it have been content that he should make no replies to criticisms? No one can say.

Lord Beaverbrook has suggested [1] that he could not have worked with politicians because he "had no realization whatever of the political temperament". If that means he had no liking for politicians, it is true. If it means that he did not understand politicians, it is a long way from the truth. It was because he understood them that he disliked them. Himself straightforward, he mistrusted their devious ways. Himself quick to decide, he despised their infirmity of purpose. For him, if a thing was right or necessary, it was a thing to be done without hesitation. The politicians' fear of public opinion, fear of weakening their hold on office or their chance of it, fear of offending powerful interests, moved Northcliffe to derision. Their ingrained insincerity filled him with disgust.

"He often told me", says Lord Beaverbrook, "that he was better off as a journalist because he did not consort with Ministers or ex-Ministers, and that for his own part he never wanted, as a private individual, to have anything to do with them." Yet at this period, the period following his return from America, he is certainly contemplating what seems to be the natural development of his exciting career, a place in the Cabinet—perhaps, it is suggested to him, the principal place. He contemplates it because there appears to him to be need for more energy in carrying on the war; he does not see who can supply that energy save only himself. He is not ambitious for office. He shrinks from the thought of the toil, the fatigue, it must lay upon him. But if he is the required man. . . .

He does not see all that is involved in the choice he has to make. He does not see that he has come to the turning-

[1] *Politicians and the War.*

point of his life. If he now takes his share in the direction of affairs, the Man and the Opportunity will have come together. What he may write on the pages of history no one can say. He will have found his proper sphere, the sphere in which the greatest influence on human activities can be exercised. If he refuses, his career is almost at an end. All that he can do in his private business has been done. He can make what he has created larger. He cannot create new *Daily Mails,* new Amalgamated Presses. He must choose between progress and stagnation, between going forward and slipping back.

The moment for deciding came very soon after he reached England. Lloyd George asked him to join the Cabinet, to take charge of the new Air Ministry. He had strongly urged the creation of this department. It seemed to be a post for which he was peculiarly well fitted; it was certainly one to which he felt peculiarly drawn. He was inclined to accept. Why he did not will for ever remain a mystery. The reason he gave in his letter to the Prime Minister declining the offer was that he believed he could do more useful work as a critic than as a member of the Government. That may have been the genuine and sole reason. It was certainly urged upon him by some of those who held high positions on his newspapers.

There were others, again, not in his employment, who put a different consideration before him. Why should he take a secondary post? If he managed the affair with ingenuity, he could obtain the highest of all. What these advisers did not allow for was Northcliffe's total lack of the kind of ingenuity they meant. Intrigue was distasteful to him. He would assuredly not scheme and conspire for power. His idea, so far as it can be reduced to exact terms, was that the nation wanted more vigour and more "concentration of mind" in the conduct of the war, that it might be looking to him to supply these qualities. He was ready to do so if the call came. But there was no thought in his mind of pushing and plotting his way to the Premiership.

He was not ambitious. There was nothing in the world he wanted less for its own sake than heavy responsibility coupled with prominent position, yet he was willing to shoulder it if it were laid upon him. What he did not understand was that in the sphere of government, as in every other, men get only what they strive after. He fancied vaguely that a demand had arisen for his services and that public opinion might blow him into office. In this he was so far correct. It was public opinion which prompted Lloyd George to offer him the Air Ministry. Had he taken this, he might conceivably have become in a short time head of the Government. But he did not care to use it as a stepping-stone. He declined it in this way:

Dear Prime Minister,

I have given anxious consideration to your repeated invitation that I should take charge of the new Air Ministry. The reasons which have impelled me to decline that great honour and responsibility are in no way concerned with the office which is rightly to be set up.

Returning after five months spent in the virile atmosphere of the United States and Canada, I find that while those two countries are proceeding with their war preparations with a fervour and enthusiasm little understood on this side of the Atlantic; while the United States has instantly put into operation Conscription, over which we wobbled for two years, and is making short work with sedition-mongers; while Canada has already given such proofs of thoroughness as the disfranchisement of all enemy aliens and conscientious objectors, and the denationalization of all enemy aliens who have been naturalized during the last fifteen years; while we, for our part, are asking immense sacrifices from these people, there are still in office here people who dally with such urgent questions as that of the unity of war control, the eradication of sedition, the mobilization of the whole man and woman power of the country, and the introduction of compulsory food rations.

I have had personal experience myself of the obstruction and delay in certain departments in London. I find that the Censorship is still being misused and that men in various positions of authority who should have been punished have been retained and in some cases elevated. We have in my belief the most efficient Army in the world led by one of the greatest generals, and I am well aware of the fine achievements of many others of our soldiers, sailors and statesmen; but I feel that in present circumstances I can do better work if I maintain my independence and am not gagged by a loyalty that I do not feel towards the whole of your Administration.

I take this opportunity of thanking you and the War Cabinet for the handsome message of praise sent to me as representing the 500 officials of the British War Mission in the United States, many of them volunteer exiles. The fact that their work and that of their 10,000 assistants is not known is due to the absurd secrecy about the war which is still prevalent. Everything that these officials are doing is known to our American friends and of course to the Germans. I trust I make no breach of confidence in saying that some of the documents which have passed through my hands as Head of the Mission are such as if published would greatly increase our prestige in the United States and hearten our people at home.

May I also take this opportunity of giving a warning about our relations with that great People from whom I have come? We have the tragedy of Russia, due partly to lack of Allied propaganda to counteract that of the Germans. We have had the tragedy of Italy, largely due to that same enemy propaganda. We have had the tragedies of Serbia, Rumania and Montenegro. There is one tragedy I am sure we shall not have, and that is the tragedy of the United States. But from countless conversations with leading Americans I know that unless there is swift improvement in our methods here, the United States will rightly take into its own hands the entire management of a great part of the war. It will not sacrifice its blood and treasure to incompetent handling of affairs in Europe.

In saying all this, which is very much on my mind, believe me that I have none but the most friendly feelings towards yourself and that I am greatly honoured by your suggestion.

That letter, written on November 15, 1917, was published at once. It gave Lord Cowdray, who was then at the head of the Air Service, the first intimation that his office had been offered to someone else. Lloyd George had not expected Northcliffe to make the offer public. That Northcliffe did so made many people believe he intended his refusal to be a bid for the Premiership. He was—and said that he was—very sorry for the hurt to Lord Cowdray's feelings, but he was undoubtedly glad to make known his opinion about the British management of the war. He did not word it as a politician would have done, wrapping up what he had to say so carefully as to conceal it quite. Nor did he write as a journalist writes a leading article, choosing phrases politely, blunting the edge of any expression that might cut. He spoke out his mind with no reserve nor with any aim but to advance what were to him his country's interests. This was one of the occasions which Lord Beaverbrook must have had in his recollection when he spoke of Northcliffe "lecturing eminent public men as if they were somewhat refractory schoolboys". This habit was not due to conceit or irritation. It was a consequence of the passion which consumed him—the passion for "winning the war". He could not be aware of anything left undone which might hasten victory without denouncing those who neglected to do it.

That he feared he might not be any longer free in this direction if he entered the Cabinet is certain. In that fear may have lain the reason for his declining to do so. There may have been other reasons. All we can do now is to guess at the state of his mind and to register the result of his decision. It definitely closed his career. From it, as those who were closest to him saw, his decline began.

Possibly that decline must have come whatever he did. Its cause may have been physical. The seeds of it may have been in his body at this time. But it is not impossible that his renunciation of the wider opportunity offered to him was the chief reason for his melancholy end. There were moments when he seemed to feel himself that he had thrown away the chance of greatness. After reading an account of his career which he had encouraged a friend to write, he exclaimed impatiently: "It is like looking at a man through the wrong end of a telescope." He seemed to himself, as he seemed to others, so much bigger than the things he had created, than the occupations which had absorbed nearly all his tremendous power of will.

For the moment the result of his renunciation was to leave him at liberty to attend to his newspaper business. The politicians shrugged their shoulders. A good many thanked Heaven for his refusal. None of them made any further advances. Whether he expected a popular clamour to arise, a national demand for him as War Premier, it is impossible to say. What can be said is that the absence of it did not disappoint him. He turned to the work from which he had been absent so long, threw himself into the task of screwing his newspapers up to larger circulations and greater influence, and especially into the agitation for unity of control on all fronts by means of an Allied War Council.

He had worked out plans for this with M. André Tardieu, French representative in Washington, while he was in the United States. Mr. McAdoo, President Wilson's son-in-law and a member of his Cabinet, was strongly in favour of them. President Wilson gave his support. Here was the explanation of Northcliffe's remark about "incompetent handling of affairs in Europe". He maintained that the absence of "the co-operative principle" had caused the Italian and the Rumanian disasters, and would ruin any private concern, no matter how big, "even the United States Steel Corporation", in a few weeks. That showed the difference between Northcliffe and the politicians. He wanted to apply to war-making the principles which had been tested and found useful in business. The politicians had no conception of business and considered it beneath their dignity to inquire into its methods. However, they were forced to create an Allied War Council; its meetings at Versailles soon produced good effects.

When he returned to England after his first visit to Newfoundland, enthusiastic about the vast enterprise in which he was engaged there, some felt it a pity that he should devote his abounding vitality and power to the smaller tasks of newspaper and magazine management. They regretted still more to see him now, after his valuable work in America, revert to his old occupations. With all his old vigour he discussed with his numerous editors the state of his publications, great and small. "No good printing long articles", he says to *The Daily Mail*. "People won't read them. They can't fix their attention for more than a short time. Unless there is some piece of news that grips them strongly. Then they will devour the same stuff over and over again. You can put it on every page, slightly varying its appearance and wording. They will read it all. But unless there is something very big, they prefer shortness to length. The war with its strain on the nerves has intensified this preference, which is the result of modern life generally. We can't afford to overlook it." So instead of column articles on the editorial page each column must contain three little ones. A number of the first of these he writes himself to show how they should be done.

An American journalist sits in his room while he disposes of a morning's work. He upbraids the editor of a comic paper for boys with "not putting paunches on policemen".

The public expects this. "Comic policemen ought to be fat. And the hen-pecked husband should always be thin. That fellow doesn't look hen-pecked. He looks as if she fed him well. Now be careful," he warns the editor as he goes, "be careful or we shall get too refined." Women's papers, religious papers, boys' story papers, all get their share of attention, and then off he goes to the office of *The Times* to lecture and chaff them there. That is his method always, save on the rare occasions when he is angry: to mingle ridicule with reproof.

It may have seemed to the American journalist that Northcliffe was no more interested in *The Times* than in *Comic Cuts,* that he considered the success of *Home Chat* to be as important to him as the prosperity of *The Daily Mail*. He may have given that impression to many who only saw him in his offices. It was very far from correct. He concentrated his energy on whatever he did. "If a thing is worth doing at all," he would say, "it is worth doing well", and if he did not think a thing worth taking trouble over, he would have nothing to do with it. He did not waste himself, as most men do, on occupations to which he was indifferent. His success, "as people called it", he attributed "to seeing ahead". "I did not think my schoolfellows were stupid, but I could always see farther than they could."[1] At other times he seemed to know that his gift of being able to pour himself into whatever he wished to accomplish had a good deal to do with it. One day he turned to an opponent at golf and asked abruptly: "Why haven't you done as well as I have?" He did not wait for a reply. "It's because you have not concentrated", he said. In his life there was no dissipation of energy. He was always occupied with something he intended to do, putting all his energy into it. Yet he was quite well aware that

---

[1] *The Real Lord Northcliffe,* by Louise Owen.

many of these things were insignificant. For the little publications which he had created by the score he had an odd sentimental affection (incidentally they made a great deal of money). But they gave him no such satisfaction as *The Daily Mail,* no such pride as he felt in owning *The Times.*

This pride did not deter him from ridiculing its old-fashioned ways. "Six hundred years ago", he was fond of saying, "there was near the site of *The Times* office a monastery, the home of the Blackfriars, recluses who lived remote from the world. The same kind of men inhabit Printing-house Square to this day." He tells these men that they need an Alert Ideas Department, and enjoys the self-pitying, bewildered looks they exchange. They find it hard to understand him. One day he chaffs them about a statement that a representative of *The Times* was "received" by an archdeacon. "I don't like that word 'received' ", he says. "It savours of the old flunkey attitude of Fleet Street—the tone adopted by the Door Steppers and the Shirt Money men. For the benefit of those who have not worked as reporters, as I have, let me add that a Door Stepper is one who hangs about Government offices and the houses of the great, hoping for crumbs of news, and that the Shirt Money man is the reporter who receives so much extra a week because he goes to report public dinners in 'full' or 'immaculate' evening dress, to use the term employed and so beloved by the scribes of Grub Street." At this the important persons on *The Times,* who have mostly joined the staff straight from Oxford or Cambridge, look down their noses and wear an expression of disgust at being told of such things.

Another day Northcliffe complains pathetically that "getting anything done at Printing-house Square is almost impossible. I told a very nice reporter, who shall be nameless, that a number of *The Times* blunders—and I am sorry to say there are a great many such blunders—were the result of the reporters' trick of writing numbers in figures instead of words. He took no notice whatever of my instructions."

One morning appears an article in which some fun is poked at Jews and Scots. Northcliffe sends next day a diary of the trouble this brought on him.

12 *noon.* To a meeting in the City where to my astonishment an American citizen of Scottish birth suddenly attacks me about the Jew and Scot article. I said it was obviously a joke. He was unappeased and violent. "*Times* going downhill, not what it was in Delane's days", he said. I left the room.

3 *p.m.* Back to Printing-house Square. Sir A. C., another Scot, brought a copy of *The Times* and complained. I told him that the Scotch had no sense of humour.

3.10 *p.m.* Sir Campbell Stuart mentioned that a Ducal Scot had complained of the Jew and Scot article.

5 *p.m.* Editor being out, wrote to him about the Jew and Scot article.

5.10 *p.m.* Attended important meeting. Proceedings disturbed by telephone calls from Jews and Scotsmen.

8 *p.m.* Left for home.

8.30 *p.m.* Arrived home tired and cross. I have no time for Jews and Scotsmen.

Next morning. The Jews and Scots have evidently wasted no time in leaving us, for the paper is down to the lowest it has been for a long time.

He enjoyed this sort of thing, but often in his most humorous remonstrances there was an undertow of irritation. He called the effort to put *The Times* on a self-supporting basis "the toughest proposition" he had ever faced. He had installed an editor of his own, but did not find it easy to work with him. He was conscious of an obstinate, unexpressed feeling against him. He knew that he was sneered at sometimes, sometimes quietly ridiculed as ignorant or inexperienced. He did not always know when he displayed these defects. He once objected to the French "Tant pis" being correctly translated "So much the worse", and declared that it "meant Kismet or Fate", which was nonsense. He once issued instructions about the use of the words "morale" and "moral", which showed that he did not know how they should be used. These slips caused amusement. He was aware of it and of latent hostility to his ideas.

Harassed by the daily worries, the mint and anise and cummin of the publishing business, he thought longingly sometimes of the larger atmosphere which he had lately breathed in America. There he was dealing with great issues, there he was in contact with men who were shaping the world's history. He said he never regretted anything; he "had no time to waste on wishing that things had been otherwise than they were". But there are moments now in which he asks himself whether he ought not to have taken the Air Ministry. He would have been in the thick of it then, instead of feeling, as he does now, "a little out of it", a little on one side. He has tried official life and found it much more to his liking than he imagined possible. He has been one of the important workers in the war, not merely a critic of what others did. He is still at times as devoted as ever he has been to his business with its varied ramifications, its contacts with life at many points, its daily fluctuations and vicissitudes. When he took it up again after leaving it for five months he exclaimed, "I am so glad to get back to my dear work!" He dwelt, half in fun, half in earnest, on the danger of "the old man" being away for so long. He plunged with zest, as we have seen, into the struggle which produced daily and weekly papers of so many kinds and in quantities so enormous. But now he has hours of lassitude. More surprising, he has moments of inclination to throw up these exacting and exhausting tasks. Yet when the offer of Cabinet rank is renewed, he rejects it again.

Lloyd George asks him in the summer of 1918 to go to the War Office. He declines. Telephones the Prime Minister's secretary (Mr. J. T. Davies) thanks and regrets. No letter now to explain why. No hesitation. Yet he lets the reason for his refusal be known. He has no taste for an office that would tie him down, force him to handle masses of detail. What he would readily accept, he makes known later through Lord Reading, would be an invitation to become Minister without Portfolio (say Lord President of the Council) and a member of the War Cabinet. He does not present this as an ultimatum, but he finds a way to have it conveyed to the right quarters. Nothing comes of it. Lloyd George at this period of the war feels himself strong enough to do without Northcliffe.

From the time of his refusal to go to the Air Ministry dates the coolness between him and Lloyd George. It is more on the politician's part than on the journalist's. Prime Ministers do not like to have their offers rejected. Nor is Northcliffe himself exempt from that failing. To one whom he offered to make a knight and who declined the honour, he was never quite the same again. "Must be a Bolshevik", he said half in fun, but half in earnest too. "Must be aiming at something higher", thought Lloyd George when Northcliffe declined office. There is no open breach as yet between them. Northcliffe feels no pique. He would like to be useful, feels sure (as so many feel) that he could be useful. He knows, too, how he could be most useful. It is a pity, he thinks, that they should not let him go where he could do the best service. But he does not fret, nor feel any personal pique.

For one thing he has his hands full enough already. In May (when Lloyd George was not feeling so confident in himself) he had been asked by the War Cabinet to undertake a piece of very urgent war work for which no man had qualifications equal to his. Northcliffe agreed to that. Not a Cabinet office this time. A post of high importance, nevertheless. Opportunities which, if used to the best advantage, might shorten the war.

CHAPTER XV

"A MASTER OF MASS-SUGGESTION"

> Lord Northcliffe organized at Crewe House the most effective scheme of propaganda known to modern history.
> PROFESSOR CHARLES SEYMOUR,
> Provost of Yale University

> Lord Northcliffe's War Publicity Department contributed perhaps more than ammunition to the defeat of the Germans.
> THE HON. SIR MANMOHANDAS RAMJI
> in a speech at Bombay, Dec. 3, 1927

MINISTER for the Destruction of German Confidence: that is the office Northcliffe now accepts.

After long delay, after much dubious debating, the War Cabinet has decided to engage in a campaign of propaganda. For six months they had been urged by Northcliffe to this decision. He discussed with Colonel House in the United States the spreading in Germany by all possible methods of news about "the immense expenditures and preparations being made in America." He did not cease from August 1917 onward to impress upon the British Government the necessity for "effective propaganda". Now his advice is at last acted upon. It is the moment to take advantage of every discouragement. The direction of the new campaign must be given to one who understands how the mass mind works, who has appealed to it successfully. Clearly Northcliffe is the man—if he will accept. Since his refusal of the Prime Minister's invitation to him to become a member of the Government, he has held aloof a little from Ministers and their satellites. They have begun to imagine that he is vexed, resentful, when, in truth, he has been busy with everything that he left to others while he was in the United States. But their doubts are at once resolved. When he is asked to be Director of Propaganda in Enemy Lands, he agrees without hesitation. It is the task for which he is pre-eminently fitted. Frequently he has urged upon Ministers the necessity of such Propaganda, such efforts to depress the spirit of the enemy, to put the truth about the war before all the enemy nations. He has no belief in an early ending, but he is convinced that, if an end can be made this year, it must be by means of "paper bullets" as well as leaden ones.

No hesitation, therefore, about accepting the post of "Minister for the Destruction of German Confidence", as General von Hutier in an angry Army Order called him, calling him also "the most thoroughgoing rascal of the Entente", calling him forger, falsifier, assassin. His mere acceptance was of value. It made enemy governing men and army leaders nervous. They feared him; they feared his ingenuity, his power.

But his appointment fell during one of his periods, a longer one than usual, of depression. He seemed tired, incapable of the reckless, joyous exertions in which he would at one time consume seventeen hours a day without fatigue in either body or mind. Fortunately he had by his side the same capable assistant, quietly vigorous, resourceful, at once methodical and enterprising, who had done so much to make the American stay successful. Lieutenant-Colonel Campbell Stuart, as Deputy-Director of the new Department and Deputy-Chairman of its Advisory Committee, composed chiefly of experts in publicity, was equally helpful in carrying through this fresh task.

He took off Northcliffe's shoulders all the daily detail work of the office which he was able to install in Crewe House, one of the most famous of London residences. He established the happiest relations between the staffs there and all the other Government agencies for dealing with propaganda. Northcliffe very quickly discovered that he could safely leave to Stuart the organization of the very important and very difficult campaign now to be begun in his name.

His was the inspiration, his the personality, which gave confidence to the British nation and its allies, while among enemies it spread uneasiness and alarm. He was able to secure for the Department the men most competent to influence German and Austrian imaginations. But, thanks to Stuart's devotion and hard work, he was not compelled to undergo the daily drudgery which was the hard fate of other men at the head of Departments of State.

His genius for picking the men he needed and "grappling them to himself with hoops of steel"—by unconsciously exercising upon them the charm and power of his personality—was never of greater service to him. He was seen at Crewe House very little. He was able now, as he had been in his own business, to do his thinking undisturbed by the trifling duties and irritations of an office. He could watch what was being done from a distance and get a far juster, more correct view of it than would have been possible to a Director in the midst of his subordinates, sharing their labours, their hopes, their fears.

The first victories of the new commander are won against the Austrians. Northcliffe's divisional chiefs in this field are Wickham Steed, foreign editor (afterwards editor) of the London *Times,* a man unrivalled in his knowledge of the politics of Eastern Europe, and Seton-Watson, another authority on the problems of that part of the world. After attending a congress in Rome of representatives drawn from all the nationalities which made complaint of Austrian oppression, they set to work to tell the Slavs of Bosnia, Croatia, and Herzegovina, the Czechs of Bohemia, the Slovaks of the Western Carpathians, the Rumanians of Transylvania, the Poles of Galicia, that if they want liberation from Austria-Hungary they must do all they can to hasten the victory of the Allies.

A printing-press works night and day, turning out leaflets, pictures with a religious or nationalist appeal, a weekly newspaper in four languages. Aeroplanes drop these in parcels over the Austrian trenches and in villages where troops are resting. They are shot across No Man's Land in rockets; they are thrown in hand-grenades. Patrols composed of Slav, Polish, Rumanian, and Czech deserters are sent out laden with "literature" to get into touch with enemy patrols and urge others to desert.

One device which specially delights Northcliffe is the performance by gramophones of Czech and Serbian national songs. At many points the trenches of the two armies are so near to one another, that words as well as music can be plainly heard by the soldiers who, against their will, are wearing Austrian uniform, defending the Austrian cause. Moved by the familiar melodies, large numbers desert. They go over to the Italians, not merely "single spies", but in parties. Once a whole company is led in to surrender by the company commander. There are mutinies as well, ammunition dumps are blown up, there are "incidents" during battles which puzzle and alarm the Austrians. They suffer less from the Italians than they do from the distribution among their troops of a million subversive leaflets a day.

The Italians incur Northcliffe's anger by their "stupidity" (so it seems to him). They hold back from the acknowledgment that the races in subjection to the Hapsburg Empire must have the bait of freedom dangled before them. He persuades, protests, to little purpose. Nevertheless the work goes on. Brave men are always ready to go among their compatriots in the Austrian ranks, to tell them how near is the break-up of the Hapsburg Empire, to urge them that the hour has come for them to strike their blow against it. Some of these brave men never return. They have been denounced and shot. Northcliffe is saddened by their fate. But not for a moment must the intensity of the effort slacken.

Not until long afterwards is the effect of the successful appeals to the disloyalty of three-fifths of the population of Austria-Hungary known to more than a very few. The many are ignorant to this day of the part which propaganda played in breaking down the resistance of Germany's chief ally. The weakness of the Hapsburg Empire was the unwillingness of thirty millions out of its fifty million subjects to remain in subjection. This weak point was the one towards which Crewe House directed its whole endeavour.

Until Wickham Steed explained to him the nature of the Hapsburg System, Northcliffe knew little about it, but he grasped at once the necessity for making every attempt possible to drive wedges into that system. "What we have to do, then," he said, "is to make the oppressed nationalities realize that they are fighting against their own interests. Once we get that into their heads Austria will have to go out of the war." This was exactly what happened, though at the time only a very small number of people had any correct idea as to the cause of Austria's collapse.

The German Headquarters Staff were among this small number. They spoke, with fierce contempt, of "Northcliffe's Poison Gas Factory", but could not help admiring the vigour and the cleverness of the "paper campaign" against the ally whom they despised, whose liability to fall asunder they had realized from the start. They did not look for any such campaign on their own front. Disruptive tactics could not be employed against German armies. Even Northcliffe, they declared, would waste his time if he tried to enfeeble the spirit of the troops of the Fatherland with lying leaflets, to destroy their belief in victory by supplying them with news of the general progress of the war.

For several months Crewe House allowed the German High Command to lay this flattering unction to its soul. H. G. Wells was the first director of propaganda against Germany. Northcliffe asked him to undertake this duty in May 1918, after he had received from Lloyd George a letter in these terms:

It seems to me that you have organized admirable work in your Austrian propaganda.... I trust that you will soon turn your attention towards German propaganda along the British and French Fronts. I feel sure that much can be done to disintegrate the *moral* of the German Army along the same lines as we appear to have adopted with great success in the Austro-Hungarian Army.

Propaganda "along the same lines" was clearly out of the question. What Northcliffe now began to study was the possibility of other lines that might, using entirely different methods, have an equal chance of success. Something was being done by the Military Intelligence Department at the War Office. It was dropping over the German lines and behind them a small number of leaflets, not very convincing or stimulating in character. Parcels of these were tied to small balloons fitted with fuses which as they burned through let the parcels fall.

For a short time aeroplanes had been used for the purpose, but the Army leaders were intimidated by an angry protest from the Germans, and (not liking or believing in this new kind of warfare) they declined to let airmen distribute leaflets. Against this surprising and pusillanimous decision Northcliffe fought for some time without making any impression on the military mind.

"If we could by any possibility be beaten", he had groaned earlier in the war, "it would not be by the genius of German Generals, but by the dullness and pig-headedness of our own." Now he had stronger reason to take that view. He was not astonished by the Army leaders' attitude towards "a campaign of paper". They were against everything new. They had not seen the need of gas-masks, steel helmets, or tanks, each of which they opposed as long as they dared. But it did puzzle him that, having agreed to the use of "the leaflet arm", they should refuse to adopt what was by far the most appropriate and the most effective means of carrying on this new kind of warfare. In the end he broke down their obstinacy by an appeal to the War Cabinet.

The problem of influencing the minds of German soldiers was different altogether from that which had been so triumphantly solved on the Austrian Front. It was far more difficult. While the Austrian armies contained large numbers of men who were already disloyal, who were anxious for the war to end on any terms, and who hoped to see the Hapsburg Empire defeated, the German troops were all of the same nationality, all belonged to the same racial stock. They were all proud—or they once had been proud—to be German. They were most of them still believers in the Kaiser legend.

"If Lloyd George supposes", said Northcliffe, "that we can drive wedges into German unity as we have done into Austrian, he must know very little about the matter. What we have to do is to frame an entirely different kind of appeal. Our biggest asset is the fact that American troops are arriving. We must make the most of that. We must harp on it all the time. *'You are almost at the end of your resources in man-power. The Allies have only just begun to pump men out of an enormous new reservoir of inexhaustible depth.'* That is what we must tell the German soldiers. But we need not be in a hurry. It is no use warning people of danger when they are full of hope and courage. Wait till they see how little they have gained by their offensive this spring (1918). Wait till they are feeling discouraged and doubtful of their leaders. That will be the time to strike despair into their hearts by showing them how their situation is hopeless."

For a time, therefore, Crewe House concentrated its energy on sending into Germany every sort of information that could depress the nation. Wells drew up statements of the aims which supporters of the League of Nations idea had before them; of the advance made by British manufacturers in lines such as lenses, scientific instruments, dyes, which hitherto had been left to Germany; of the difficulty the Germans would have in recovering their trade and their shipping. By many ingenious channels news was sent into Germany, mostly by neutrals, either sympathetic or subsidized, whose business took them in and out of the country.

For example, there crossed the Dutch frontier every morning a large number of Dutch workers who were employed on German soil. Every evening they returned to their homes in Holland. An envoy from Crewe House mixed with them, won over a certain trustworthy few, and thus found a means of disseminating either by word of mouth or by printed matter information designed to prove to German minds that their interests were being betrayed.

Before the summer of 1918 had passed came the moment foreseen by Northcliffe at which the paper war could be loosed against the German troops with good hope of success. At the beginning of July, H. G. Wells resigned his post. He had for some weeks, indeed ever since his appointment, been disputing with Northcliffe over the discrepancy between the views which the Director of Propaganda was supposed to hold as to the right method of making Germans dissatisfied and the tone adopted towards them by the Northcliffe newspapers. These were full of threatenings and slaughters; nothing would serve but the extermination of the German race. Their frantic denunciations were in comical contrast with the lofty, reasoned arguments of the Memoranda which had been fathered by Northcliffe and approved by the War Cabinet as a basis for the operations of Crewe House.

It was curiously characteristic of Northcliffe that he was not disturbed by this contrast, that he did not even notice it until Wells brought it to his attention. It was equally characteristic of Wells that such a discrepancy should annoy and even infuriate him.

To Northcliffe the only thing that mattered was "getting on with the job". He never at any time in his life tried to think far ahead. His intellectual processes were not logical; they were intuitive. His imagination, limited in scope, was violent in its vigour. At this period he could see nothing but the necessity of beating the Germans: to this end any and every means should be employed. What did it matter if this means and that means clashed, if they could not be comprehended within the terms of one formula?

In his newspapers he would treat the Germans as the lowest of criminals: that was the way to keep at boiling-point the public indignation against them. In his Propaganda he would be reasonable; he would promise that, if they turned from the Hohenzollerns, they should be received back into the comity of nations; he would say anything that seemed likely to induce them to end the war. To

Northcliffe the result was all-important, any methods by which it could be obtained were justifiable. He considered Wells fussy and meticulous for maintaining that all methods ought to square with one another, for expecting him to lay down for his newspapers the same basis as that on which he was willing to build his Propaganda.

The two activities, he declared irritably, had nothing in common (that was his genuine belief). He "would not allow Wells to dictate to him what he should publish in his newspapers". Wells's high voice rose higher and higher in the endeavour to make him appreciate the shocking illogicality of his position. The writer simply could not understand the man of action. Wells thought Northcliffe unprincipled; thought that he deliberately signed Memoranda in which he did not believe. Northcliffe did believe in them—for their purpose. To Wells, words seemed to be acts: they were binding, they were real. In Northcliffe's view they served merely the purpose of the hour. Nothing could bridge the gulf between minds so far apart. Wells shrugged incredulous shoulders and withdrew. I was asked to take his place.

I had just returned to England after spending six months as a War Correspondent in France. Service during four years on five different fronts (including the Russian, Italian, and Rumanian) had taught me something of soldier psychology. Northcliffe in the United States introduced me to audiences as "the man who had seen more of the War than any other living soul". That was kindly exaggeration, yet he was convinced of my unique experience and told me now that he expected me to bring forth the fruits of it by "hitting the Germans where they'll feel it most". Roughly he sketched the lines which should be followed. "You get the right stuff out", he said, "and I'll see that it reaches its destination."

At once we began to prepare leaflets of a different character. The idea was to convey to the men who might pick them up and look at them their purport at a glance. We illustrated them, we gave simple diagrams, we chose the simplest phrases, the most direct forms of statement. The tone adopted was one of friendly counsel. The intention was to make the leaflets read as if they were the work of Germans who had realized the hopelessness of going on.

The reason for the failure of most of the efforts to influence the German mind was that those who made them did not try to imagine themselves German. They wrote from the British or the French point of view, which at once aroused antagonism. Now the attempt was made (and, as German Generals testified, successfully made) to adopt the German point of view and from this to present every argument against continuing the war.

Northcliffe saw that military effort alone would never end the war. He saw that the Home Front of one side or the other would have to be broken. He understood better than any man in high position on the British side that Armies alone could not win a victory; their successes must be accompanied and aided by ceaseless and energetic assaults on the spirit of the German People. Long afterwards when Prince Max of Baden's *Memoirs* appeared it was seen that the German Supreme Command had, at all events for one short period, a clear recognition of the necessity for this double offensive. In a memorandum which Prince Max calls "an earnest request", German Headquarters thus addressed the Government in Berlin:

How can we deal a blow at Britain in the field and at the same time utilize this blow to bring about the collapse of the British War Machine at home?

The answer is: Germany must employ an adroit, unflagging political propaganda to convey the suggestion to the British people that Lloyd George's "knock-out policy" is alone to blame for the continuation of the war, that it is following imperialistic aims of conquest, while a peace consonant with Britain's honour and security could have been had earlier by negotiation without further bloodshed.

The British Commanders in the field made no such suggestion to the Government in London. The Government acted without their prompting—also without any clear notion of what had to be done—when it appointed Northcliffe Director of Propaganda in Enemy Lands. It was a fortunate choice. No one else would have pierced to the heart of the problem so surely and at the same time have known so well how to take the measures needful for its solution.

It was useless, he saw, to try and depress the German People and the German armies so long as those armies were gaining ground. He waited for the moment when they began to lose ground. Then, he knew, both the soldiers and the population at home would be wavering, uncertain of the issue, depressed. Arguments must be laid before them to prove that the Hohenzollerns were alone to blame for the continuation of the war, that they were following imperialistic aims of conquest, while a peace consonant with Germany's honour and security could be had by negotiation without further bloodshed. At the same time the American numbers and effort must be emphasized, so as to convey the impression that, if the Hohenzollerns were not thrown over, fresh millions would appear in the field every few months until Germany lay in ruins and its inhabitants starved.

Northcliffe could with certainty anticipate the effect of such arguments and information, rehearsed in simple terms and reinforced by pictures. He had spent a lifetime studying the psychology of crowds. That was his business;

he had been successful as a publisher of newspapers and magazines because he understood it better than any other man of the age. The Generals sneered at our leaflets, they made difficulties about scattering them. When the sudden collapse of Germany came, they claimed all the credit for themselves. But it is worth recalling the fact that during the final month of the war, while the German spirit sank lower and lower, to flare up at last in fierce anger against the Hohenzollerns, the successes won against the Germans were not many; in a purely military sense they did not gain a great deal. But throughout that final month the Paper Offensive was in full swing; it had been gathering force since July, when Foch's offensive began to make itself felt; it cracked the German power of resistance; it ended the war.

In support of that statement I will quote here only one piece of evidence. As early as August 15, 1918, Crown Prince Rupprecht of Bavaria wrote to Prince Max of Baden: "Masses of propaganda leaflets have been thrown over to our troops by the enemy and are having a damaging effect on the *morale* of our exhausted soldiers." That was the effect which Northcliffe had confidently anticipated. It became more and more marked as the weeks of autumn went by. Soldiers on leave took it home with them. Soldiers returning to their units carried with them the gloomiest tidings about the miseries in store for all Germans if the Hohenzollerns remained. The "adroit, unflagging political propaganda" was doing its work. Three and a half months of it saw the German Home Front pierced in hundreds of places. The Hohenzollerns were sacrificed. The war was over.

One of our enterprises which greatly amused and pleased Northcliffe was a German trench newspaper. We made it look exactly like the real thing. We filled it with stories and articles interesting to read. An officer picking it up would have had to scan it carefully before he discovered anything suspicious about it. Here and there harmless-looking paragraphs gave the German soldier information which he received from no other source. In the middle of an article otherwise highly patriotic would be slipped a sentence or two intended to startle the reader and make him reflect.

We worked with whole hearts in the spirit of the documents submitted by Northcliffe to the War Cabinet as the outlines of the policy to be followed. We told the truth. We addressed the Germans in the accents of comradeship; there was not one of the staff at Crewe House on whose lips those accents were false. What was emphasized and insisted upon was that guilt lay upon the Imperial Government and that if this Government were overturned the German People would not be held responsible for its misdeeds. When the Peace Conference met, all that was forgotten.

The War Cabinet forgot it; Northcliffe himself forgot it. He did not appear to recollect that such a policy had ever been laid down in documents signed by him. They had served their purpose. The German resistance had been weakened. They had been compelled to ask for peace. That created a totally different state of affairs.

So the man of action again put words aside as unimportant. He did not see that the Germans had been deceived, that Crewe House had been employed to deceive them, that the undertaking offered to them had been repudiated as soon as its purpose had been served. He saw only that the propaganda weapon had done its work well, had created a new situation in which new issues arose, which called therefore for a fresh adjustment of ideas. He made the adjustment accordingly. There was no dishonesty in this.

He did not gloat over the deception practised; did not even perceive it. He simply passed on from one task to another, leaving behind him everything that had to do with the past.

Had he not been capable of this concentration, of this refusal to look at any aspect of a problem save "How can I find the answer to it?" he would not have been Northcliffe, he could not have done a tenth part of what he did. Such is the character of men of action. Among those of his generation he stood pre-eminent, for in him this character was developed to a degree far beyond the common.

It certainly helped the work of Crewe House to get itself done with less delay and friction than other departments met with. At first the printing of leaflets was slow. We could not be sure of keeping the German troops supplied with news. We wanted them to have the latest. Often, we felt, our intelligence must be stale when it reached them. Sir Campbell Stuart, with Northcliffe's authority behind him, arranged very soon for specially quick work both in the Government printing-office and in the transport of parcels to the Front. Half a million copies of the trench newspaper were sent over every week. Of leaflets we were distributing 100,000 a day. "This was a new weapon," wrote Field-Marshal Hindenburg pathetically in his book *Out of My Life,* or rather, he added, "a weapon which had never in the past been employed on such a scale and so ruthlessly." And as to its effect in deepening the demoralization of the troops he went on:

"In the shower of leaflets which was scattered by enemy airmen our adversaries said and wrote that they did not think so badly of us; that we must be reasonable and perhaps here and there give up something we had conquered. Then everything would be soon right again and we could live together in peace, in perpetual international peace. . . . There was, therefore, no point in continuing the struggle. Such was the purport of what our men read and repeated. The soldier thought it could not be all enemy lies; he allowed it to poison his mind and proceeded to poison the minds of others."

It was through proclamations of Field-Marshal Hindenburg and other German Generals that Northcliffe first learned what the value of the Paper War was. We worked on, editing our trench paper; making our leaflets more and more pointed; sending "London Correspondence" to neutral newspapers (Swiss, Dutch, Swedish), which sent copies into Germany; putting slips into books which were going to German buyers through neutral lands; announcing daily the figures of the American divisions which were now taking the field. But we worked in the dark. We could not tell whether our arrows were hitting their target. We did not even know for certain that our productions were being read.

Then suddenly was published an Army Order by Hindenburg deploring the results of the new phase of warfare.

The enemy bombards our Front, not only with a drumfire of artillery, but also with a drumfire of printed paper. Besides bombs which kill the body his airmen throw down leaflets which are intended to deaden his spirit.

And the Field-Marshal was obliged to say that the spirit of the men in field-grey uniforms had been noticeably deadened by this attack. General von Hutier, commanding the 6th German Army, was not less emphatic. He it was who conferred on Northcliffe the title "Minister for the Destruction of German Confidence". He complained vehemently of the "constantly increasing number of leaflets" and declared that Northcliffe was spending "billions". Here he was ill-informed. The expense of Crewe House propaganda was trifling.

It was evident from these testimonies that "the drumfire of printed paper" was producing an effect which alarmed the German Commanders. But few had any inkling of the nearness of the German collapse. Northcliffe had declared at Elmwood in July that it was futile to hope for an early ending of the war. "Mark this," he said, "none of us here will see the end. No people of our age will be alive at the end." In that there sounded the overemphasis which had become so much more common in his pronouncements since his stay in America. But he was not by any means alone in his opinion that the war would last another winter at any rate. Professor Gustave le Bon has shown that Marshal Foch did not anticipate success during 1918. The Marshal himself wrote: "Little by little, as we saw success coming, the front of attack was extended." Foch had not planned the general hail of blows under which the German armies gave ground. General Mangin has told how he was instructed in July to "go forward softly and occupy only positions in which you could pass the winter". Nor had any of the Allied statesmen or generals suspicion that the collapse of the German Home Front was so near. Within less than three weeks of the Armistice Lord Balfour said the end was not yet in sight. "We have no reason to suppose that our enemies, or at all events the most formidable army there, are on the point of disaggregation." He did not know, only a very small number even in Germany knew, how rapid and effective the propaganda from Crewe House had been. "What damaged us most of all", a Staff-officer at the Front wrote in the *Cologne Gazette* of October 31, 1918, describing the state of the German Army during the retreat, "was the paper war carried on by the enemy, who dropped daily among us 100,000 leaflets which were extraordinarily well distributed and well edited." The same newspaper said of Northcliffe after his death: "His particular achievement was the moral collapse of the German people." In another Cologne journal, the *Volkszeitung,* a correspondent at the front said in September: "Our enemies have been very busy distributing leaflets from the air. I have had two of these in my hands and it is not to be doubted that our enemies are in this superior to us, for the leaflets are so well produced that anyone not on the look-out is likely to fall a victim to them."

No wonder the German Minister for War, General von Stein, admitted that "in propaganda the enemy is undoubtedly our superior". No wonder the *Deutsche Tageszeitung* said: "We have a feeling that our enemies' General Staff cannot hold a candle to our General Staff; but we also have a feeling that our enemies have a brilliant Propaganda General Staff, whereas we have none."

That was testimony to "the great services" which Northcliffe had "rendered to the Allied Cause", more striking even than the Prime Minister's letter containing this phrase, written after the Armistice on receipt of Northcliffe's resignation. "I have had many direct evidences", Lloyd George added, "of the success of your invaluable work and of the extent to which it has contributed to the dramatic collapse of the enemy strength in Austria and Germany."

Here was a piece of direct evidence given later. In July 1919, the German writer Arnold Rechberg, said in the *Tägliche Rundschau:* "It cannot be doubted that Lord Northcliffe very substantially contributed to England's victory in the world war. His conduct of English propaganda will some day find its place in history as a performance hardly to be surpassed. He correctly estimated the character and intellectual peculiarities of the Germans."

General Ludendorff in his *War Memories* paid a like

tribute to the director of the operations which caused the moral collapse of the German troops and robbed the nation of its confidence. "Lord Northcliffe", he said, "is a master of mass-suggestion." That was the secret of his triumph in this, the last outstanding labour of his life.

CHAPTER XVI

THE YEARS AFTER THE WAR

He never received the credit due to him in the winning of the war.

Colonel House

So the war ends—shortened, so the Germans declare, by Northcliffe's paper bullets. And so once more "the most powerful man in England" returns to his private affairs. He has had his chances to remain in public life. He has refused them. Because he could not get what he wanted, the position of Minister without Portfolio, he would not take any position at all.

He has abundant vigour left in him, though it is no longer inexhaustible. He is at fifty-three as striking in appearance as he was in youth. He is handsome in feature; his eyes, though they do not open quite so widely, are lustrous, beautiful; his head is massive, set back upon his shoulders with defiant poise. A little too massive his body also, so he complains with a flash of the old humour. Still there is in him at times the schoolboy love of fun, the touch of comical exaggeration, the satirical insight into pomposity or pretence. A man, it seems, with abundant life and energy: a man fit for great employments. Yet no great employment is his.

He might have been going now to the Peace Conference in Paris, one of the British plenipotentiaries, one of the prominent figures in the drama which was meant by the French to be a tragedy for the Germans, but which now in the light of Germany's swift revival is seen to have had the nature of farce. He would like to be going. He feels that, after all the work he has done, his place is there. Perhaps Lloyd George will ask him to go in some capacity or other. "I ought to be there", he says, "to keep an eye on him." And when there is raised the possibility of Asquith's being asked to join the Peace delegation, Northcliffe declares himself immovably opposed to it. "Asquith had his opportunity and failed to make good", he declares. So Lloyd George drops the idea. He is anxious up to this time, the end of 1918, not to quarrel with Northcliffe. He knows quite well Northcliffe's opinion of him; he resents it. But he fears the combined attacks of *The Times* and *The Daily Mail*.

He goes so far, in the endeavour to placate their proprietor, as to suggest to him that he should take a house in Paris, near to that in which he will himself live during the Peace Conference. Nothing more definite than that. Northcliffe, however, considers that he has been invited to be a Peace delegate. He prepares accordingly for a long stay in Paris. Yet, when he goes to see Lloyd George to inquire about credentials, the Prime Minister says, "Oh, I had a purely unofficial position in view for you." Had thought, in fact, that Northcliffe might "manage the Press". Now the quarrel cannot be avoided. Northcliffe is furious, says he has been tricked. The breach, once made, rapidly widens.

The two men have never been more than acquaintances. They did not understand one another. Therefore they did not respect one another. Northcliffe had a contempt for politicians. You could never depend on them, he said. They never went straight out for anything. They shilly-shallied, beat about the bush. They had no pluck, no imagination. It was hard to get them to do anything; they preferred to talk.

In Lloyd George he declared that he saw all the politician's defects magnified by the undoubted genius of the man. He made no allowance for the Prime Minister's difficulties; he did not admit them. "If he took a line of his own and stuck to it, he would get through. But he has no courage, no backbone."

This was no new discovery of Northcliffe's. He had often spoken of what he considered Lloyd George's weakness of fibre during the crisis which ended in his succeeding Asquith as Prime Minister. "I had to push him and hold him up all the time", was Northcliffe's description of that incident. Within a few days of the Armistice he was prophesying that Lloyd George "was going the right way to create Bolshevism in Britain".

"He talks progress, but he is taking in the Old Gang who will prevent progress from being made. I have warned him without effect. He is afraid to stand alone. He has no idea beyond making these combinations in which he always gets the worst of it, as he did from the blackmailers, Arthur Balfour and Austen Chamberlain, Walter Long and Carson, in that momentous week at the end of 1916."

That prediction was within four years exactly fulfilled. The Old Gang did prevent progress from being made, and in 1922 the Conservative elements in the Coalition threw Lloyd George overboard and seized power for themselves.

In an article written a few months later (*The New Illustrated,* February 1919) Northcliffe indicated what line he would have had Lloyd George follow, were he beside him in the Cabinet instead of the Conservatives whom Northcliffe so well knew. "I am assuming," he wrote, "that he would, if he were a free agent, be in favour of a square deal all round, justice for everybody, and an end to profiteering and privilege." But "nothing can ever bring the Tories to embrace willingly such social reforms as those which the soldiers now returning to civil life are contemplating", and Lloyd George, "has not that high moral courage which enables a man to stand alone. The most perilous defect in his character is that he is not sure of himself."

That was a penetrating criticism, and there were other things into which Northcliffe saw clearly at this time in addition to the Prime Minister's character. Ireland, he predicted, would be one of the toughest problems for the combination to tackle. Here he proved himself again an accurate forecaster of events.

I believe I could settle the Irish question in a week if I had power over all parties. Divide Ireland into North and South—that is the only way.

That way was adopted in the end, but only after unimaginable horrors had sowed bitter memories. Had it been decided on at this time (November 1918), Ireland would have been spared civil war; the English People would not have on its conscience the eternal infamy of the Black and Tans.

It was the statesman in Northcliffe who pointed to the solution of an age-long difficulty. It was the journalist in him who added:

And I would make Ulster spend a million pounds in propaganda in the United States to let the American People know why they don't want Home Rule with the South.

The world after the war occupied his thoughts frequently. He had no fixed views about anything, he did not reason anything out. In his more reflective moments he reached by sudden jumps many of the conclusions to which sane people everywhere have since come. But when he felt sore against Lloyd George, or when he was providing his newspapers with "talking-points", he seemed to be the

Photo] [Ira Hill, New York
LORD NORTHCLIFFE AT THE HEIGHT OF HIS FAME

crudest, most frenetic of Jingoes. He would say in a quiet private talk:

I hope this will be the end of standing armies. A force of, say, 100,000 men provided by the nations jointly and highly trained would be necessary, but beyond that no armies should be allowed.

Yet into the public expression of his opinions nothing of that kind was allowed to creep. The line taken by his newspapers filled the minds of their readers with entirely different ideas—ideas of revenge, of "keeping Germany down", of rebuilding the world as it was before the war instead of reconstructing it bit by bit on new foundations.

What these foundations should be he saw—at times—clearly enough. Before the war ended there was drawn up at Crewe House a Peace Policy. This was aimed at removing as far as possible causes of prolonged enmity, at laying bases for friendship among nations more genuine and permanent than the relation which had passed for friendship and had prepared catastrophe.

Among his staff in the department of Propaganda in Enemy Countries there was doubt as to how he would view this effort to direct the arrangements for Peace towards conciliation, away from short-sighted resentment. He appointed a day for the reading of it. He listened with attention, nodded approval now and then. When the reading ended, he made no comment; he turned to his chief private secretary and said: "I want this to appear in all the principal newspapers of the world on the same day. Make the necessary arrangements, please."

Yet his own newspapers continued to shriek for a policy totally different, demanding that the Kaiser should be hanged and the Germans forced to pay the whole expense of the war. "He has not said it" was one of their slogans, repeated day after day as a reproach to Lloyd George for not immediately endorsing these demands. For months a warning to the British People that the Junkers would "have them yet" was printed in large type and prominent position.

Did he then appraise everything as a newspaper stunt? Did he consider the Peace Policy to which he put his name useful merely in that sense, and the slogans equally useful? That is part of the explanation, no doubt. Allowance must be made also for his irritation against Lloyd George; his feeling that he ought to be in the Cabinet, and one of its most influential members; his inclination to put his views forward and force the Government to follow. Most of all must we attribute the inconsistency between the expressions of opinion in his newspapers and the tone of his conversation, which so often astonished persons meeting him for the first time, to that fatalism already remarked on as the strongest element in his mind. It did not seem to him to matter greatly what he or anyone said or wrote about anything. *Che sarà sarà*. What will be, will be.

For a man of action it was a surprising creed. That one who has shaped his career by his own exertions and won spectacular success can believe in destiny is hard to understand. Yet so it often has been; so it certainly was with Northcliffe. Hence the capriciousness, the irresponsibility, the unsteadiness of opinion which marked him as a newspaper man. He did not value consistency. He lived for the moment; he changed with his surroundings, taking on their colour, accommodating himself to whatever mental atmosphere he found himself in. "Which is the real man?" was sometimes queried. "The one who talks quiet good sense with penetrating insight, or the one who fills his newspapers with wild nonsense calculated to sell vast numbers of them to the unthinking and the ill-disposed?" Both were the real Northcliffe. Which of them came to the surface depended partly on his mood, partly on the company in which he happened to be.

Thus, although his newspapers appeared to hinder reconstruction, he himself had a clear notion both of the necessity for it and of the lines which it should follow. He declared that the policy of "crushing Germany" was "idiotic". He wrote to an acquaintance who had protested against the appearance of German advertisements in *The Daily Mail:*

MY DEAR LADY ——,
    I am sorry I do not agree with you about Germany.
  We have to extract from the Germans an immense amount of money. One of two things is possible. We must either (1) encourage German trade, or (2) relinquish the hope of their being able to pay. Which do you prefer?
  Personally I encourage the German advertisements, in the hope that we, and our Allies, may be able to get the reparation that is due to us.

Here again, to illustrate the strong good sense which marked his talk, is a note of a conversation with him about the apprehensions many felt at the end of the war concerning the attitude of the workers and the possibility of attempts at revolution:

N. talked about labour difficulties. Syndicalism arose chiefly in businesses of the second or third generation, in which there was inefficiency, often harmful to the workers, and lack of sympathy.
  The best way to keep men in good humour was to go among them. He had always adopted this plan, though some of the heads of his businesses were always against it. He never put in force a new time-table or began a new development (such as a new edition) without asking the Fathers of Chapels, that is to say, the Shop Stewards, how it would affect the men. The

men were able to see the heads of the business. If they wished it, he would see them himself. The consequence was that he had never had a strike in any of his offices.

Strikes were usually due to bad management, sometimes to monotony of occupation. If people were engaged week after week and year after year in making some small part of a machine or manufactured article; never saw the finished products; had only enough of their attention taken up to keep them from getting their fingers cut off, they would certainly in their spare time take to drink or betting or the wilder forms of political excitement.

One way to counteract this monotony and stimulate imagination was to show them by means of films all the processes and the finished articles and the uses to which they are put. He had done this in the Newfoundland Pulp and Paper Works with excellent results. The workers there would take an interest in what they were doing, even if it was monotonous, when they saw that their operations were part of a chain which began in the forests and ended in the hands of newspaper readers all over the world.

It was absurd to lump all the labouring classes together and speak of them as if they were terrible, unreasonable people, quite different from the comfortable classes. There were grades among them and individualities just as distinct and diverse as among the well-to-do. They responded to the same stimuli and behaved in the same way.

Too little allowance was made for the high spirits of young men among the workers. They had their "rags" as University undergraduates had. Yet the undergraduates' pranks were leniently dismissed with "Boys will be boys", while the others were told they behaved disgracefully, like hooligans and blackguards.

Go among the people who work for you, talk difficulties over with them, treat them as fellow-creatures, and more than half the labour troubles disappear. I told Winston Churchill this when he was having trouble with the munition workers. I said, "Winston, go among them." What did he do? He went about the country making speeches. That is all these politicians can think of.

Few men great in action have clear and decided ideas. Either they carry out the plans of others or, like Napoleon, they try one thing after another until they blunder into catastrophe. Northcliffe sees plainly at this time that the defects of politicians are especially harmful in a period such as the world is passing through. He knows that, whatever his faults may be, he had never hesitated to grasp nettles, never fancied that talking could make up for being afraid to act. Yet for the lack of clear, decided thinking he has rejected the chance to play the part for which he believes himself competent. He will not climb the tree to pick the fruit. He expects it to fall into his mouth. His attitude has been that of Macbeth:

If chance will have me king, why, chance may crown me, without my stir.

"I have observed", wrote Lord Haldane, "that people get things in large measure by insistent demand for them": Northcliffe knew this was so in business life; he did not know that in politics (where solid merit counts for so little) it is even more so. Therefore he is now but a critic, where he might have been a leading actor—and a critic with a personal axe to grind.

Sometimes he feels the weight of responsibility press heavy on him as a newspaper owner. "Yesterday", he writes of a journey to Scotland, "I travelled north and watched people reading the papers in a corridor train. Gracious, what a preponderance we have over the others! I never realized it before, as I travel little by train. The responsibility makes one think and think and think, and I always do think about this responsibility."

Partly to this, partly to the wish to annoy Lloyd George, was due his ready acceptance of the suggestion that he might offer the Labour Party, which had then no organ of its own, space in *The Daily Mail* for two weeks before the General Election of 1918, so that its programme might be put before the voters. He did not hold a high opinion of the Labour Party, but he thought it deserved fair play. With the workers he was always in sympathy, but he did not consider they were ably led. He paid higher wages than other employers and he made conditions of work as agreeable as might be. But he fired up when trade union officials offered any interference with his business. During a railway strike in 1919 a protest reached him from some of the men in *The Daily Mail* office against what they called the unfair treatment of the strikers by that journal. He wrote in reply:

I have no intention of allowing my newspapers to be influenced in this or any other matter by anyone.

For a long period my Press was assailed by the Asquith Government, its suppression was continually threatened, it was persecuted in the law-courts and proscribed in Parliament again and again.

During the war it was attacked by ignorant members of the public, burned in the streets, boycotted by advertisers, and banished from most of the principal clubs and reading-rooms.

Lately it has been bitterly and vulgarly assailed by Mr. Lloyd George because of its independent attitude at the Peace Conference.

I am entirely satisfied with the attitude of my journals towards this national calamity, and rather than be dictated to by any body of men I will stop the publication of these newspapers.

There was no hostility to Labour in that; he simply resented interference with what he claimed as his prerogative.

The same double motive which had impelled him to give the Labour Party space for the statement of their election policies led him to show whirlwind energy in organizing a reception for President Wilson in England.

"The neglect of Lloyd George and Balfour to go to Paris to meet Wilson", he says (December 23, 1918), "nearly led to the President's not coming to England at all." Finding that no plans had been made, he became very active. The Royal Family "entered heartily into the scheme suggested and did everything they could to make it successful". The President's welcome was all that could be desired.

Northcliffe had no personal interest in bringing him over from Paris. He was not attracted by Wilson as a man. But he felt that it was desirable that the President should visit England and be well received. His sense of responsibility as a guide of the public was aroused.

Yet there were moments when he seemed to lose this sense or deliberately disregard it, and these, unfortunately, were the moments at which his doings caused the more stir. When Lloyd George, taking courage at last to turn and rend his critic, spoke scornfully and derisively of him in the House of Commons, there was a general feeling that Northcliffe had brought this on himself.

It was on April 16, 1919, that the Prime Minister, provoked by almost daily pinpricks, was moved to retaliation. He had been angered by a telegram sent to him in the name of a large number of M.P.s who feared, or pretended to fear, that British interests were in danger at the Peace Conference. One of the signatories interrupted him with the excuse that their information came from "a reliable source". At once Lloyd George saw his chance and took it. He knew what this reliable source was, he declared scornfully. A man who was "here to-day, jumping there to-morrow. I would as soon trust a grasshopper." And then he went on to reply savagely to Northcliffe's attacks on him:

I am prepared to make some allowance for even a great newspaper proprietor, and when a man is labouring under a keen sense of disappointment—however unjustified, however ridiculous, his expectations—a man under these conditions is apt to think the world is badly run.

When a man has deluded himself, and all the people whom he permits to come near him help to delude him, into the belief that he is the only man who can win the war, and he is waiting for the clamour of the multitude that is going to demand his presence to direct operations, and there is not a whisper, not a sound, he is rather disappointed. It is upsetting that the war is won without him. There must be something wrong, and of course it is the Government.

At any rate, he is the only man who can make peace. Yet nobody comes near him to tell him so. The only people who got near him challenged and contradicted him. So he published the Peace Terms in advance, and he waits for the call. But the call does not come. He retreats to his sunny clime, waiting. Not a sound reaches the far-distant shores to call him back to his great task of saving the world. What can you expect? He must feel it. He comes back and says, "Well now, I cannot see the disaster, but I am sure it is there. It is bound to come."

Under these conditions I am prepared to make allowances, but when that diseased vanity is carried to the point of sowing dissension between great lands whose unity is essential to the peace and happiness of the world, then I say that not even that kind of disease is a justification for so black a crime.

The Times, Lloyd George went on, was still on the Continent regarded as a serious organ; many still believed it to possess a semi-official character and to be inspired by the British Government. Not everyone knew that it was "a threepenny edition of *The Daily Mail*". This, the Prime Minister concluded, was "his only apology for taking any notice of the kind of trash of which these newspapers have been full for the last few months".

That was a skilful, an effective reply. It admitted of no rejoinder, except, indeed, the rejoinder that twice Lloyd

George had offered Cabinet positions to the man whom he now disparaged. Northcliffe was too magnanimous to retort upon his assailant thus. Like Sir Robert Peel on a more famous occasion, when Disraeli attacked him in the House of Commons after soliciting office unsuccessfully, he forbore to use the *argumentum ad hominem*. The attack did not disturb him. Lloyd George had compared him to a grasshopper. He shrugged his wide shoulders and said: "If we must be entomological, he is a tiresome, buzzing fly, fond of garbage; not a mosquito, because he has no sting."

The onslaught was unfair, in that it took no account of Northcliffe's striking war services, acknowledged so handsomely on other occasions by Lloyd George himself. It suggested personal ambition as Northcliffe's motive for wishing to be a member of the War Cabinet and a negotiator in Paris: that was grotesquely untrue. The speech was also ungenerous. Yet in politics all weapons are considered fair, if they are used adroitly and if the moment for using them be well chosen. Nor had Lloyd George been generously treated by Northcliffe. Most people were therefore amused by the episode and inclined to admire Lloyd George for standing up to "the great newspaper proprietor". They were a little tired of the Colossus of journalism. His power appeared to many to be mischievous, others found it irritating. A satiric saying passed from lip to lip: "Have you heard? The Prime Minister has resigned and Northcliffe has sent for the King." There was sympathy with Lloyd George. It was felt that he had been harried and worried without sufficient cause. His popularity was prolonged by what were so plainly vindictive onslaughts, and by all intelligent readers the attitude of the Northcliffe newspapers was contemptuously condemned. They championed all the lost causes. They failed to catch the after-war spirit, failed even to discover it in the air. Yet he himself was by no means so insensitive. He said that the world would never go back to the conditions that prevailed before the war. He agreed with those who saw peril in government by the Money Power. He had no belief in the possibility of restoring monarchy in Russia. But while he was reasonable, and at times farsighted in his talk, his public attitude seemed to mark him as a fanatical reactionary.

Such justification as there was for this estimate arose in some measure, though neither he nor anyone else yet perceived it, from loss of balance due to the disease already at work in his brain. He was becoming more violent in his likes and dislikes, in his judgments and comments. He narrowed his circle of intimates, surrounded himself with flatterers and parasites, grew intolerant of those who did not agree instantly with anything he might say.

There were exceptions to this. He still paid genuine respect to his mother's views, and, having formed the highest opinion of Sir Campbell Stuart's ability, he was inclined very often to be led by him in matters concerned with his business and his social activity. The young Canadian had been knighted for his work at Crewe House. His value was fully appreciated by Northcliffe, who put him into very high positions on *The Times* and *The Daily Mail*, leaned on him more and more. He appeared to have found for only the second time in his newspaper career someone whose advice he would within limits accept without hesitation, whose activity he did not constantly check by interference or explosive criticism. This had been his relation with Kennedy Jones. Already before the war that had come to an end. "K.J." had given up his positions in the Northcliffe organizations, had given up journalism, the only occupation he understood or cared for. He went into a furniture business, set up a stable of race-horses, got himself elected to Parliament. Nothing interested him as newspapers had done. He sold out of the furniture firm, his race-horses never won, in the House of Commons he made no mark. He had often gibed at men who were tempted away from Carmelite House and expected to set the Thames on fire, men who sank at once into obscurity, thus proving that the strength of the chain did not in this case depend on any particular link in it. Now the same gibe was, unjustly, directed at him.

Northcliffe felt his loss, though he never said so. He knew "K.J.'s" value. He respected his judgment. "K.J.'s" place could never be taken by anyone. Yet from Campbell Stuart he received help not less valuable, though of a different kind.

This association certainly lightened the burden of Northcliffe's last four years, the years between the ending of the war and his death. During those years he was scarcely ever free from troublesome ailments. In 1919 he wrote from Mentone: "I'm told to do nothing but raise sufficient strength to get rid of my ill-behaved larynx, now in the thirteenth month of its wickedness"; and a few days later: "I have to maintain absolute silence—except for an hour's dictation of letters and telegrams. . . . I have to be alone and not use my voice. . . . My wife has come out to join me and it is very disappointing that I cannot talk to her." Again in a pencilled note: "I have now to be as moping mum as a Trappist and must not even dictate letters. 'Help, help!' cry the unfortunates who get letters from me. However, I am learning typewriting . . . I chafe for my printing-presses amid my sunlit orange-groves."

Being forced to go into involuntary exile, he was relieved to find that there was at last someone who could represent him in his absences. He could travel, he could direct from a distance. He felt, he said, that he could leave the actual day-by-day steering to Stuart. Yet the strain he imposed on himself was none the less a very heavy one. *The Times* gave him unceasing anxiety. He called himself its Chief Mule. He had to struggle against methods, traditions, prejudices, which stood in the way of its becoming a useful newspaper and of its getting enough advertisements to enable it to pay its way. When he and the Editor (Geoffrey Dawson, formerly Robinson) disagreed, he could express his displeasure and procure the Editor's resignation. This occurred in February 1919, when Mr. Wickham Steed was appointed, a man of distinguished personality, acute intellect, and very wide acquaintance with European affairs. But Northcliffe could not change the entire staff; he had to undertake the difficult task of instructing them in journalism. He found it very hard, for instance, to introduce order into the make-up of the pages. "A thing we newspaper folk often forget", he wrote, "is that the public do not understand newspapers as we do. They do not know how to find things in newspapers, and they prefer the journal that gives the same feature in the same place every day."

His attention was focused on the smallest as well as the largest points in the conduct of the paper. One day he would send an account of the topics that came up in the conversation round a dinner-table, another would bring a hope "that the Editor will be able to get some of the exclusives that Delane (the most famous Editor of *The Times*, 1817-79) used to obtain. I learnt a good deal about him from his old friend, Lady Dorothy Nevill. He was the champion—to use the modern phrase—'scooper' of the time. He learnt the art from John Walter the Second."

Then there would be suggestions for the advertisement

pages, an inquiry as to delay in reviewing some book of the hour, satirical remarks at the expense of the Personal column. He often spoke and wrote of the difficulty of his task.

Those who imagine that conducting newspapers is an easy task for the idle rich—oil millionaires, shipping millionaires, chocolate millionaires—should have realized by this time that long years of watchfulness and energy, much industry, and technical knowledge are essential to victory.

He resented the intrusion into the newspaper field of men who pursued financial or political gains; he even wrote a pamphlet about this, speaking his mind plainly.

Reference is sometimes made to the Northcliffe period of *The Times* as if it had lowered and injured the property. That period did, in truth, save it from extinction. Before he died it was once more making money; its prosperity since his death is due mainly to the changes he made and the spirit infused into it by him. He left it a vastly better newspaper and a far more attractive advertisement medium than it was when he took it over.

There were eccentricities during his management, but these were the result for the most part of the poison in his system: it made him liable to sudden impulses, even frenzies, and under such influence he issued sometimes strange instructions. Often these were disregarded. The staff of *The Times* behaved all through with discretion and good sense, and as it was in the main the same staff during his ownership and during that which followed, the difference in the paper could not be great when his hand was removed from it. Actually it was very slight and in some directions the change was not for the better. But it was the fashion to sneer at Northcliffe, a fashion set by some who had not scrupled to ask favours of him. To say that he had "almost ruined *The Times*" was easy; few knew enough to be able to query the truth of the indictment.

No doubt most of the abuse muttered against "the Northcliffe *Times*" during his life, and muttered more loudly when he lay dead, was the result of the ill-feeling aroused during the years after the war by *The Daily Mail*. It was stimulating fear and suspicion, sneering at the League of Nations, opposing anything calculated to restore friendliness in Europe. To compare with it *The Daily Mail* of later years is like "appealing from Philip drunk to Philip sober". It stood then for almost everything that people of good will were trying to get rid of. To the alarm and annoyance of these people its circulation grew, its proportions swelled with more and more advertisements.

In May 1921 Northcliffe was spurring on his staff "to the hard work of getting up to our two millions a day". This, he added, could only be done "by getting plenty of exclusive news, plenty of good pictures, good serial stories, and by intensive publishing".

By that sentence he showed what he considered the elements essential to the success of a daily paper appealing to the Many as well as to the Few. He did not mention policy, opinions, leading articles. He knew they did not matter. He knew what the mass of newspaper readers wanted and he gave it to them. He broke down the dignified idea that the conductors of newspapers should appeal to the intelligent few. He frankly appealed to the unintelligent many. Not in a cynical spirit, not with any feeling of contempt for their tastes; but because on the whole he had more sympathy with them than with the others, and because they were as the sands of the sea in numbers. He did not aim at making opinion less stable, emotion more superficial. He did this, without knowing he did it, because it increased circulation.

He played skilfully on the inbred snobbishness of English men and women. He knew they liked to suppose that the paper which they read was read by the Best People. He was well aware that, if advertisers could be made to believe this, they would compete eagerly for space and willingly pay high rates. From the first he had seen the value of letting it be known that *The Daily Mail* did everything on the grand scale. He liked stories to be told of the large salaries it could afford to pay. He liked to impress on the public its wealth and enterprise by sending correspondents to the ends of the earth; sometimes to get news, sometimes merely to write articles. He expected these correspondents to assist in creating the impression that his newspaper treated them in a princely way.

One of them being commissioned for the first time was given this single instruction: "Stay at the best hotels." Another who had put into an article a remark made to him by a barber while he was being shaved was told by the Chief in a letter: "All *Daily Mail* correspondents are supposed to travel with a valet", and this was not entirely a joke.

No one understood better than Northcliffe how large is the element of snobbery in the English character. He had learned from Kennedy Jones that this could be made profitable and never forgot the lesson. They planned the *Mail* to look as unlike a "halfpenny rag" as possible. Northcliffe continually urged the staff to remember that they must produce a paper which appeared to be "for the Best People". Everything had been done from the beginning to create that illusion. He did not find the task of keeping it up easy, but he never missed an opportunity to emphasize its importance. One of the papers had a Beautiful Child Competition. "It seemed almost impossible", he says, "to vulgarize this, but the Editor has succeeded in doing it. Vulgar people naturally dress children vulgarly, and the first children selected were so attired. It is a pity that —— (the Editor) mars his excellent ideas by blemishes which reflect upon the whole of our business. If I have told him once, I have told him twenty times that what he needs is a supervising sub-editor of education and refinement." On another occasion: "I do not think the common-looking women at the Bargain Sales in the *Evening News* will do that paper any good, any more than the common-looking babies did the *Weekly Dispatch* any good."

His own naturally fastidious social taste inclined him to be severe on such lapses, as well as his understanding of the effect upon advertisers of making them suppose that his newspapers went among people with money to spend. By this time *The Daily Mail* actually had this kind of circulation. The response to advertisements in its pages was very much larger and more valuable than that which any rival could show. The Best People did read *The Daily Mail*. It was now seen in first-class railway compartments as much as in third-class. It had made its way from the kitchen and the butler's pantry of the big country house up to the hall table. It sold a larger number of copies daily than any newspaper in any country had ever sold before. And daily he watched over it, daily bent his thoughts to the problem of making it more attractive, daily sent to the staff a detailed criticism of their efforts and their delinquencies. He did this also for *The Times*.

What chiefly strikes those who look through these criticisms is their exceeding good humour, their friendly tone—as of one comrade to others; the absence from them of irritation, severity, harshness. It is impossible to read them and not experience the charm by which Northcliffe fascinated almost everyone with whom he came into close touch. He could be harsh, he was at times irritable. But he never inflicted pain or humiliation willingly. When he did inflict it he was ill or angry, impatient or suddenly provoked. "Now and then", says one of his secretaries, "he would dictate words in the course of these daily messages which when they were read over to him sounded cruel or bitter. He always softened them. He never let any expression of that wounding kind remain." Even when he has to complain of being misreported in his own paper, or of a photograph which slanders his still handsome features, he uses phrases studiously gentle. "Please do not publish that picture of me any more", he requests. "My mother dislikes it."

"I cannot help noticing", he writes, "that in my reply to Admiral Scheer the main and vital part has been taken out—the vital part being my express disbelief that Britain would ever join Japan against the United States. I would be greatly obliged if matters concerning myself were referred to me before publication." That mistake vexed him sharply, for it laid him open to be misunderstood in America. Yet he gave vent to no expression of annoyance. "I would be greatly obliged", he said.

Here is another mild protest concerning himself:

There are in to-day's issue two references to myself, in both of which mistakes occur. On page six I am said to have written a letter. I wrote no such letter. *The Times* has a correct report of what happened. On page three I am said to have congratulated the organizers of the "first" trade parade ever held in the City of London. The word that I used was "finest" (see *The Times*). Such an obvious error as the last I cannot understand.

That is all. No hard words, no demand for anyone's head on a charger. An outsider who had been misrepresented would have been warmer in his language than this. Once someone asked Northcliffe if he was not angered when he saw mistakes in his newspapers. He replied: "I know how difficult it is to avoid mistakes." Abuse of himself he treated as calmly as he treated errors about himself. Yet when a famous legal advocate (Sir Edward Marshall Hall) introduced the name of Lady Northcliffe into a law-case without necessity (as her husband considered), instruction was given to mention his name as little as possible in any Northcliffe newspaper. The barrister's offence was rank. An action was brought against *The Daily Mail* by an actress who had by accident been called the mother of another actress almost her own age. Marshall Hall had to make the most of a thin case. In his speech to the jury he said: "My client may have to work for her living, but her reputation is entitled to the same consideration as that of any lady in the land—including Mrs. Alfred Harmsworth." Some while after the boycott had been in operation the K.C. met the Editor of *The Daily Mail* in the Garrick Club; he complained that his practice at the Bar was suffering badly. As the result of their talk, he offered a formal apology; he was invited to call on Northcliffe, they talked in a friendly way, the ban was at once lifted. In several important suits after this *The Daily Mail* employed Marshall Hall; it also allowed Sir Hall Caine to praise him warmly in an article on a case in which he had appeared. The quarrel was entirely dropped.

Such vindictiveness appears rarely in Northcliffe; very seldom indeed is it the outcome of any personal grudge. Always readier to speak a pleasant word than a harsh one, always wishful to see everyone around him happy, he had nevertheless in his earlier years given way to an impatience, an irritable humour, a roughness in moments of tension which he found it hard to check. Now he has mellowed; grown kindlier, gentler, quicker to make allowances. He has come to value affection more highly than he did in youth. He seems to take pleasure in making the relation between himself and those who work with him agreeable and, if possible, affectionate. "Our two Toms", he says one day, "are sailing forth on a holiday trip, one to California, the other to Canada. They have been instructed to spend as much money as possible and then come home. The Directors have decided on these trips as a reward of special merit."

The "two Toms" were Mr. Tom Clarke (now managing editor of the *Daily News*) and Mr. Tom Webster, the caricaturist. "The Directors" was a figure of speech. Although Northcliffe retired from the chairmanship of the Company called Associated Newspapers Limited in the early spring of 1919, when he was ordered to take a long rest at his favourite Valescure on the French Riviera, he was still Autocrat of all the businesses he had brought into being. Giving members of the staffs opportunity to see the world was his idea; "the Directors" secretly considered it wasteful and ridiculous excess. His generous impulses were often a trial to them.

To a special correspondent who had been unwell he wrote: "I do beg you will go away on a sort of roving commission from the office or, if they will not do that, at my expense. And that you and Mrs. —— will not return until you are thoroughly well. . . . Now please remember that you are not in the *writing* business but in the *getting-well* business."

One morning he says that he "thought continually last night of the Night Make-up Editor, he must have had a very heavy time". Another day he says that this same Editor, "who has been working under great difficulties and is very tired, is to receive a bonus of fifty pounds and to be sent off with a companion for a holiday".

"I want", he writes, "a bonus of fifty pounds to be sent to Jimmy Dunn" (who was in Ireland during the Civil War). "He has stuck to his task, which is that of a War Correspondent in a dangerous country, loyally. He has done his work even when ill and has had very little holiday."

For being unsparing in efforts to push a block (illustration) through quickly an Overseer of the Engraving Department is specially mentioned. "Will the Cashier please see that he receives my thanks and a bonus of five pounds? I am informed also that the make-up men on duty and the electrotypers put in good work. Will the Cashier see that they receive a bonus of fifty pounds between them?"

The death of a man who had been for a short time on the editorial staff moved him to write: "S——'s sudden end is one of the saddest things that have happened in our little circle for a long time. He always looked to me very healthy, but nothing would stop his overworking. The last time we met I had to give him a serious talking-to about it. I trust that we shall be properly represented at the funeral and that Mrs. S. will be looked after."

When men who had long been with him retired, he spoke of them with warm feeling. "Everyone who knows the history of Carmelite House will be sorry to hear of the resignation of the doyen of our staff, Mr. W. J. Evans, who retires on a very well-earned pension and emolument." (Evans was Editor for many years of the *Evening News*. His pension was fixed by Northcliffe at £2,500 a year, his "emolument" at £10,000.)

"It is quite easy for those who, with well-packed pockets, bustle in and out of Carmelite House in 1922 to forget about those who fought the fight 20 years ago," Northcliffe continued.

"I do not know any more nerve-racking task than conducting an evening newspaper. In my opinion no evening newspaper editor or make-up man should work more than four days a week. People do not sufficiently consider that bringing out an evening paper six times a day (six editions) is at least twice as fatiguing as bringing out a morning paper. Mr. Evans played a great part in the building of the *Evening News*."

And after the farewell luncheon:

"Yesterday's ceremony brought lumps, I am sure, to the throats of many of us as we looked at one who has played so great a part in the upbuilding of Carmelite House. Mr. Evans is one of the very few men to whom I would leave the complete control of that building. There are only two others."

Frequently the daily message began with what he called "bouquets", compliments on the excellence of the paper. "The staff has sent me a very pleasing birthday present," he says on July 15, 1921, "in what I call a perfect issue of *The Daily Mail,* with the largest gross sale figure on record." When he returns from his world-tour he writes: "I wish to thank my colleagues most heartily for the splendid way every Department has co-operated during my absence, and especially for the fine paper this morning." On December 24, 1920, he concludes a *communiqué* in which he had pointed out certain defects with the playful remark: "I must have a little Christmas grumble, you see."

It is true that when the Chief went away and remained far from the office, there was still a sense of relief among most members of the staff. But it was less profound than in former days. He bound men to him now with a firmer tie. However often he might worry them with telephone inquiries or suggestions, even though he dragged them out of bed in the morning or, if they were day men, disturbed their rest at night, he inspired their devotion; he made up for lack of consideration one day by excess of it the next.

He never refused to listen to explanations if those who

offered them took the right line. He never resented being "stood up to". Indeed, he despised those who did not stand up to him (the number included some who held very high positions about him). He was always ready to make amends if he had been unwittingly unjust.

A clever young man named Vernon Bartlett,[1] with a fine sense of independence, was sent to a foreign capital as correspondent. He had been engaged originally as secretary to the Managing Editor, but Northcliffe, dropping in on him, plied him with queries such as "What's the price of paper?" "What's the price of ink?" and discovered in thirty seconds that he was unfitted for the job. He therefore found him another. Just after he had installed himself in his foreign residence he left for a few days to fetch his wife and child. His substitute was instructed not to use the cable if he could avoid it.

During the regular correspondent's absence a bad accident occurred. The substitute did not cable an account of it because a news agency was doing so. Northcliffe cabled to the correspondent: "Very bad beginning. Must not occur again." In replying, the correspondent explained and took rather a high line, mentioning also that he had not been able to obtain repayment of certain expenses incurred on behalf of the paper. At once he received a very pleasant letter from Northcliffe and another from the manager offering him an increase of salary! He certainly had no reason to regret his brush with the Chief.

[1] Now representative of the League of Nations in London.

CHAPTER XVII

THE BIG AND THE LITTLE

Northcliffe was one of the most interesting and inspiriting men I have ever met.

C. F. MOBERLY BELL,
Manager of *The Times*

GOOD humour, then, as examples have shown, was the prevailing and the prominent feature of his daily messages or, as they were called in the office, *communiqués*. They leave on the imagination a picture of a sunny-hearted, fun-loving, boyish-natured man. But there was far more in them than that. They reveal a closer knowledge of the public mind than had been possessed by any public man before—or has been possessed since. They show the workings of a many-sided intellect. They would serve, if they could be published with necessary annotation, for a handbook of popular journalism.

He did not pretend that the comments he made were all his own. He frequently attributes them to his "ferrets", men and women who were employed to read all the productions of his presses and give opinions upon them. But in the main what he dictated were his own reflections on the papers he himself had read. They were alive with the vigour he alone could impart to them; they were the expression of his vivid personality, his interests, his humour.

One day he reads in a French journal that M. Clemenceau is wearing a new shape of hat. "Why not get a specimen of these hats from Paris?" he suggests. "It is about time men had a new hat. Why not offer £100 for the best design for a new hat? There is at present only the silk hat, the pot-hat or bowler (what in America is called a Derby), the straw hat, the felt hat of various shapes (usually referred to as a Trilby—I do not know why), and the universal cap."

"A new-hat-for-men competition would be most amusing", he continues, warming to the idea. "Let somebody draw up the rules who understands such things. Do not let anybody handle this who has not framed the rules of such competitions before or he will miss out some vital rule. Let reference be made to hat monotony."

In course of time the competition is launched, a prize hat is chosen. A picture of it is published, but not the kind of picture that would attract general notice. The wearer is too clearly not one of the Best People. "It is a pity", Northcliffe says, "that we did not have it photographed on the heads of well-known and good-looking men. As we have none in the office (when I am away), I suggest that people like Owen Nares, Gerald Du Maurier, and others who combine good looks with popularity should be photographed with the hat on, but, of course, it must on no account be treated in a facetious fashion."

Next day he returns to the unfortunate picture "of the bounder who was put on the main page wearing the hat."

"I heard some nasty remarks about it", he says. "It is this kind of lack of worldly knowledge which hurts the paper. I should have supposed that the humblest member of the staff is well aware that the great *couturières* and many a leading tailor dress distinguished-looking people practically free, for the sake of the advertisement. The launching of a new mode is as difficult as launching a ship. I do not know who was responsible for the vulgar picture, but he has done the hat a great deal of harm and should go home to Hoxton" (a region the reverse of fashionable) "and reflect on his lack of knowledge of the world. Having given the hat a nasty knock, it will take some time to get it right."

A few days later he returns to the hat. "I wish you would get some good-looking men to wear it. As for Mr. Augustus John" (the portrait-painter, who had been photographed in it), "people say that he is as ill-dressed as they say I am. Personally, I consider that tweed is not suitable for this type of hat. The best material for it is undoubtedly brown or grey felt."

And then again: "The hat propaganda refers to 'professional men's orders'. Do the men who write about this matter realize that what the public want to know is not whether professional men wear the hat, but if Bond Street wears it. If once we create the impression that the hat is for professional and business men, we will kill it."

The hat died, not because the booming of it was defective, but because it had served its purpose. It had been for some time a talking-point. It was ridiculed, but it made people talk about *The Daily Mail* and so increased circulation.

Many would suppose, after reading these directions, that the man who gave them was incapable of dealing with larger affairs. They would find that he was not less anxious at this period to keep his newspapers right in their policy on the most important international questions than he was to follow up stunts which would advertise them.

In 1920 anxiety was caused in Britain by the increase of the naval power of the United States. "One of the great problems of the world", he writes (November 24, 1920), "we are not talking about it much—we cannot—is the rise of this huge American Navy which is being pushed steadily forward. I spoke to d'Eyncourt, the Chief Constructor at the Admiralty, and he is as anxious as I am. But what is to be done about it? The Americans are building big battleships. In yesterday's *Times* Sir Percy Scott said big ships are doomed. Can we not get him to elaborate this theme? It may disconcert the Americans. He is an original man and carried his views on gunnery against great opposition. He is a disagreeable fellow, and that is why he was so unpopular in the Navy; but he was right."

A controversy is therefore started in *The Times*. A fortnight later he is writing:

"By far the most important thing in the morning newspapers is Sir Percy Scott's letter to *The Times*."

I am not inclined to accept the view of Sir D. Sturdee, a very stupid man.

I was told that Admiral Beatty had expressed the opinion that the Americans would not be able to man their ships. He tells me that he never said anything of the kind. He knows a great deal about the United States and is fully aware that they have a Scandinavian population of the first and second generations equal to the population of Scandinavia itself, and that during the war they had more naval volunteers than they could do with.

Anyone who knows the United States is aware of the fact that they would conscript sailors just as they conscripted them in the last war, and as they have conscripted drink.

This is the most anxious subject that has appeared in *The Times* in the whole of its history. Britain has never been faced before by a potential enemy with a semi-hostile population of a hundred and ten millions of people who have absorbed an immense share of the world's gold.

A week passes, and he is

. . . glad to notice the way we are following up the Big or Little Ship Controversy. One begins to hear it talked of every day. Nearly every New York newspaper has endeavoured to interview me by one means or another within the last few weeks about our alleged rivalry with the United States and the general

American belief that they have got to build against both Japan and Great Britain on account of the Anglo-Japanese alliance.

Yesterday I gave an interview to the United Press. I first stated that I knew nothing about battleships big or small, but I did know that Fisher told me more than once that the day of the big battleship was over—and that was as far back as 1915. I pointed out that Sir Percy Scott in 1914 told us much about the submarine and was laughed at by those who thought it was an under-water joke.

I pointed out further in my interview that any attempt on our part to combine with Japan would lose us Canada, Australia and New Zealand at once. To my knowledge anti-Japanese feeling in Western Canada is as intense as it is in Oregon and Northern and Southern California. Australia shares these feelings.

Just before the end of the year (1920) he urges that, although he may be going abroad, the discussion on Great Ships or Little shall continue.

It is in my opinion the only way that we can stop the creation of a giant American Navy. If these irresponsible people get a Navy they will use it.

"I suggest", he adds, "that we reprint the correspondence in pamphlet form when it has run its course."

And then, the practical side of him coming uppermost:

It should be neatly printed, with an attractive but not sensational cover and sold at one shilling.

That was the authentic Northcliffe, the man of big ideas who was not above attending to the smallest details.

When he called the population of the United States "semi-hostile" he was not speaking at random. In Paris one day he bought thirty American reviews and magazines. "Without any exception they each contained anti-British propaganda such as

belittling matter,
suspicion-arousing matter,
gross ignorance and mendacity matter;

also many references to our alleged anti-American attitude on everything—shipping, oil, cables, films, books, plays, and sport, even golf."

Again:

I am getting seriously disturbed at the volume of anti-British feeling in the United States. One very level-headed Englishman who knows America intimately writes to me in the following terms: "Whether it be within twelve months or twelve years, I am very confident that this country is consciously or unconsciously preparing for war with Great Britain."

A little later:

I am very glad to read the leading article (in *The Times*) on the American *idée fixe* that we have a secret agreement with Japan to join her in fighting the Americans. It is a mistake to suppose that this idea is confined to readers of the Hearst newspapers. The discovery of the existence of the Pact of London was a great shock to the whole American people. The whole atmosphere of Washington and that of the American newspapers is one of suspicion about Great Britain—an intense suspicion like that which many people in England feel about the Jews. A letter from a friend in New York this week says: "My position as an Englishman here is almost unbearable. I am distrusted even by friends of ten years' standing."

I think that if this leading article is sent to America—I presume some endeavour is being made to send it there—it will do a great deal of good.

Northcliffe reminded his staff frequently that American news needed careful and well-informed handling.

"Why should we call Mayor Hylan of New York Hylam?" he inquires. "I know why. Because the sub-editor who handles the American copy does not take the trouble to read the American newspapers. The other day he called him Hyland. Why should we refer to Coney Island as Coney? Surely we have more than one Irishman in the office and surely they know how to spell the well-known Irish name Hylan?'"

He impressed upon all writers and editors in his service that they must not talk about "our American cousins". He spoke of "the anger aroused in the United States when English after-dinner speakers say: 'We do not regard Americans as foreigners.'"

"Oh," replies the American, "then you regard us as fellow-subjects of George the Third. We are not a separate nation!"

I have heard an English speaker howled down—which is very rare, for they are a most polite people at public gatherings and theatres—for making such a remark.

The Americans should always be referred to as foreigners —and they are foreigners, though, thank God, there are many happy links between us.

He did not neglect opportunities to strengthen these links. When a team of American athletes is expected in London, he says:

It is very short notice, but we must make a success of it. Find out the leaders and interview them. Let someone go to see them who understands how to talk American and speak to them in an American way.

The importance of understanding Canada and showing respect to its prominent men was emphasized by him with equal force. He was "sorry that the first letter I have ever seen from the Canadian High Commissioner" was not given the position it deserved, and he added a hit at the "second-rate schoolmasters" whom *The Times* delighted to honour when they wrote letters to it, a scholastic tradition that tried his patience. He looked on Canada as The

Interpreter's House which could help people in Britain to understand the United States. This was in his mind, he said, when he appointed Sir Campbell Stuart to high positions both on *The Times* and on *The Daily Mail*.

The flexibility of mind displayed in his daily messages helps to explain both his successes and his limitations. He was as ready to discuss the smallest office details of journalism as to fix his thoughts on the "weightier matters" of world concern. He rings up a News Editor at seven o'clock one morning to know "what he is doing about Lady Diana Cooper's skirts", which are attracting attention at the moment. He sends a telegram suggesting as a good subject for discussion "Do women eat enough?" There is a feature for children in *The Daily Mail*. Morning by morning the adventures of a mouse are related and pictured. He watches this with the same alert attention that he gives to naval policy or Anglo-American relations.

"I am receiving many complaints about Teddy Tail", he writes. "Fresh animals should be introduced—comic monkeys, elephants and frogs." Again: "Let us get back to the important subject of Teddy Tail. Some years ago we printed riddles. We cannot increase Teddy Tail's space, but we can reduce the size of the pictures and introduce some other characters and give riddles. Let someone who understands about children get busy with Teddy Tail."

Evidently there was improvement, for later he says:

I must say a word for Teddy Tail. A tiny mite of 2½ years, the granddaughter of a very distinguished person, was brought to me yesterday so that I might tell her all the private life of Teddy Tail, in whose existence she implicitly believes.

Men who have built up large businesses often continue to watch the smallest details, aware that on them prosperity is founded, as well as on the broader lines of management.

Northcliffe was more than anything else a business man, a newspaper proprietor. How to sell his products was his chief concern, not for the sake of the riches they returned to him, but because huge sales were evidence of success and gave him power. No matter for surprise, therefore, that he should give his attention chiefly to the increasing of those sales. "Let us," he never tires of saying, "touch life at as many points as possible, cover a wide field."

In 1921 he points with the satisfaction of a prophet whose counsel has been proved sound to the result of a concentration of insurance canvassers in a northern city of Britain. "We leave a copy of *The Daily Mail* in a thousand houses every day, free. At the end of a week the householders are interrogated. As a result we are taking readers from all the Lancashire papers. The answer invariably given by these new readers is that they like the variety *The Daily Mail* gives them."

He knows, too, they like it because it is easy to understand. "We are writing for about five million people. There is another forty millions who have no acquaintance with what we write about. We must explain, explain, explain." He wants always "to do big things big and little things little", but he has no illusion about the relative value of the two in the daily presentation of news. It is in the little things that the mass of people are most of the time interested. "I hear a lot of talk", he writes one morning, "about the Whaddon Chase dispute. It seems to interest many people much more than the Coal Strike." His judgment was correct. As a "talking-point" a quarrel between fox-hunting aristocrats and squires was worth more than the struggle between miners and colliery owners with its effect on the nation's prosperity and future. He noted this, shrugged his shoulders, and gave the public what it liked. His conception of a journalist's duty did not include systematic efforts to turn that public's attention from the trivial to the significant, from gossip to great affairs.

Often he would touch in passing on some subject of the utmost importance. At one moment he was in favour of setting the unemployed to work on roads instead of compelling them to eat the bread of idleness. At another he "would like more attention paid to the performing animals question. There is an abominable lot of cruelty behind these totally unnecessary performances. Personally, I hate to see performing animals, and I remember when I was a reporter finding out a good deal of the cruelty involved—especially in the matter of performing birds. We must also continue to keep our eye on the Plumage matter until it is really through" (a proposal to get rid of the killing of beautiful birds for the adornment of women's hats).

Frequently he dwelt on the necessity of protecting those who walked the roads from careless or criminal drivers of automobiles. "So long as magistrates regard driving by drunken men as a kind of joke, so long shall we have accidents caused by these people. There should be no fine for drunken motorists and no imprisonment in the second division (where conditions are lenient) for men who drive motor-cars when drunk." He was strongly in favour of "the rigorous treatment of road-hogs". It was "a scandalous thing that any person can get a motor licence in England" without giving proof of competence. "Report as many accidents as possible", he directed. "An American friend who motored from London through Canterbury to my house at St. Peter's told me he was horrified at the danger of our highways with their hidden side roads and cross roads, to which he was unaccustomed in the United States."

He himself is horrified at the increase of reckless driving. "I go by train wherever possible. Send out a man who understands motoring to some of the danger-spots on a Saturday afternoon and see the helpless endeavours of the unmounted police to cope with these devils on wheels, feminine and masculine." A police-sergeant at one of the danger-spots said to him: "What can we do with them, my lord?" "On the other side of the Atlantic", replied Northcliffe, "you would be mounted on a ten-horse-power motor-bicycle and you could catch them." But no systematic effort is made to get the law altered.

All very well to run campaigns against this or that abuse in favour of that or the other reform, in the years when the reason for the existence of newspapers seemed to be news, including comment, and the protection of the public welfare. Now the reason for their existence is seen to be —Advertisements. The Advertisement Director has to make the profits which are distributed in dividends growing larger and larger year by year. He claims the right to a voice in the discussion of news. The reading-matter must be of a character to soothe and exhilarate. The great thing is to persuade people that all is well, that they can spend money safely with an open hand. Dilating on evils which call for remedy makes them uneasy. Serious treatment of social problems is disturbing. Men will not acquiesce in their wives' lavish outlay on dress, on furniture, on household appliances, if there is hint of trouble in the air. Keep the contents of the news pages light and cheerful, therefore: that is the demand of those whose business it is to secure more and more advertisements at ever-soaring prices.

Dramatic the change from the days when Northcliffe began to know daily newspaper offices. Then the humble Advertisement Department was disdainfully tolerated by the Editorial grandees. Now the wheel is come full circle, the change is ruefully contemplated by the man who has done more than anyone else to bring it about.

"It is not pleasant to think", he says (November 30, 1920), "that, owing to the gigantic wages paid in newspaper offices and the high price of paper, newspapers are now for the first time in their history entirely subordinate to advertisers." He does not add to high wages and dear paper the distribution of large dividends, though he does not forget it. "The situation", he concludes, "is such as should make everyone in a newspaper office think."

He thinks a great deal about it himself. "I have held out as long as possible", he declares, "against devoting more space to advertisements." But the crushing increase of expenses makes it imperative either to raise the price of the paper (*The Daily Mail*) or to enlarge the amount of advertising. "Of the two expedients I am decidedly in favour of giving more advertisements." But he makes no attempt to hide his feeling that this is merely the lesser of two evils. "The advertisements are beginning to spoil the paper", he cried a few days later, the journalist in him revolting against so flagrant a departure from the way in which he has always walked. Encroachments on news space fill him with misgiving. "The leading article now begins below the fold, which robs it of its importance. There is an increasingly large advertisement at the bottom right-hand corner of the editorial page. In a few days the advertisements at the bottom of the main page will be increased; that will be the end of that."

Gone the idea of "the busy man's paper", the small, compact *Daily Mail*. From eight pages to twelve, then to sixteen, with twenty and twenty-four looming ahead—that is the outcome of putting the production of newspapers on a level with other profit-making concerns. The making of the profit has become all-important: the whole organization must be regulated by that. No one better aware of this than the revolutionary who threw down the old system and set up the new. If advertising falls off, he is quick to ask why. When it is found to be difficult to print sixteen-page papers without new machinery, he fiercely inquires why this has not been foreseen and provided for. "If the thing is not done within a reasonable time, I shall see to it myself", he shouts at his dummy Directors. Yet he cannot bring himself to look complacently on his own work.

"I am sorry to see so many top-heavy advertisements", he grumbles. Whole pages are spoiled, he says. There is a "beastly big bottle" in one of the "displays" to which he cannot be reconciled. He frequently speaks of "bludgeon advertisements", meaning that they are intended to knock people down. How can he keep them out? "For twenty-five years I have been writing letters and sending telegrams to the Advertisement Department, holding long, wearisome meetings with them, inviting the heads to my various residences at home and abroad, and always emphasizing, 'Do not let the advertisements rule the paper.' After a quarter of a century my patience has become exhausted."

Threats, remonstrances, appeals have no effect. Shareholders are greedy for larger dividends. Profit must be the first consideration. He knows it all the while. He is a Frankenstein. He has created a monster which he cannot control.

Perhaps it is this uneasiness which sets him against an Advertising Exhibition that is held in London. The leading spirit in this effort is a brilliant advertising man who has been with him and taken other employment after some disagreement. One of the features of the publicity for the Exhibition was a parade through London. Northcliffe shook his head. "Sure to rain", he growled.

The day turned out fine and the parade was a success. While it was passing along the Strand, Northcliffe in his car came up one of the streets leading from the Thames Embankment. He was compelled to wait at the top of the street for a long time while the procession wound its slow length along. He fumed, but there was amusement in his eye. The irony of it diverted him. He had to admit the value of the "stunt". And when he got to his office he wrote to the brilliant advertising man that he couldn't stand out any longer. Soon that man was back with him. There was magnanimity in that as well as business clear-sight.

A fertile field of disagreement between him and the Advertisement Side is Insurance. Offering to pay a sum of money to the relatives of persons killed in railway accidents with copies of his periodical in their possession was one of the devices by which Mr. Newnes pushed the sale of *Tit-Bits*. Others adopted it. After a long interval it reached the daily newspaper Press. One journal insured registered readers against travel accidents before the war. After the war, Northcliffe took up this mode of increasing circulation with headlong energy, forced his rivals to follow, and started a costly competition in benefits which enormously increased the number of newspaper buyers. This made it possible to increase in proportion the charge for advertising space, but Advertising staffs did not like Insurance; they found that many advertisers denied the value of the additional circulation secured by this means. It was not easy for Northcliffe to overcome either this reasoned objection or the prejudice which, as he often said, he always encountered when he proposed anything new. In this matter, he complained, "the elder statesmen and die-hards of Carmelite House could not see beyond their own noses". He remained confident to the end that Insurance was both legitimate and effective. Was it not helping to lift the circulation of *The Daily Mail* towards the two millions of his constant desire?

He had instituted long before this the net sale certificate, which showed advertisers exactly how many copies were sold and enabled them to judge whether space was worth to them what they were asked to pay for it. Until these certificates were offered they had been obliged to content themselves with a vague statement as to "circulation"; this might mean copies printed, of which large numbers were returned unsold. Northcliffe maintained that the advertiser had a right to more exact information, and, as he could show larger figures than anyone else, he introduced the practice of supplying, and even publishing, this information. His aim from the start of *The Daily Mail* had been to reach the point where he could give a Million Sale certificate. This he was able to do soon after the ending of the war. Then at once he fixed his ambition on reaching two millions. He believes now in Insurance because it is helping him forward towards this end.

What is his motive? What spurs him on? Not greed of money. He has all he wants; "more perhaps than is good for anyone", so he says sometimes, so he told the Middle West editors at Kansas City in 1917. He is not extravagant in his tastes, profuse in expenditure. When he is paying a visit, he remarks on the number of flunkeys and says, "There is so much luxury, which, personally, I don't think is good for anybody." As for desiring great possessions on their own account, that has never been his way. He points sadly to men who have been ruined by riches. "Poor K.J." he says, for K.J. is one of them. After he has quitted the newspaper trade (which, he admits, he "found a profession and left a business") he tries shop-keeping, horse-racing, and House of Commons—and finds satisfaction in none of them. He dies before his time, a disappointed man. Mere wealth was not his aim; he wanted something—he did not know what it was he wanted—which wealth might mystically bring him to make him happy. "Alf" had no illusion of this kind. He estimated riches at their true value. He knew what they could bring—and liked it. Otherwise, to be wealthy was nothing to him. Those who set their hearts on riches, heap up their gold, are fearful about losing any of it, love it for itself, are chary of spending. Northcliffe has no use for money save to spend it. He is not interested in the size of his fortune nor in the way business advisers invest it. He could do without it, he says confidently. He can always make a living by his wits.

"Some of my brothers are afraid of revolution. They think their money may be taken away from them. I have no concern at all for mine. Whatever state of society might be substituted for the present one, there will have to be newspapers. I should never starve." Nor does he now desire advancing circulation for his journals because it is tangible, palpable evidence of success. Once he did so desire it, and won it. Now his success has been so long acknowledged, it needs no further proof.

Where, then, must we look for the spring of this endeavour in his later years? Partly in the vital force of him, as yet little weakened, still imperiously demanding outlet and employment. Now that he has missed the chance of a part on the stage of government, he can give that vital force no other work to do. After his short and successful experience of public life he has turned back to tasks which seemed to have been laid aside for good. He "does the thing that's nearest". He is uneasily conscious that these tasks are unworthy of one who has easily and competently handled great affairs. He must therefore accomplish them with startling results; must let the world know that his vigour is unabated; must force it to say, "What a man has been lost to the work of rebuilding after the war!"

How, then, explain the striving of some of his newspapers to hinder this rebuilding? Why did he fail to discern in their ravings a fatal hindrance to the growth of that conception of him which he wished to implant in the public mind? The explanation may be found by contrasting the line taken by *The Times* with that of *The Daily Mail*. In *The Times* there was apparent (in spite of its vagaries) the mind of a man (Wickham Steed) who always looked forward to the reconciliation of past enemies, to the restoration of a true peace. *The Daily Mail* had no such steersman. The direction of its policy was in the hands of smaller men. Northcliffe left it almost entirely to them. In his daily messages he seldom even mentioned their treatment of the matters which concerned the welfare of nations; he confined himself almost entirely to the technical side of their activities.

In truth he did not think it much mattered what was said in leading articles, nor how the public were misled by the colouring and suppression of facts. He himself had no doubt that hatreds would soon be forgotten; he saw the nations eager to emancipate themselves from the tyranny of war and preparations for war. But he did not feel called upon to try and hasten the process. He did not, indeed, believe that possible. What would be would be, no matter what was written or said. If *The Daily Mail* readers liked its attitude, as its steadily climbing circulation showed they did, why change it? It could make no difference to the unfolding of Destiny's plan.

This, then, was one motive for his effort to increase sales: the wish to show that he could still make the world open its eyes in astonishment at his feats. And mixed with that was a curiously defiant and spasmodic personal vanity, a new element in his character, an element due undoubtedly to disease of the brain, of which the seed had been sown in America, mixed with the flattery that for the first time disturbed his mental poise. Until a late period in his career he had no wish to be in the public eye. He made it a rule that he should not be mentioned in his newspapers. He disliked appearing in public. He discouraged even the printing of his portrait. In a letter to one who asked him for a photograph to reproduce, he said in the early days of his fame: "I don't want to appear in your Gallery of Famous Journalists. I object to publicity. I am like the small boy who at a Sunday-school treat was asked, 'Tommy, would you like some jam?' 'No, ma'am,' he replied, 'I works where it's made.'"

He remained of this mind for many years. During the war his attitude towards publicity altered. He now seems to seek and to enjoy it. One of the strangest illustrations of this is given in 1921. He invites thousands of the men and women employed by him to a luncheon at Olympia, an enormous building used for exhibitions. He addresses them with the aid of a loud-speaker. He allows an eccentric clergyman to offer up prayer, referring to him as "Thy servant Alfred". He positively courts the homage of crowds that he once took pains to avoid. The gathering was held on a Sunday, May 1st. A few days before that he wrote: "My doctor is emphatic that I should not be present at all, and that I certainly should make no gramophone records for the occasion. However, I am just off to the large gramophone works at Hayes to see if I can bear the strain, and I shall be present on Sunday for an hour and a half, and will be accompanied by my lady and my mother." He did not make the records, but he appeared at the luncheon and spoke with some difficulty. He was heard little better than he had been in the Madison Square Garden, New York.

However, the occasion gave him genuine pleasure. "Yesterday's moving function greatly stirred those who have been at our daily task a quarter of a century", he wrote the next morning. "It was a magnificent piece of organization in every detail. I am quite certain that when I said such an entertainment could be provided in no other country I was right. . . ."

A hint of megalomania in this and in other of his sayings and doings makes some of his friends anxious and unhappy.

A year later this new fondness for being in the centre of the picture has become stronger. He resolves to make a tour round the world, not for rest, recreation and health, but in a sense an official tour. No sooner is his intention known than invitations are showered upon him. There is, it seems, a curiosity everywhere to look at a man about whom everybody has heard so much. Kings, princes and governors shared this with the common people. Each of the States of the Commonwealth of Australia proposed to honour him with a banquet. New Zealand could not be left out. The French Government hoped he would visit French Indo-China. The Dutch Government offered him entertainment in Java. The American Government assumed that he would wish to see something of their administration in the Philippine Islands. The Viceroy of India, Lord Reading, asked him to be a guest at Delhi.

Thus the planning of the journey was a difficult task. So many invitations had to be refused. It was like a puzzle, he said, to fit the others in. At last all was ready. On Saturday, July 16th, he left England, and one of his last messages expressed the hope that "no one would give up his Saturday holiday to shake hands with me at the railway station", though "I need hardly say I shall be happy to see any of my friends there".

A characteristically thoughtful touch from one who knew what, to newspaper men, Saturday holidays are.

CHAPTER XVIII

ROUND THE WORLD

Nobody could exchange half-a-dozen words with him, nobody could even cast a second glance at him, without being aware of something unusual. . . . With his clear-cut features, his large and beautiful eyes, and his naturally dominating manner, he was bound to command attention wherever he went.

E. T. RAYMOND
in *Portraits of the New Century*

AFTER his death some of the notes which Northcliffe dictated day by day during his travels and sent home as letters to his family were published.[1] They made an interesting book. Interesting not alone by reason of his colourful descriptions and shrewd comments, but because of the self-drawn portrait it contains. A portrait drawn unconsciously, without any posing. He had no thought in his mind but to bring before his "little circle" (the affectionate phrase was very often on his lips), as vividly as his power over words permitted, the scenes unrolled before him, the incidents of his tour. That is evident on every page. That is the chief value of the book. It helps greatly towards an understanding of the man who spoke it at odd moments in sweltering steamer state-rooms, in bare hotel suites, in official residences where it was hard to snatch a moment to himself.

He could not say that it was "at any time a pleasure to write it". He had to dictate much to a secretary who could only write longhand, and "longhand is maddening to one whose home typists can take down accurately at 150 words

[1] *My Journey Round the World*, 1923.

a minute and read their notes correctly months afterwards". Also there was "an absence of that leisurely solitude which makes for good authorship". The Diary was "thrown at my various secretaries and strangers or scribbled by myself in baths, cabins, and trains, in stifling heat very often". His notes were flung together without any idea that they might appear in print. He said he had no intention to write an account of his tour. He replied to publishers who offered to publish his book that there would be no book to publish. The notes were unstudied jottings, made for one purpose only. Whatever else he left undone, he never failed to write home. Daily he sent a cable to his mother, daily he added a little to his home folks' travel-diary, no matter how tired he was.

Thus the first impression registered on the imagination after a reading of this book is identical with that made by the messages or *communiqués* to his staff: the impression of a warm-hearted, sympathetic, generous nature. As soon as he settles in a state-room he arranges at the end of his bed "what I call my shrine: photographs of my family and my friends which I look at every morning and evening, and all the little keepsakes that were given me for the voyage". Another day he says: "I would like those who gave me little 'keepsakes' before I left to know that among the most used are Mother's little book and the case of scent-bottles—nothing is more refreshing than eau-de-Cologne and lavender water in the tropics—and the medicine chest, which is used every day, the thermometer and barometer, and the automatic 'dater' given me by my wife's mother. This morning, owing to the skipping of a day, everyone is at sea as to what day it really is. My little dater tells me that it is August 21st."

"Mother's little book" was *Daily Light on the Daily Path*. The "little book full of wisdom which Mother gave to guide me", he calls it after he has been familiar with it for some months, and quotes from it the saying: "It is good for a man that he bear the yoke in his youth", adding the unexpected comment: "I do often ask that my early 'success' may not have spoiled me; but I did bear some yoke, a good deal more, in fact, than I like to talk about."

On December 24th he dates his notes "Christmas Eve—Mother's Birthday". And on New Year's Day he writes: "I woke at exactly seven minutes to six this morning, which was seven minutes to twelve last night in London. I thought of every one I am fond of, all the great armies of people who work for me on the St. Lawrence in Canada, in Newfoundland, Paris, Manchester, London, Gravesend, and everywhere else. Not one single department forgot me this Christmas and New Year." Weeks before he has mentioned sending off "our New Year's cards and letters". "Those who don't get cards from me will know they have been stolen in the post, for I have missed *nobody*."

He tries hard to put work ("my dear work") out of his thoughts, but he cannot help recollecting that it goes on. "This Monday, August 8th, we are exactly seven hours behind London summer time. It is five minutes past four in London—*The Daily Mail* conference is beginning." He feels that he must not be away too long. "It is time", he says in January, "that I relieved those who are carrying my burdens at home."

At a place in Queensland called Indooroopily he visits family connections and finds very interesting "the process of tracing family likenesses to their kinsmen at home". He mentions often that people in the crowds at railway stations hold up copies of his publications to show him that they penetrate to the ends of the earth: this pleases him. He frequently speaks, too, of what he calls the "ghosts" who arise everywhere to greet him. Old schoolfellows, men who have been in his employment, men who worked with him in his early, inconspicuous days, "people who have been entertained at our houses", a "next-door neighbour in Hampstead in 1888". He has a friendly word for every one of them. He is glad to see them; they "remind him of home." "Are we homesick?" he says in one letter. "No, but I don't say we should not be if we were not on the way home and getting nearer to it every day."

Nothing more grotesquely remote from the truth than the belief so oft encountered that he is cold, self-centred, with no time for anything but his business, and no aim in his business for anything save making money. In all the Diary not a sentence to suggest that he had money in his thoughts. He notices wherever he goes what birds there are, is delighted when he discovers one that is new to him. A bird sanctuary gives him keen pleasure. "These wild things, which fly from the gun when afield, literally feed from the hand when here." And then he adds: "I saw a very tame rhino. Who wants to shoot these poor beasts?" He remarks continually on the flowers that he sees, has a quick eye for unfamiliar trees. "How nice it is" (in Cairo) "to be back again among the roses and violets and oranges after tropical flowers and mangoes!" On the first morning of his stay at the Viceregal Lodge, Delhi, "I woke up and found that this low, quiet house is set in lovely English gardens with hollyhocks, roses, lavender and dephiniums".

He never fails to describe the landscapes, the nature of the country he is passing through. Fujiyama fills him with wonder. He speaks again and again of the unearthly loveliness of Japan's wonder-mountain. Of "that superlative work of art, a noble Japanese garden", he gives an exquisite tiny picture.

A Japanese garden is, above everything, a Place of Peace. No sounds save those of the falling water and rare voices of birds spoil that utter silence which envelops it as with a gossamer veil. Silence! You cannot guess at the meaning of the word till you have roamed amid the flaming maples, leaned over the little bridges which connect lake-island with hillside, and have watched for hours a couple of medieval figures in a medieval punt scouring the bottom of the lake. A beautiful wood-and-paper Japanese house crowns one of the hills in this perfect garden, a house where my friends and I drank out of frail cups the finest Japanese tea.

The actual tea and the honourable method of drinking it are but symbols of one of the most beautiful doctrines in history. Properly to drink and appreciate tea, you must drink it in a beautiful garden. In order to appreciate both it is necessary to attune your mind to beautiful things—and, say the Japanese, none are more beautiful than Gentleness (which means kindness), Good Manners (which, to my mind, is the same thing), and the Courage which makes the Perfect Knight. Some of us (most, I believe) would say that we have here a Trinity in Unity. . . . In such surroundings, under such a cloud-flecked sky, amid such blue-green hills, who but a churl could fail to acquire the alleged essentials of Japanese chivalry—Gentleness, Good Manners, Courage?

He does not reserve his interest for Nature and the beauty contrived by man: he looks into industries, he visits especially newspaper offices. But he is clearly not of a mind to inquire how much this cost, what profit that is making, whether there are openings for profitable investment. And, showing none of the acquisitiveness of the Rich Man, he does not display either the usual characteristic of the Powerful Man. He will never take advantage of his position, never claim privileges or exemptions on account of it. At Honolulu, "after our visit to the newspapers we made a dash for the boat and arrived there at 2.59, the sailing time being three o'clock. The captain would have 'held' the boat for me, but I am determined I will not set a bad example to the other passengers." When noisy passengers disturb the ship, and "sing hilariously at 2.30 a.m.", other passengers "suggested that I should complain to the captain. I know all about ships' rows and feuds, and I shall complain of nothing." When he makes a railway journey in India, "the dustiest journey I have had for a long time", without any special accommodation, he says: "There was no private car for us, but I think it does people good to come down a peg. We got on very well indeed."

He is at times oddly modest about the wish of so many people to see him. "I think one of the reasons for the intense curiosity shown is that in these places they hardly ever see anybody." Sometimes he laughs privately at the attentions paid him, though he is very careful not to let those who pay them think he is anything but grateful.

When the Warden of a District in Tasmania tells him that receptions have been arranged at every place on the road, he smiles and gives no sign of dismay, but ruefully writes in his Diary: "He thought I should be pleased about it!" Approaching Marseilles, he mentions the reception he is to have there and then says thankfully: "After that it's private life for me. I've had enough and to spare of fusskins." He records an entertainment towards the end of the tour which he was obliged to attend, "and where, for the last time, I hope, on this circumnavigation, I was the Prize Pig of the Show". When the *Egyptian Gazette* calls him "Northcliffe, the King Maker", he says slyly: "Perhaps a teeny-weeny bit overdone."

Nor is he at all the kind of Great Man who resents being taught. Wherever he goes, he picks up information. "I had no idea of how much I didn't know. If you want to find out something, go yourself; if you don't want to, send someone else to look." He makes a note to get a history of Penang when he gets home. "We know nothing about other peoples", he laments. "What thousands of little things one has to learn in order to be successful with Eastern people!" (The particular "little thing" which prompted this reflection being that the natives of Ceylon must be called Sinhalese, not Cingalese, if one wishes to avoid giving offence to them.)

Again: "The value of our trip has been to counteract some very prevalent thoughts. It has taught me that Orientals don't like Western rule. An eminent Filipino said that, 'It is better to have our own disorderly government rather than be interfered with by Americans.'"

Would he have tried to beat this salutary truth into the heads of the readers of his newspapers if his life had not been so soon cut short? Who can say? He did not seem always to connect learning with teaching. He was "mighty keen to be back in that very small circle in which I live and mighty keen to help with my newspapers", but he records no keen desire to tell the world what he had been finding out about it and about the people in it. He has never had didactic impulses.

From fellow-passengers he "learns more than by almost any other means". On the ship which takes him from Hong-Kong to Singapore, "I have talked", he records, "with the following people: Portuguese; Bombay Mohammedan merchants trading with Japan; Australian commercial travellers; a Norwegian mining engineer; an Englishman living in South Africa who is taking a holiday in China, Java and Japan; the British consul at Kobé (Japan); Americans going round the world (two ladies); Japanese going to Scotland to fetch a ship; and people of whom one knows nothing and who give away nothing as to their affairs. There are always these on every ship, just as there are people who see nothing. There are always people who see nothing and can't understand why they came. Also there are prejudiced people, such as Englishmen, who object to everything everybody says. Americans are as bad. We met one American who said, 'Whenever I meet an Englishman, I make a point of telling him what I think of his little ant-heap.' But travelling in the Far East is a revelation as to Britain's greatness, and our vast possessions make Uncle Sam 'sit up and take notice', as he says."

Thus, although he assures his mother, who has asked anxiously when he means to take a holiday, that "the greater part of this tour is cabin and deck-chair—ample holiday for anybody", his mind is seldom at rest. He is for ever listening, talking, reading. "I'm learning more and more about *The New World of Islam,* which book all should read." Clearly he enjoys himself, except when the "fusskins" become too wearying. From all whom he encounters there is some information or some entertainment to be drawn.

"On one side of me at table (Bombay to Suez) sits an Australian millionaire who lets me know at every lunch-time of some fresh development of his wealth. On the other side there is a young wife going home to increase the population. She has her mind running upon a future Etonian. Being chained up with a number of one's own species at close range is instructive. In your circle at home you pick your associates, avoiding people you don't like. Here you are up against folks, whether you like it or not. I hope the experience is making me more tolerant of others."

He resists the temptation to shut himself off from the rest. He enters good-humouredly into the fun of life on shipboard. "A nice Mrs. Jay busied herself and provided Prioleau and me with costumes for the fancy-dress

Photo] [*Ernest H. Mills*
LORD NORTHCLIFFE AS HE WAS TOWARDS THE END OF HIS LIFE BEFORE ILLNESS ATTACKED HIM

ball. I had a beautiful silk mandarin robe two hundred years old. I am getting quite frivolous."

John Prioleau was his principal private secretary on the trip. The last words in the Diary are these: "Let me finish by saying that my chief companion, Prioleau, and I went round the world together without a cross word. It says a great deal for Prioleau." It said also a great deal for Northcliffe. He knew that he was inclined to be exacting sometimes, sometimes short-tempered. He resolved to keep these faults in check. He was not afraid to say that, as he might get tired now and again of those who went with him, so they might get tired of him. At the start he arranged with his little staff that

they should keep apart in ships so that we shall not get tired of each other. I told them the old joke of the butler and the master. "You give me notice, John? What's the matter? You have been with me many years, you have been treated like a friend, received good wages, good living, and had plenty of spare time to yourself." "Quite true, my lord," replied John, "but the fact is I hates to see yer faces." This is a good motto for a companion, especially as the arch-traveller is a man of irritable disposition when aroused by politicians, autograph-hunters, reporters, cinematograph operators, camera fiends, admirers, cranks, financial schemers, and leg-pullers in general.

Not many prominent people know themselves as well as Northcliffe knew himself; very few admit their own failings as he did, or show the same brotherly consideration for those who serve them.

Tolerant of people, he showed, too, a refreshing lack of national prejudice as he journeyed. "It is good to see ourselves as others see us", he says. He sympathizes with the complaint of Australians that houses in England are seldom "equipped with the modern conveniences of life and are nearly all of them dark inside". He agrees that

English carpentry is inferior to American. In a Japanese train he passes, on the way to the restaurant car, "a severe-looking English party", and adds the caustic comment, "My goodness, how English we look when we are abroad!" He reflects, when he is in Australia, on the wretched manner of existence to which great numbers of people are condemned in Britain. "I cannot bear to contrast our vast slums with the sunshine and plenty here." He was taken to see "what they call slums, but there was no slum about them. They resemble our poor suburbs and are no worse." He cannot understand why anyone "who has the money to get here with" should be content to stay in England. He listens to New Zealanders who tell him why they or their parents would not stay there. "The squire and the parson" drove them out, and drove out very fine people. He finds it "no wonder these young people are very different to the peasants of Essex and Wiltshire. Their attitude is more like that of Scotch people (but with no respect for the laird). They are independent but polite." On the other hand, the titled folk who have gone to New Zealand have been "very bad specimens". "Even now each town has its little coterie of well-born remittance-men —those who live on doles from England."

He goes to Japan firmly opposed to renewing the Anglo-Japanese Treaty. He is not inclined to like the Japanese, yet in all his comments he is fair and friendly towards them. He separates "the Japan whose brutality is notorious, the Japan who is obviously trying to rule China in order that she may rule the world", from the other Japan of charm and beauty and nobly attractive ideals. He is grateful for the politeness of the people in the streets. "I was told that they stare, but they don't stare as they do in Germany or Spain, where one is followed about in small towns by crowds. Here the little staring I have seen doesn't seem at all offensive." Again, at Osaka, "Japan's Manchester", he sees "none of that rude staring we have been told about. I wonder how much staring there would be at Liverpool Street Station about the same time of day (11 a.m.) if a party of Japanese in decorated cars turned up and had to face a gang of cameras." In the hotel at Kyoto he is made to feel "rather ashamed of some of the hotels in our large provincial towns when I compare them with this one". The railways are "as good as any, and the meals served in the restaurant car are quite up to those in England, with a very quick service". The same fairness of mind towards people he does not care for makes him admit that it was the Germans who developed ships into sea hotels. "To be honest, it was they and not we who gave the world the promenade decks, abundant baths, single-berth cabins, and varied diet."

One custom of the Far East he cannot speak of without disgust; he dislikes intensely being pulled about by men in rickshaws. It offends his sense of human dignity. Singapore displeases him for several reasons; it is a "hustling, noisy, cocktail- and stinger-drinking" place ("stinger" being the local word for whisky-and-soda). Also, he remarks, it is "rickshawing". He notes with pleasure when he reaches the Dutch East Indies that "there are none of the hateful, man-pulled rickshaws here". Another habit that jars on him is "the drinking in the Far East" among British and Americans, especially the drinking by women. "I am told it is no uncommon thing for a woman to have three or four cocktails before lunch. At a reception given to me the other afternoon I saw the women drinking cocktails at five o'clock. The climate here (Peking) has nothing to do with it; it is habit." But he pulls himself up for thinking that it is "unladylike" in women to walk about on deck smoking. "Well, if they sit about smoking, why should they not walk about smoking? A distinguished general's girl walks about smoking with her father. Why not?"

If she had been a woman, not a girl, he might have felt less indulgent towards her. He has an instinctive sympathy with the young. He has not "grown up" himself in the sense of becoming static instead of dynamic; he does not talk pompously, praise the past with fatuous complacency, hate change. He likes to be with young people. He puts himself on a level with them, does not assume airs of omniscience or superiority. Children arouse a protective tenderness in him. He laments the late hours "little mites of two or three years" are allowed to keep on a French ship; he wishes "they were put to bed in the afternoon". On another voyage he notes that "there is a three-months-old baby on board. I notice that as we get farther and farther into the tropics the little mite gets paler and paler." On a P. and O. steamer he finds every specimen of humanity represented, and mentions some of them, leading off with "a number of delightful children whom every one loves, with their audacity in climbing in dangerous places". Also there are "crowds of healthy young people who play games all day, to the annoyance of the older people". Clearly he rather enjoys the contemplation of that annoyance.

With satisfaction he remarks, between China and Singapore, that "the children on the whole look very well and seem happy." Some of the tiny ones whose English mothers are taking them home from China for the first time "speak nothing but Chinese, having been brought up by Chinese servants. I say to them 'Chin chin' (How are you?) and 'Chow' (food), the only Chinese I know." Buddha loves the little ones, he learns in Japan, watching a child of four float a prayer in the sacred pool of a temple. "Of all the holiday folk who thronged its courts the children were the happiest and the most at home. Whether at twelve months he crawled painfully on his fat tummy along the gravel, or at the immense age of six lorded it among those who fed the wheeling clouds of pigeons, the child was the person who mattered in the Temple on this Day of Flowers." Wherever he went he had an eye for children, thinking no doubt of his unofficial family in England, which partly made up in his latest years for the disappointment of childless marriage.

It was his vivid enjoyment of the interest in human life which kept him alert and cheerful during this long tour. That the formality and the hurry of his visits on shore tired him was plain. As much as possible was done to spare him fatigue. The Chinese put a train at his disposal. The Suez Canal Company made every arrangement for his convenience when at their invitation he passed through the Canal in a yacht. But "travelling in this fashion, one gets all the annoying experiences of royalty. One has to be up at all hours to receive people, to grin and bow, make inane talk before cinematograph operators, and enjoy mighty little privacy." He was always glad to get off to sea again. "Be it ever so humble, there's no place like—a ship", he says. Just after the New Year, when he has still nearly two months of travel before him, he lets it be seen that he longs for the settled routine of his English existence. "There are lots of things we circumnavigators would like, but which we very often don't get", he writes. The following, for example:

1. A nice cup of tea or coffee on waking, with a newspaper less than a month old.
2. A bath with hot and cold taps and not a barrel full of water, a tin dipper, and a concrete floor.
3. A climate where you are not wet through by one or two

swings at golf, and where you need not change your clothes all day long.

4. A telephone and regular daily work.
5. A lunch which doesn't need two or three tablespoons of Lea and Perrin's sauce to help it down.
6. An afternoon nap with no flies to bite you.
7. No black, yellow, and other polyglot reporters asking, "Will master kindly say few words?"
8. An evening paper. My! what a treat an evening paper will be.
9. A little twilight.
10. A dinner without punkahs or electric fans or black servants.
11. A bed, not a mosquito cage. Smoking inside mosquito bed netting is dangerous. It can only be done if Frederick sits by with a bucket of water ready, as he has done.
12. A bedroom in which you don't have to search for snakes before going to bed.
13. A night without noises, such as that of the lizards up and down the ceiling calling each other, the distant tom-toms, the flapping of wings of flying-foxes—those horrible bats as big as turkeys.

Towards the end of the trip, too, he complains of feeling chilled and weary. He has lost the zest with which he set forth. When he got to Melbourne in September he was described as "looking the embodiment of energy and good spirits". At Sydney the newspaper men saw "a powerfully built man with sun-tanned face, eyes that twinkled with good humour, a broad brow, a massive head, a strong profile dominated by an impressive chin and a Napoleonic nose". Now he is shrunken, withered. He stoops.

"Every ship has its odd characters", he says sardonically in the record of his last day but one. "Among those on the *Egypt* (Port Said to Marseilles) is a former fat man, now in skeleton class, who, beginning life as a reporter at sixteen, is now said to have more papers than he can count and more money than brains. Is finishing whirl round world and ready for another to-morrow."

That is cheery bravado. He could not in that hour have borne the thought of further travels. A curious, childlike touch reveals how glad he is to be approaching home. "For the first time since July 16th of last year my watch is keeping the same time as your watches, and that makes me feel very, very near England." Next day he is even less attracted by the notion of another whirl. "I have resolved", he says, "that I was not built for any kind of public life and that I hate crowds, demonstration, ceremonial, and, curiously enough, although I am one myself, reporters."

No one who knew him could expect him to feel otherwise. It was hard to imagine him going through all the "fusskins", as he called it, so patiently. In every respect save the most important of all, that of his health, the tour had been entirely successful. Did the Australian newspapers go a shade too far in calling him "the most influential journalist in the world and the best-known man in the British Empire"? He smiled at the description himself. Yet would any other journalist in the world, would any other citizen of the British Empire, have aroused so much interest, have been received and entertained as he was? One or two British statesmen might have been accorded as much Government recognition, one or two film or boxing celebrities might have stirred to the same pitch the curiosity of the crowd. No one could have combined as Northcliffe did official and popular welcomes. No name so widely known as his was connected with achievements so spectacular and yet so solid. Around no other public man in any country had clustered so many legends, none was credited with so much of that elusive possession, Power.

The object for which he was persuaded in the first instance to go to Australia had been forgotten. It was to urge the Australians to keep their country white and to make this secure by encouraging people from Britain to settle among them at the rate of 250,000 a year. If they did not fill up their vast territories, he told them, other races would. But he very quickly learned that the Australians do not want any large increase of their population. They fear wages might go down. Before he left the Commonwealth he wrote: "The White Australia ideal seems to me to be impossible."

That was his way. He never tried to escape from his conclusions. Just as he had accepted the failure of *The Daily Mirror* as a newspaper for women and set to work to turn it into something else, so now in this great matter of the future of Australia he gave up his theories and preconceptions, admitting that he had made a mistake. This was no effect of illness. He wrote the sentence quoted above just after he had sailed from Queensland for Borneo, while he was still fresh and mentally vigorous. Indeed, there was at no time during the tour any indication of the insanity which declared itself after his return. The assertion printed by Lord Oxford and Asquith in his reminiscences that Northcliffe cabled to King George "I am turning Roman Catholic" and that the King replied "I can't help it", was malicious gossip.

It was characteristic of one who was above all else a realist that he should go across the world as the champion of a certain view and policy, and that, finding when he got there they were visionary, he should admit that he had been deceived and say no more about them. It was such open-mindedness that unfitted him for politics. The outward side of public life, as we have seen, with its artificiality, its meaningless parades and mummeries, its substitution of the husk for the kernel as the important thing, had no attraction for him. But there was a deeper reason for the unlikeness between him and the politician. He could not be content to mouth platitudes. He would not continue to murmur shibboleths from which all significance had been stripped. For him black was black and white white. Things either were so or they were not so. He could never have inhabited comfortably that borderland between Actuality and Shadows in which for the most part the politicians pass their lives.

CHAPTER XIX

"A MIND DISEASED"

I have suffered from a curious illness.

"NORTHCLIFFE *is going mad.*" This was the rumour which began to circulate soon after his return from the world tour. Not mad in the usual sense of the term. His brain was affected by the mysterious malady of which he had shown symptoms since his return from the United States towards the close of 1917. Symptoms slight at first, scarcely noticeable save by those who saw him every day. Symptoms growing each year more grave. Now they grew alarming.

It had become known at once, when he was back in England, that he was a sick man. His appearance made this plain to all who saw him. He had complained much of the cold during the last stages of his journeying. He felt "the terrific change," for instance, from tropical Colombo to the cold Delhi climate of January. He recorded also in a letter home a strange attack; it constrained his movements and left him weak. The ship's doctor called it "something sciatic" and attributed it, after the manner of doctors, to "lying in a draught". He now began to find "every place very cold and draughty". Clearly something had gone wrong.

He was changed in mind as well as in body. He grew irritable, unrestrained in his talk. He surprised many who knew him well by outbursts of rage, sometimes physical in their manifestations. Thus one day on the seashore near Elmwood, his house on the coast of Kent, he struck down a seagull with a heavy stick which he carried and beat it furiously as it lay on the sand. The friend who was with him saw in this act, so utterly at variance with Northcliffe's usual interest in and kindness to birds, a sinister symptom of disturbed mental balance. If, as many said, there was death in his face, there was in his thought and speech melancholy evidence of brain disturbance.

Yet he continued to work as usual. He resumed at once his early morning study of newspapers, his dictation of messages to the staffs of *The Times* and *Daily Mail*. For a little while these messages did not strike any unusual note. They were a trifle querulous. But then he always had a good deal to find fault with when he returned after long absences. Had he not said that he came back from America in 1917 to find his *Daily Mail* almost ruined? Besides that, his criticism was admitted to be in the main just. "A paper of things, not of people" he sighed (which sentence should never be forgotten by journalists eager to supply the public with what it wants); or "it seems ridiculous that having been away for eight months I should have to start all over again teaching you how to print pictures"; or "I think the best thing we can do about this morning's paper is to forget it". All true enough, the wiser members of the staffs admitted to one another. "The Old Man might be a bit grouchy, but he was right all the time."

Still, they were not sorry when after a week of an English March he went to the Pyrenees for sunshine and warmth. "I am leaving to-day", he wrote on March 8th, "for a climate in which I can go out of doors. I have not been out of doors, owing to the cold wind, since I arrived in England."

"I have left Sir Campbell Stuart complete control with

power of attorney," he continued, "and I hope there will be a complete investigation of financial affairs at Printing-house Square" (*The Times* office), "and that all obstructionists, Die-hards, passive resisters and 'passengers' will be removed from the vessel." The long struggle he had had to make *The Times* self-supporting had worn a furrow in the tired brain. He raged at the "squandermaniacs" of Printing-house Square, although at this period every effort was being made to cut out needless expenditure. All this angry talk sounded unlike him; he was not accustomed to be so brutally outspoken. Nor was the mysterious, melodramatic ring of this in keeping with his usual manner: "As to the policy of *The Times,* Sir Campbell and Mr. Steed know my views: I have told them privately of certain things that are going to happen in the great world." Frequent mysterious references were made to his movements, his acquaintance with matters hidden from the rest of mankind.

Early in April he was back. He had soaked himself in sunshine, his spirits were good, he felt a different man. He was pleased with the papers. Everyone had done well. "I am especially grateful to Sir Campbell Stuart for bearing the weight of my power of attorney during my absence." *The Times* is "admirable in every respect". *The Daily Mail* he finds "much the best morning-paper in London". Yet he very soon begins to find fault. His messages grow longer. They are curiously discursive, at times irrelevant. His mind seems to be jumping here and there, like a clock that has got out of control. Something in the news columns about Mr. Pierpont Morgan, jun., prompts him to this: "The Morgan family have been readers of *The Times* for generations. Years ago the old man told me in his beautiful office in New York that he only read two papers—the London *Times* and the New York *Eve-*

ning Sun." He sees a few lines about a City of London Debating Society: "Fancy the old Urban Club getting a notice! My Father was a regular attendant thereof." Every message now includes the warning, "I am not responsible for errors in these *communiqués* which are telephoned."

The messages include also complaints which he receives from all sorts of sources, letters which were formerly passed on without comment to the departments concerned. Now there is nothing too small for the Chief's personal attention. He thinks "people rarely communicate direct with me unless there is something radically wrong". As a consequence of this, he takes up every trifling grievance, every hint of anything amiss with the machinery of the business. He goes out "to investigate the delivery of the *Evening News*. It is faulty everywhere." Unless the circulation manager goes about more and sees what is going on, he will be asked to resign. Then: "There is a curious misunderstanding of feminine psychology by *Daily Mail* leader-writers and, having found out who they are, I know why. I do not want any women leaders written again by old women in trousers."

All this is disquieting. Clearly he is either intentionally or unconsciously eccentric. Which is it? That doubt is dissolved by the incident of *The Daily Mail* hall porter. A tall, good-looking soldierly man in uniform, he has always been sure of a pleasant word from "his lordship". Now "his lordship" suddenly declares to him that he is to be head of the "so-called Advertisement Department". Northcliffe has complained much about the paper being disfigured by displays too blatant which obscure the news. Now he will put a stop to it. "Some of the Directors may think I am joking in the matter. There is no joke about it. Mr. Glover is well-educated, speaks French better than any one else in the building, writes well, and has excellent manners. He is coming to see me shortly and I know he will comport himself among my other guests with proper decorum and bonhomie." The shareholders, he rambles on, are not going to tolerate the ruin of the paper by the Advertisement staff.

Mr. Glover bears his difficult burden with dignity and humour. The Chief is convinced he has done the right thing. "When he was appointed, some people thought it was a kind of joke. In fact, one of my 'Eyes' in the office heard someone remark: 'Really, I think the Old Man is a bit off his head.' Well, the Old Man, 'Mr. Alfred' of earlier days, may be off his head, but he has stopped for ever big-bludgeoning advertisements getting into the paper. He had long consultations with Mr. Glover before giving him this important appointment and was profoundly impressed by Glover's horror of advertisements that destroy the news columns and, I may add, by his remarkable chest measurement and reach. To the best of my belief no appointment of authority is ever made at Carmelite House" (the then *Daily Mail* office) "without great thought and consideration as to its effect on the happiness of the whole office."

Mr. Glover lunches in due course at the house in Carlton Gardens where Northcliffe settled down after the war. In the afternoon he is invited to address some thirty of the younger men in the Advertisement Department. He "thought very well of them and in his excellent speech pointed out that he proposed dealing gently but firmly with any future transgressors with regard to bludgeon advertisements. . . . He strips in the ring at 18-stone and has a reach longer than Dempsey's."

The same obsession against a certain kind of advertisement shows itself, though not so genially, in Northcliffe's criticism of *The Times*. He is looking for "a strong personality to strengthen the managerial staff". He dislikes many things in the conduct of the paper. "I dislike the fact that though I have spoken to Mr. —— again and again and again and again and again and again and again and again and again and again, and though we desire to make *The Times* the best-printed paper in the world, it accepts advertisements like that of X and Y, most of which is illegible except with a magnifying glass. . . . Will Sir Campbell kindly send this message to-day in my name: 'Lord Northcliffe presents his compliments to Messrs. X and Y, and regrets that in their interests as well as the interests of *The Times* he cannot accept illegible advertisements.' "

These were the first clear indications of the disease which was rapidly affecting his brain. They multiplied every day. He became convinced that *The Times* would ruin everyone connected with it. "I beg those who go about saying that Northcliffe has a deep pocket to realize that it is a public Company, and if my pocket be deep, which may or may not be true, that does not help the situation of the proprietors of *The Times*. Let some of those who draw large salaries and who endure slackness in the management of our affairs picture to themselves the tears of the mothers who have been obliged to withdraw their children from school as the result of the absence of dividends on the shares of *The Times*. I sometimes wonder if anything will move Printing-house Square."

All this was merely exaggeration of anxiety felt for years, just as the appointment of Mr. Glover was due to the magnifying of a dislike long cherished against unsightly displays. He spoke of his life being threatened; it had been threatened during the days of the struggle for Irish self-government. He imagined he had been with the British Army in France during August 1914, an embroidery natural enough upon his real experiences in the war's later periods. But there begin soon to be original delusions, fresh imaginary causes of complaint and fierce recrimination. He undertakes a campaign against a tendency which he fancies he has perceived to make *The Daily Mail* office "a family party". He professed to have discovered that "two men who have been in the office for years are brothers, masquerading under different names". He found that "someone in the Cashier's Department is a relation of a man in another department, and there are many such cases. The office is a honeycomb of relations and relationships."

One day he announced to *The Times* staff that he had received "an anonymous communication from someone who calls himself X", revealing a scandal. This was that "Mr. ——'s sister-in-law is in the Insurance Department; Mr. J—— B——'s daughter in the Atlas Department; E—— of the Intelligence Department has a brother in the Atlas Department; Miss T—— of the Registration Department, who used to have two sisters in the Subscription Department, has only one there now; the son of G—— of the Stationery Department acts as office-boy in the Weekly Edition office; L—— of the Back Door has a son in the Canvassers' Department, and so on." Then he made a statement which aroused much comment: "As I never myself employ friends or connexions, in justice to the other proprietors, it is grossly unfair to me that there should be such underhand business going on." At once memories flew back to the early days when he had an office full of his brothers. Possibly it was a subconscious realization of the mistake he made then which now stirred him to this strange madness.

It grew by what it fed on. "Any persons employed in

the office, however humbly, can help the proprietors by stopping this scandal. Six persons have been dismissed to-day as a beginning." He was soon eager for "the cutting down of certain sections of the staff by over twenty per cent. Everybody who hears the size of the staff is amazed —and so am I." A number of people actually had notice to leave given them. Some left their places, bewildered as to why this misfortune had fallen on them. Almost all were reinstated when the management of affairs was taken into other hands. One or two who were put out preferred to stay out. The novelist, Valentine Williams, for example, was told to choose between remaining Foreign Editor of *The Daily Mail* and writing novels. He had already made a name as author of sensational stories. The edict went forth that no one who carried on any other occupation should remain on the staff. Valentine Williams decided at once to give up journalism. His Chief's crazy whim did him a good turn; as a novelist, he prospered exceedingly.

Then, before Northcliffe had done with men like Williams, he was attacking "the young women who carry teapots about all day at Printing-house Square" (he had seen the preparations for tea one afternoon), and others who used office notepaper—"the very Carmelite House notepaper I personally designed twenty-five years ago". He reports "somebody" as saying to him "about the teapot party", as he had heard it called: "If these young women are necessary and if they must have tea, cannot you supply them with a general teapot and stop their waste of time in wandering all over the office and making us ridiculous before all the foreigners and others who come to see *The Times?*"

"Carmelite House", he feels, "is out of control. Some new element is required in the directorate to stop these abuses. . . . I shall try to find a new director who will do nothing but co-ordinate the whole thing and watch." He fancies that his efforts are being hindered deliberately.

Some heads of departments seem to think that they are running a Government office in which the juniors, as they call them, are allowed to know nothing. We are not running a Government office; we are running a public institution in which there shall be no secrets. If heads of departments cannot maintain their dignity by their own efforts, they should not remain heads of departments. Certainly they should not hide the chief shareholder's views from those concerned. The only position I have in this undertaking is guardian of the shareholders' interests and I find that I am being continually obstructed by little men in big places. I name no names.

Often, however, he did name names and caused much resentment. Fratches with prominent members of his staffs and with his fellow-directors became frequent. He made known a serious disagreement that had arisen between him and Mr. John Walter. A little later he wrote about two directors of *The Daily Mail,* Walter Fish, afterwards its able editor, and Sir Andrew Caird, in such a tone that they issued writs against him. Yet he continued to put into his messages sensible, masterly comments on the quality of the papers as well as these clearly unbalanced onslaughts and insane charges.

There were moments when he grew reminiscent. He spoke about his early experiences as a reporter. He deplored the drop in the consideration given to reporters. He attributed the blame for this to the National Union of Journalists, although for many years he had encouraged it and even urged men who worked for him to join. He sent the Union in 1912 a message in which he said:

In the last twenty years our craft has risen from a humble, haphazard and badly paid occupation to a regular profession, which must, in the future, offer increasing opportunities to men and women of ability. It has therefore become all the more necessary that newspaper workers should adopt the methods of other professions and form a society for mutual protection and encouragement.

The introduction of all manner of time-saving machinery within the last few years has made the work less arduous but more nerve-exhausting, and it is incumbent upon journalists to unite for the obtaining of longer annual holidays and better pay. It is my proudest boast that the changes and competition which I have introduced into English journalism have had the effect of increasing the remuneration of almost every class of newspaper writer as well as greatly adding to the number of those engaged in journalism.

It is not, in my opinion, wise or politic for newspaper proprietors and journalists to belong to the same institution, and I have been much pleased to notice that there is nothing of the cap-in-hand and beanfeast business about your society.

Now he attacked the National Union of Journalists for "lowering the tone and *morale* of Fleet Street". He felt that newspaper reporters were not treated with the same courtesy and consideration as they received when he was young. He had attended a meeting at which they were placed behind the speaker so that they might be out of the way. He suggested, "although I was only a guest", that they should be moved forward. Lord Burnham, another newspaper proprietor, the host on the occasion, agreed. But it had not occurred to him, as it occurred immediately to Northcliffe, that they ought to be where they could do their work properly. He had never been a working journalist, had not the mind of the newspaper man.

"Since the advent of the N.U.J.", Northcliffe commented, "reporters have become more and more humble. When I was a reporter sitting alongside George Augustus Sala and many others, I can imagine what would have happened if we had been put behind the speakers. We did on one occasion write a short polite note to the head orator of the meeting saying that as we could not hear him we were going to leave and there would be no report. . . . I hope that any reporter connected with my newspapers, assigned to a back seat, will politely inform the chief guest who wants to get reported that, as he cannot hear, there will be no report in *The Times* or *The Daily Mail.*"

Next day he reverted to his grievance against the Journalists' Union. "When I started reporting in 1881, we reporters sat in order of price. *Times* reporters at 3d." (that was then the price of *The Times*) "would speak to nobody. The *Morning Post,* which had then only a sale of a few thousand a day, tried to carry out this arrangement, but, as their reporters were shabbily dressed, it did not go down. The twopenny *Standard* sat alone, and then came the penny newspapers, which the others treated with contempt. The last time I saw Mr. Sala we had a merry laugh over this matter and I noticed he made reference to it in some memoirs of his. But, as I said yesterday, we were a flesh-and-blood lot in those days, and not a lot of buns-and-milk-fed 'Nujjers'." (Members of the N.U.J.).

Feverish and exaggerated as this was, it represented a real part of Northcliffe's nature. He was always and before anything else a newspaper man. He resented any rudeness to his colleagues, any slur upon his profession. He once objected to the use of the word "received" in the statement that a Church dignitary for the purpose of an interview had received a representative of *The Times,* "as if he conferred an honour upon a member of the staff. . . . I do not like our representatives to adopt a cap-in-hand attitude in dealing with an Archbishop or anyone else."

As a newspaper man, he had resented the intrusion into journalism of rich men who bought newspapers for purposes far removed from the intention of increasing their enterprise or their legitimate influence. Now this resentment blossomed fantastically in his imagination; he wrote and published a pamphlet called "Newspapers and their millionaires, with some further meditations about us". This was in its origin a reply to the suggestion that the wages of mechanical staffs in newspaper offices might be reduced by common effort. It developed into a half-humorous onslaught on several men whose portraits were given, the intruders into a field where he considered they had no business.

"Behind every newspaper in London," he said, "with the possible exception of some sporting journals and a labour publication of which I know nothing, there is a multi-millionaire, a millionaire, or a very wealthy colleague, a Shipping King (Sir John Ellerman), a Cotton-waste King (Sir John Leigh), Coal Kings (the Berry Brothers), an Oil King (Lord Cowdray), and the rest of them." Each of these was clearly recognizable and to some of them, so that there might be no mistake, he attached names. For example: "I told Lord Cowdray that his newspaper" (the *Westminster Gazette,* run as a morning paper at a heavy loss to carry on a political vendetta against Lloyd George) "was about as good as my first oil-well and pipe-line establishments would be." There spoke the journalist, jealous for the reputation of his craft, incensed against any who entered the newspaper business without either knowledge of or enthusiasm for it. He had used a like illustration when a cotton-factory owner started the *Tribune* and came heavily to grief with it. "If I went into the spinning and weaving business," he said, "I should expect to fall. I know nothing about it."

Another matter which had long been in his thoughts came uppermost now, magnified by disorder in his brain. He had often spoken of the number of appeals for money which were published by *The Times,* many of them, he believed, for the benefit mainly of secretaries and their assistants. Now he said: "As I am going away, probably for a long time, may I say that during my absence it is my special wish that no appeal be inserted of any kind whatever, unless it be personally addressed to *The Times* by the King's Secretary, the Queen's Secretary, Queen Alexandra's Secretary or Princess Mary's Secretary. To this rule I wish no exception whatever to be made. . . . All appeals should appear as advertisements."

A few days after this he wrote: "Before this reaches you all I shall be out of England on a very interesting mission, of which you will hear later and of which you know nothing now, though you may think you do." This caused no merriment. All knew now that the rumour in Fleet Street had truth in it. Northcliffe had been "going mad" for some time. Every day furnished fresh proof of unbalanced wits.

One such piece of evidence had caused much talk. At a dinner-party he claimed that *The Daily Mail* could "make or break" any theatrical offering, and undertook to prove this. A play called *The Gentleman in Dress Clothes* had just been produced. He went to see it. He pronounced it without hesitation the best play he had ever seen. He sent for members of *The Daily Mail* staff to join him in his box. He said: "These gentlemen have been instructed to boom this play. There will be a photograph of it in every edition of *The Daily Mail* for a month and a paragraph every day in the *Evening News,* telling London that London has got to see it." Here again he was doing what he had once done skilfully, usefully for his purpose (as he did with *The Miracle*), in a fashion violent, exaggerated, unbalanced. The readers of his newspapers were not impressed; they were bewildered. They supposed that he had an interest in the play.

Day after day it was praised, puffed, written about from all points of view. Even the actor whose enterprise it was (Mr. Seymour Hicks) admitted that he felt embarrassed by this overwhelming publicity.

Yet Northcliffe was not yet, in the common usage of the word, insane. No doctor would have certified him incapable of managing his own affairs. It became very difficult indeed for those about him to know what they ought to do. That he was under the influence of delusions seemed clear at times, yet at other times it appeared to be possible that he was merely giving rein to a grotesque form of humour. Mixed up with startling comments, violent personal attacks, fanciful complaints and curious recollections was so much wisdom in newspaper matters, so much acute insight into business methods, so much sound judgment of public affairs as made it hard to believe that reason no longer held its seat in his disordered brain.

Yet it could be seen that the malady of mind gained upon him, and as soon as he began to send to *The Times* the articles about Germany which were the outcome of his "interesting mission", all doubt as to his condition was lamentably dispelled. It was clear to all who saw him on his journey to Cologne and during his stay there that, as Lord d'Abernon, British Ambassador in Berlin, wrote in his diary, "his powerful brain was already affected by illness". He had sent "a secret messenger" to reach Cologne ahead of him and "make the necessary arrangements". This man was to be recognized by his "grey Tyrolese hat". He said he knew he was running the risk of assassination. "But I am not afraid for my life," he added; "I shoot from the hip." He carried actually an automatic pistol. This he was persuaded to give up. As he neared Cologne explosions were heard. Some forts were being destroyed. Northcliffe listened, then he muttered, "As I expected, the fighting has begun." Yet there were hours in which he seemed sane.

"He talked incessantly," was Lord d'Abernon's report, "but not foolishly."

In his articles to *The Times* there was the same variation between sense and nonsense, absurdity and reason. Two of them were printed, conveying to a wider circle knowledge which up to then had been possessed by a few only. They were read with amazement. He told how he had travelled to Germany under an assumed name, that of Leonard Brown. He declared that he did "not shake hands with Germans". He described his diet. He inveighed against German women for having "the ugliest legs in the world" and against England for tolerating what were, in comparison with those he found abroad, "our horrible hotels". The style of the writing was jerky; he was more discursive than ever, more irrelevant; italics were frequent.

"Why did *The Times* publish the articles?" was the query on many lips. The reason was plain. He was still chief proprietor of *The Times;* in these last days he became indeed almost sole proprietor, for he bought from Mr. John Walter the bulk of the shares still held by that family and thus secured for the first time complete control. However eccentric the matter and manner of his contributions might be, he had ordered their insertion; inserted they must be—until the direction of the paper was taken from him. This happened very soon.

He sent from Paris on June 9th a message saying that he had "had a most interesting journey in Germany, but had suffered from a curious illness since. Some people think I was poisoned there. Personally I cannot believe that, but I know I have been very bad." To this he added:

I wish this *communiqué* to be prominently posted in a hundred different rooms, because Mr. P——, my private secretary, who is doing important work of which Carmelite House does not know, is being hounded to death by certain people in the office, most of them enormously paid.
There's an idea that Mr. P—— knows my views. He does not know my views and many mistakes occur through asking him. Any person who in future asks Mr. P—— any question whatever will incur my grave displeasure.
As for my whereabouts, Mr. P—— rarely knows. When I am abroad, it is known only to my family. I hope I shall not have to say this again.
The telephone people have orders to keep a list of those who try to get through to Mr. P——. A list is being kept of all such calls and I'll see this list on my return, which will be very shortly.

But when the second article had appeared with the words "to be continued on Friday" appended to it, he lay in an alarming and distressing state; he was beyond question out of his mind and suffering also from a dangerous heart affection. The articles were not continued. His return to the office was not made "very shortly". He never saw his work-rooms or attended to his "dear work" again.

CHAPTER XX

THE END AND AFTER

He felt he had been commissioned to do something and he could find no practical outlet for his powers and energy.

FIVE years had the trouble in the brain taken to mature and to overwhelm him. He had not been in full health and strength since the end of the war. He wrote in 1919: "It is unlikely I shall ever be able to return to full tide of work." Early symptoms appeared while he was in the United States. Hailed everywhere as "the most powerful man in England", he began to ponder for the first time in his life upon his own importance. From that time on, as this narrative has shown, he was never again the man he had been. He lost in great part the playful, boyish humour which prevented him, until the war came, from taking himself or anything very seriously. It was not vanity which attacked him: no trace of that defect appeared in him at any period. He had far too wide an outlook to be vain. No one who understands, as he did, what a flash the longest human life is, how trifling the largest achievements of man in any age, viewed from the distance of even a few hundred years, can fret himself about the attention paid (or not paid) to him, can pride himself upon his intellect, his energy or his wealth.

What, then, if vanity be ruled out, was the cause of the change in Northcliffe which began in 1917? It was a mystical belief that he was the man appointed to clear up the chaos into which the world had fallen. That may seem strange to those who knew him but slightly, who supposed him to be a cynic, without ideals, without vision of the unseen, without faith. Such supposition did not merely betray lack of acquaintance with Northcliffe; it could be founded only on defective knowledge of the human character and mind. Had Northcliffe been a cynic lacking faith, he would not have created newspapers, he would have made no stir in the world. He was able to do these things because he had an unshakable faith—in his destiny. From boyhood he had seen in his mind's eye "the forms of things to be". He aimed high, always as high as he could see. That his ideals were not more lofty was due to the defective early training of imagination and intellect which he so often deplored and which made him later on set exaggerated value upon education at Oxford and Cambridge.

From the moment when he saw in George Newnes's office the opportunity offered to enterprise and vigour by the existence of a vast new reading public which had nothing to read, he believed himself the man appointed to seize that opportunity. When the war came, he felt for the first time that a further call was made upon him. He rose to the fullness of his stature. Many who knew all that he did held with Colonel House that he "never received the credit due to him in the winning of the war", for the "tirelessness of his endeavours to stimulate the courage and energy of the Allies", for his "success in bringing them to a realization of the mighty task they had on their hands". Grappling with each task as it came in the spirit of a devotee, the belief grew upon him, as one after another his labours were accomplished, that his was the hand preordained to straighten out the tangle, to end the war and restore peace to the Peoples. He did not exult in this. Rather he was inclined to exclaim with Hamlet:

*The times are out of joint—oh, cursed spite
That ever I was born to set them right!*

Yet he did not attempt to shirk what he considered to be his destiny. He would not spare himself. He had a suspicion that he might be shortening his life; that weighed with him not at all.

It was during his stay in America as head of the British War Mission that the certainty of his Call came to him. The reason for this was the recognition by Americans of the part he had already played in the war and the position he occupied in England. That position was weighed outside his own country more justly than within it. His influence was better understood even in Germany than it was by the mass of his own countrymen. Prince Max of Baden in his Memoirs, among his estimates of the force by which Germany was opposed, wrote: "Lord Northcliffe occupied a position apart. He not only prepared and co-operated; his was often the directing will." In another part of his Memoirs Prince Max said: "As early as July 1915 it had been foreseen (in Germany) that in the end Lloyd George would be ready to accept the national leadership from Northcliffe's hand." Very few foresaw that at so early a date in England. Many are still unaware that it was the hand of Northcliffe which forced the Premiership upon Lloyd George.

In America he was hailed openly as the strongest force in England. No such tribute had been paid to him at home. Though at first he was inclined to put this aside as an exaggeration, the frequent, continual repetition of it worked upon his mind. Before he left the United States he was convinced that there was laid upon him a mission far greater than that of setting in order financial relations between the two Governments. He went back to London prepared to receive an offer of the Premiership and resolved to accept it.

The pity of it is that, had he filled the place which he looked on as his, he would probably have kept his health of body and mind both. This would no doubt have happened if he had accepted, as an instalment of power, the post which was actually offered to him, that of Air Minister. He was probably dissuaded from accepting it by those who suggested that, unless he became Prime Minister, he could do better service by refusing office and using his newspapers to keep Ministers in the right path. Very soon he was troubled by doubts as to whether he had acted wisely in refusing. He tried to reconquer serenity by attending busily to his newspapers and periodicals. But he was haunted by a sense of having failed to seize the chance which destiny held out to him. So, when Lloyd George invited him to set up the Department of Propaganda in Enemy Countries, he at once agreed; he threw himself into his task with as much energy as he could muster—not by any means the energy of former years.

Then, after the Armistice, belief in his mystical Call grew strong again. He was to fashion the peace, he was to heal the wounds of the nations and usher in a new age. But again he waited, Macbeth-like, for "chance to crown him". Again he expected that he would be summoned to his task. He did not know that in public life the highest places are seized, not offered; the highest tasks undertaken by those who happen to be nearest to them and can snatch at them, not by any, however well qualified, who are outside the ring. Therefore again his hopes were dashed, his faith in himself and his destiny shaken. This time the effect was more painfully marked.

"He felt he had been commissioned to *do* something and he could find no practical outlet for his powers and energy."

That was written of another famous man, different in every way, save one perhaps, from Northcliffe. What Henry Larkin wrote in *Carlyle and the Open Secret of his Life* (1886) may have been true of the epic poet of the French Revolution, of the biographer of Cromwell and Frederick the Great. It was true of Northcliffe and it ruined his life. The frustration of what seemed to him to be his mission strangely warped his intellect and may have brought upon him also the disease of the heart which caused his death.

This disease, known as *infective endocarditis,* had been in his system for at least a year before it killed him: so medical authority declared. How the infection began was not to be determined. He himself believed that he suffered from Indian jungle fever and also that he had been poisoned by ice-cream served to him on the Belgian frontier when he was making his last trip to Germany. "There", he said, "I was unfortunately recognized." The poisoning he supposed to have been intentional. The doctors, however, waved this aside. They thought that possibly there might have been a septic condition round the roots of the teeth. "However this may be", said the *British Medical Journal,* "there can be no doubt that he had a general streptococcal infection and that eventually the blood was invaded." There was a slight weakness in one of the valves of the heart; this was attacked by the streptococcus. Then the poison swiftly did its work.

When he broke down in Switzerland after his visit to Germany, Mr. Wickham Steed, then editor of *The Times,* at once went out to him and with Sir Leicester Harmsworth arranged for his removal to Paris. The railway journey through France was made in the private car of M. Poincaré, then Prime Minister. Back at home, the best medical advice was sought for, the most celebrated physicians attended him. But they could hold out no hope of recovery; the disease had gone too far. At first it was announced merely that he had been ordered to cease work of every kind because of "the unsatisfactory condition of the heart" and "troubles with sleeplessness". But soon the bulletins showed that he was near his end. He knew it himself in the intervals when his mind was clear. For the most part his days were clouded by delusions. His mind went back thirty years. He spoke and wrote then as if he were the Alfred Harmsworth of the years before *The Daily Mail*. He scribbled incoherently, with a strange inversion of his sane opinions and sentiments, reproaching and abusing some whom he most cared for, heaping praise and benefits upon others whom he despised.

In the middle of July he sent on his birthday lucid "last messages" to a number of old friends. "Give a kiss and my love to Mother and tell her she is the only one", was among them; her "little book" (*Daily Light on the Daily Path*) is buried with him. Early in August he asked Wickham Steed to give him "a full page in *The Times*" for his obituary notice, "and a leading article by the best available writer on the night". On August 14th the end came.

At once there seemed to be in the public mind an appreciation of his personality and his works more just than had been shown at any time during his life. King George expressed the general feeling by his telegram to Lady Northcliffe:

I have just heard with regret of the death of Lord Northcliffe after a painful illness and I offer you my heartfelt sympathy in your loss.

The President of the United States (Mr. Harding) and the President of the French Republic sent expressions of their grief and sympathy. From the American Ambassador in London (Mr. George Harvey) came this tribute:

Of the surprisingly few great personalities developed by the Great War, Northcliffe's will live in history as one of the three or four most vivid. It is not for an American to attempt to measure the value of his service to the Empire, but I may, I trust, with propriety bear testimony to the debt owed to him by the Republic for his unflagging endeavours in the interest of our common race.

It was a cardinal test of his faith that perpetuation of civilization could be assured only by mutuality of purpose and action on the part of our two countries, and he actually did more perhaps than any other man living or dead to attain fulfilment of this noble aspiration.

America joins Britain in full sympathy at the loss of one of her greatest sons, and I, in common with so many others who loved him for himself, grieve inexpressibly at the passing of a friend dear and faithful for thirty long years.

Mr. Hoover, then Secretary of Commerce in the United States Government, declared that

the world has suffered a great loss in the death of the great and courageous journalist who served faithfully in building good relations between our two countries.

The Pilgrims of America mourned "the loss of a great and loyal friend of the United States" who had rendered inestimable services in behalf of closer unity and co-operation of effort of the two great English-speaking Powers of the world. Mr. Edison contributed a characteristic summary of his friend's dominant quality:

He always impressed me as having a great, unique personality, with a restless desire to accomplish great results in a very limited time.

THE END AND AFTER 343

The Prime Minister of Australia (Mr. Hughes) spoke of him as "one of the great forces making for victory during the war". Another old friend, Mr. Frank A. Munsey, published in his newspaper, the *New York Herald,* a sketch at greater length, calling him "the British Empire's greatest single human force", a man who "cared nothing for money for money's sake", whose "passion was for constructive achievement, creation, the development of things". Marshal Foch deplored the passing of "one of the leading champions of the common cause during the war".

But, while all these testimonials showed the estimation in which Northcliffe had been held among the men who ruled and influenced and led, there was to be given yet a more striking proof of the impression made by him upon his age. A genuine unprompted demonstration of regard was to be offered by the mass of people. Though he had never courted the crowd, never sought popularity, the crowd was now to mark his passing by one of those spontaneous displays which are the clearest evidence of admiration and sympathy. It was arranged as soon as the news of his death had been published that a funeral service should be held in Westminster Abbey before the burial in St. Marylebone Cemetery on the outskirts of London, where his father and his grandparents lay. This service was made the occasion of a popular tribute unmistakable and unexpected. In the Abbey there had never, according to one of its experienced officials quoted by *The Times,* been so many people. "It is a bigger crowd", said this authority, "than any we had for the war ceremonials." Along the seven miles of streets between Westminster and Finchley, where the St. Marylebone Cemetery is, there were gathered, too, very large numbers of people. At some points they formed crowds, at others they were scattered singly along the sidewalks; but they were continuous all the way. He would have been pleased could he have seen the throng, but he would have been still more surprised. Neither he nor anyone else, until that day, had any notion of the regard felt for him or of the effect his personality had created among the population at large.

Still it was in the Abbey, where affection and grief were more intimate, that the most moving episodes of this farewell ceremony could be noted. Here came almost all who had been close to the dead man throughout the later stages of his career. Sincerely sorrowing for their Chief were those who had worked with him, marvelled at his vigour, valued his inspiration. Here was Sir George Sutton ("Sutkins", to use Northcliffe's playful nickname for him) who, beginning as secretary, had been made managing director of the Amalgamated Press, a baronet, and a very rich man. Here was Charles Whibley, cynic, Tory of the Tories, fastidious critic and writer, hater of all that he could denounce as "democratic" or "popular", yet a firm and faithful friend to the inventor of the democratic, the popular Press. Here was J. L. Garvin, reflecting sombrely that "a cataract of human energy, sending currents far and wide", had been dried up, feeling "as one might if Niagara itself were to cease and vanish".

Mr. Jealous, first editor to give the eager boy Alfred Harmsworth an opportunity to try his hand at reporting; Evelyn Wrench, snapped up by Northcliffe from Eton to work for him: to found Overseas League, English-Speaking Union, Association of All Peoples, to succeed St. Loe Strachey as editor-proprietor of the *Spectator;* Campbell Stuart, the prop on whom Northcliffe had leaned with relief during his last years; Louis Tracy, who, after crossing Northcliffe's path at the period of the *Evening News* purchase, took to novel-writing, fell on evil days, re-encountered Northcliffe in the United States during 1917, made appeal to him, and was at once put into a position where he was useful and well-paid: Robertson Nicoll, the witty Scotsman with strong influence among Free Churchmen, who reckoned Northcliffe "the greatest transforming force that has appeared in British journalism"; George Isaacs, Secretary of the Printers' Trade Union, testifying to Northcliffe's desire that his "workers should have the best possible conditions of employment and be so treated as to make them contented and happy"—these, with numberless others who had been at one time or another among Northcliffe's "colleagues" (as he always called them), sorrowed in the Abbey and let their minds wander through memories of him.

Filson Young, man of letters and musician, could recollect, for example, how he worked for him and became a warm friend, then quarrelled with him and drifted away; and how years later, when one who had been a close intimate of them both (Charles Furse, the painter) died, Northcliffe sent a hurried, imploring note asking for an article, telling Young to put his own price on it, which Young did, the price being nothing; and so the breach was healed. Wickham Steed could recall his visit with Northcliffe to Verdun during the attack of 1916, the hardships they endured and the smiling refusal of Northcliffe to fare in any way better than his companions, even though it came to sharing stale crusts of bread and morsels of mouldy cheese. Max Pemberton, friend from boyhood, frequent comrade in travel, reflected sorrowfully on his forebodings when he first heard of the world tour plan, and said, "Alfred, you may be signing your death-warrant."

Of those who had worked for him, produced his newspapers, his magazines and periodicals, there were hundreds, past and present members of the staffs, men and women, who pondered over their dealings with him. To a large number he was but a brooding presence, a voice that gave orders, a Will that shaped the form and pressure of their endeavours. Others could recall relations with him, personal, familiar, maybe intimate. One thought of his devastating energy when a success was to be clinched and extended; a second, of his cold detachment and frowning brow when a failure had to be admitted, a loss cut; a third, of his invariably playful greeting and schoolboy sense of fun; a fourth, of the quiet dignity with which he met and disregarded insults; a fifth, of his fierce rage at what he considered culpable carelessness or shirking of plain duty. Each had in mind some particular aspect of the dead man's personality.

There were, too, many who had served him in other more intimate, more personal ways. Frederick, the valet of later years, successor to the incomparable Paul (an Austrian who disappeared at the beginning of the war), lamented an employer whose kindliness and humour were vivid in his thoughts, whose occasional impatience was forgotten. "Sandy" Thomson, the golf professional who travelled with Northcliffe whenever he took a holiday and had taught him to play a good game, dwelt upon the thoughtfulness which his pupil always showed for his comfort and convenience; upon the good-natured patience, too, with which, as a beginner, Northcliffe drove two hundred balls one after the other at his first lesson. Pine, the devoted, limping chauffeur, remembered tearfully the countless generosities of one who liked everyone about him to be well-off, and who had built at Elmwood a billiard-room so that he and "Sandy" and Paul might indulge their passion for the game.

People to whom he had spoken once perhaps, people who had been thanked for some trifling service by a quick, courteous word, people who had merely seen him pass down corridors, enter or leave one of his offices—they could not gain admission to the Abbey; they were scattered among the throngs which waited in the streets for the passing of the coffin. Some of the multitudes who stood in the sunshine to see the hearse and the long line of carriages pass were drawn by curiosity, by that eagerness for sensation which Northcliffe had encouraged and stimulated through his Press. But vast numbers felt that a powerful influence was withdrawn, that a character with immense possibilities either for good or ill had been extinguished. Each among these probably had, also, a conception of him peculiar to the brain in which it occurred.

There was a composing-room foreman who recalled many days of pleasant fishing with "the Chief". There was another, a golf professional (J. H. Taylor), who treasured a picture post card which Northcliffe sent him from New Zealand to say that a certain club there had called a green after him. There was a little postmistress from Totteridge, where his mother lived, who had had many a present from him "because I give you such a lot of trouble". There was a taxi-cab driver who could tell of a comical pilgrimage undertaken at a period when he was employed to wait outside the office if Northcliffe were occupied there late at night. One day the still young newspaper-owner said: "I think of starting a canteen for the people working with me. I want to see what sort of eating-houses they go to. Show me some." So the man took him to one after another and at the end Northcliffe said: "They seem to me to be good places, with wholesome food at low prices. I don't think we could do any better than that." It was characteristic of him to make the investigation himself.

So there were carried to the grave at Finchley, near the

house he had bought for his mother, where he had been so constant in his attentions to her, not one Northcliffe, but countless Northcliffes. The images of him on the mental retinas of those who mourned and those who watched could not be numbered. Each reflected some fragment of him, each was true as far as it went. To gain a complete picture the assembling and the setting in order of all those fragments was required. Few men have been so many-sided; few have displayed dispositions so various. He could turn with ease from the discussion of some problem affecting destinies of nations to the consideration of jokes for boys or the kind of "chat" which would most interest women in slums and Suburbia. He would pass from analysing with almost uncanny precision the character of some public man or the nature of some national crisis to weighing the merits of rival "fashion artists" and to considering whether a page of joke-paragraphs would please the readers of a religious weekly better than a page of texts. He enjoyed both occupations equally, he gave himself to each with equal concentration. He did not appear to attach more importance to planning a *Times* leader than to encouraging a *Daily Mail* stunt or reshaping the make-up of *Answers*. But he turned a different front to his assistants in these several tasks; he was a different man to each set of them.

A different man, too, in numberless other surroundings. A character hard to apprehend unless it was studied under many lights, in relation to many another character. This explains the failure of all attempts to "put Northcliffe into books or plays". His figure attracted novelists and playwrights. Both H. G. Wells and Arnold Bennett found their imaginations affected by it. Wells sketched the young Harmsworth in the guise of Cossington (*The New Machiavelli*). Bennett has told in his *French Journal* how in the early days of Northcliffe's prosperity he "had a notion of writing a play about him. Of course," he added, "I greatly admire him as Leviathan, though I have never set eyes on him save occasionally at lunch in the Temple Restaurant." Later on Bennett returned to this idea and produced *What the Public Wants,* not with very fortunate result. Nor was J. B. Fagan's *The Earth* any more to the popular taste. In neither was the portrait of Northcliffe recognizable. He himself chuckled over both efforts. The story called *Napoleon of the Press* came earlier and caused him some annoyance. He bought up all the copies that were to be had. Of *Mightier than the Sword,* by Alphonse Courlander, still affectionately remembered in Fleet Street, he was tolerant. "Not a bit like," he said, "but never mind, he's a clever boy." *Lord London,* by Keble Howard, was satire of a cruder variety. Not one of these authors suggested Northcliffe's many-sidedness, his rapid sometimes bewildering changes of front.

Not that he ever sank his personality. He was very far from being "all things to all men". He was always himself. He did not, chameleon-like, take on the colour of anyone he talked to. He was apt, it is true, to snap up opinions here and there and to adopt them as his own. But he used these merely as aids to business, as ideas to help in making his newspapers readable, often as reproaches to his staffs for not "knowing what everybody knows". When he was not thinking about his publications, which was seldom enough, his own real opinions came to light; and they—or most of them, at any rate—remained steadfast throughout his life. At will he put them aside. What he thought did not matter. He had to find out what the mass of people were thinking; to fit his proceedings and policy in with that. Here was the explanation of his many-sidedness; of the limits also which were imposed on his success.

So he was buried, and for a while it seemed as if even his name might disappear. He left no heir, though he left children by whom his five-million-pound fortune was, according to his will, eventually to be inherited. The will was complicated; it caused litigation. Payment of the legacies he had devised for all who served him was delayed and had to be ordered by the High Court. The divulging of the fact that he had left children to succeed to his wealth came as a complete surprise even to those who had been his intimates; it was to Lady Northcliffe also an unpleasant surprise. She soon after married an old friend, Sir Robert Hudson. In his latest will, made while he lay ill, her husband had "particularly desired that my darling wife should remarry if she wishes", and had added: "She and I both know whom we desire she should marry." Lady Northcliffe became, therefore, Lady Hudson. There were, however, brothers resolved on repaying what he did for them by keeping his name alive and in honour. A new *Daily Mail* building was called Northcliffe House by Lord Rothermere, who also joined with Cecil Harmsworth in founding a Northcliffe Chair of Modern English Literature and a Northcliffe Lectureship in Literature at University College (part of the University of London).

It was Lord Rothermere who succeeded him, so far as any succession was possible. He bought control of the newspapers founded by Northcliffe; although he sold the Amalgamated Press with its many periodicals, he became the possessor of far more valuable properties than Northcliffe had ever owned. He founded a fresh chain of provincial evening journals which he named the Northcliffe Newspapers. But his interest was not, as his brother's had been, in newspapers for their own sake. As a journalist, Northcliffe had no successors. Many drew inspiration from him. None developed what he had done. He pushed his way into the field of daily journalism when it was producing newspapers for a small number of buyers, newspapers that were interested in little beyond politics and business. He made them touch life at every point. He changed them completely—from organs of political opinion to organs of entertainment. He saw that very few people wanted politics, while a very large number wanted to be entertained, diverted, relieved for a little while from the pressure or the tedium of their everyday affairs. Newspapers during the first decade of the twentieth century became entirely unlike those of the last decade of the nineteenth. That change was of Northcliffe's making. Yet in making it he did not act as an instrument of necessary change.

We can say for certain that if James Watt had not discovered how to use steam power, if Stevenson had not applied that power to a locomotive, if Cooke and Wheatstone had not invented the electric telegraph, if Marconi had not transmitted the first messages by wireless, someone else would have done these things. They had to be done. Many were working along the same lines. The time had come for advances in man's mastery of the elements. Most great inventors have thus been agents for their age. They happened to be the first to put in practical working ideas that were in many minds.

But there was in the nature of things no reason whatever why British newspapers should not have remained very much as they were towards the end of the nineteenth century. German and French newspapers have altered little. It could not be said that a revolution in journalism was in the air. Northcliffe was not one among many who were planning to improve it. He stood alone; his notions were scoffed at. He had to convert all who worked with him to faith in his revelation; he had to teach them the new technique. Thus he revolutionized journalism. He created a new type of newspaper. In no editorial particular of any moment has that type been altered since he died.

In some directions the energy that he breathed into journalism has noticeably slackened. Newspapers have settled down to doing mechanically what he did with vigour and enthusiasm. He left a mark on his age which cannot be overlooked, which never will be. For the newspaper was among that age's most prominent and powerful institutions—powerful, that is to say, in its influence on the public mind, the national character; and the newspaper as we know it was the creation of this one man. No one has yet altered his creation by any material change in reading-matter or in form. Certainly there have been changes behind the scenes, changes invisible or only dimly discernible to the reader. During the years following his death the tendencies noticeable in journalism during Northcliffe's latest years, tendencies which he had deplored, grew more and more marked. No attempt was made to conceal the dependence on devices for increasing circulation other than interesting news and sound opinions. Insurance and competition coupons were elevated to greater importance than excellence of contents, arrangement and display. Advertisement revenue had to be the chief thing aimed at. Fierce competition and huge capitalizations made this necessary. Already, a few years before he died, Northcliffe had seen his creation, the force he had released, turn like the Bottle Imp into a shape he did not like, which made him fearful for the future of journalism. He was in the position at which most revolutionaries arrive: they cannot call a halt when the changes they desired have been made. They are forced to look on while the process they began is carried farther than they meant it to go, and usually in directions of which they strongly disapprove.

He could not have checked this had he lived. He would have been too wise to try and do more than slow it down. He might have delayed the momentary triumph of finance over journalism; he knew he could not prevent it. Thus, while he could look back on a personal career of success scarcely ever broken, he deplored having made newspapers worth the attention of rich men and speculators. He believed in control by newspaper men; any other seemed to him unhealthy. For he was himself a newspaper man; his devotion was given to journalism for its own sake, not for the sake of what could be made out of it.

That was his attitude towards public employment also, and for this reason he failed to reach high political position. He imagined that, because his capacity fitted him for it, he would be called upon to accept it. He did not desire it for the rewards it would bring; he was eager only to do what required doing and thus accomplish the task with which he believed himself called on to grapple. High political position is not open to men of that type. We might reverse the familiar verdict on the Emperor Galba and say of Northcliffe that he would have shown himself *omnium consensu capax imperii si tantum imperasset* (by general agreement fit to rule if only he had ruled). As the opportunity was not offered to him, he figures in the history of his age, not as statesman, but as journalist; not so much a moulder of events (though he was that too) as one who profoundly influenced the recording of them; not a power in politics, but the creator of a force as yet incalculable in its effect upon the mind, the manners, and, it may be, the morals of the Anglo-Saxon race.

INDEX

Absent-minded Beggar Fund, 85, 113
Aden, wreck of, 109
Air Ministry, 226, 235, 339
Alcock and Brown, Atlantic Flight, 148
Amalgamated Press, 44, 350
Answers, 49
Asquith, H. H. (Lord Oxford and Asquith), 168, 175, 178, 197, 198, 202, 318
At the War, 198

Baldwin, Rt. Hon. Stanley, 221
Balfour, Earl of, 206, 254, 259
Bartlett, Vernon, 282
Beaumont, Captain, 35
Beaverbrook, Lord, 188, 225
Beck, Adolf, 59
Bell, C. F. Moberly, 122, 162, 283
Benham, Charles, 156
Bennett, Arnold, 348, 349
Bennett, James Gordon, 74
Berry Brothers, 44, 331
Birkenhead, Lord, 178
Blatchford, Robert, 151
Blériot, 144, 145
Bolton Priory, 208, 215
Borden, Sir Robert, 209
Briggs, 106
British War Mission, 205
Burnham, Lord, 29, 119, 329
Burton, Claud, 169
Butes, A., 161

Caird, Sir Andrew, 215, 328
Carlyle, Thomas, 340
Carr & Co., 32, 47
Carson, Sir E., 168, 259
Chamberlain, Sir Austen, 259
Clarke, Tom, 279
Clowes, Sir W. Laird, 87
Courlander, Alphonse, 349
Cowdray, Lord, 229, 331
Crewe House, 254
Crystal Palace, 118

d'Abernon, Lord, 190, 333
Daily Express, 7
Daily Mail, The, 45, 61, 73; circulation figures, 110; later *passim*
Daily Mirror, 90–102, 152
Davies, J. T., 236
Declaration of London, 164
Delane, John T., 53, 120, 272
de Villemessant, 37
Devonport, Lord, 185
d'Eyncourt, M., 285
Dolling, Father, 157
Dunn, James, 280

Edison, Thomas, 342
Edward VII, 37, 108, 143
Ellerman, Sir J., 331
Elmwood, 52, 157, 204
Evans, W. J., 280
Evening News, 56, 116, 280

Fagan, J. B., 349
Figaro, Paris, 37
Fish, Walter, 328
Ford, Henry, 219
French, Lord, 186
Furse, Charles, 345

Garvin, J. L., 188, 344
Gentleman in Dress Clothes, The, 332
George, D. Lloyd, 165, 183, 202, 203, 226, 258; attacks Northcliffe, 267
Glover, Mr., 323, 324
Grahame-White, 146
Grand Falls, 138
Grey, Lord, 184

Haig, Field-Marshal Lord, **177, 179**
Haldane, Lord, 176, 265
Hampstead and Highgate Express, 25
Harding, President, 341
Harmsworth, Alfred, sen., 17, 24
Harmsworth, Cecil, 95, 350
Harmsworth, Harold, *see* Rothermere, Lord

INDEX

Harmsworth, Hon. Vere, 96, 177
Harmsworth, Mrs., sen., 14, 304, 341
Harmsworth, Mrs. Alfred, see Northcliffe, Lady
Harmsworth, Sir Hildebrand, 95
Harmsworth, St. John, 95
Harmsworth, Sir Leicester, 95, 340
Harvey, George, 342
Henderson, James, 43
Henley House School, 22
Hicks, Seymour, 333
Hindenburg, Field-Marshal, 253
Hoover, President, 342
House, Colonel, 205, 217, 218, 222, 337
Howard, Sir Ebenezer, 20
Howard, Keble, 349
Hudson, Lady, see Northcliffe, Lady
Hudson, Sir Robert, 350
Hughes, Mr. (Australia), 201, 343
Hutton, Richard, 96
Hylan, Mayor, 288

Iliffe's, 30
Ingram, Sir William, 27
Insurance, Newspaper, 296
Ireland, Northcliffe's views on, 167, 260
Irwin, Will, 103
Isaacs, George, 345

Jealous, Mr., 26, 344
Jellicoe, Admiral Lord, 185
Jones, Kennedy, 56, 76, 93, 270, 297
Journalists, National Union of, 329

Kipling, Rudyard, 85, 113
Kitchener, Lord, 88, 175, 183, 191

Labour Party, 265, 266
Latham, Hubert, 144
Le Bon, Professor G., 254
Leigh, Sir J., 331
Levavasseur, 144, 145
Lipton, Sir Thomas, 78
Long, Walter (Lord Long), 259
Lord London, 349
Lucas, E. V., 149
Ludendorff, 255
Lusitania, the, 200

McAdoo, Mr., 230
Macdonell, James, 54
MacMunn, Sir G., 183

Mangin, General, 254
Marcosson, Isaac, 204
Markwick, E., 35
Marshall Hall, Sir E., 278
Mathers, Helen, 43
Max of Baden, Prince, 190, 248, 250, 251, 338
Melba, Dame Nellie, 43
Mightier than the Sword, 349
Milne, A. A., and father, 23
Miracle, The, 117, 118
Morel, E. D., 166
Morgan, J. P., & Co., 215, 322
Morton, Edward, 27
Mosley, Sir Oswald, 115, 116
Munitions Crisis, 186
Munsey, Frank A., 343
Musson, Rev. E. C., 21

Napoleon of the Press, 349
Nevill, Lady Dorothy, 272
Newfoundland, 134
Newnes, Sir G., 1, 36
New York World, 153, 161
Nicoll, W. Robertson, 149, 345
Nordenfeldt, 9
Northcliffe, Lady, 33, 49, 91, 278, 350

O'Connor, T. P., 55, 58
Olympia Luncheon, 300
Olympic Games, 113
Outing, 34
Owen, Louise, 232

Pagenstecher, Dr., 69
Paulhan, Louis, 146
Pearson, Sir A., 7, 66, 121, 133
Peking "Massacre," 107, 108
Pemberton, Sir Max, 2, 345
Pine, W., 346
Poincaré, M., 340
Portsmouth election, 87
Prioleau, John, 311
Pulitzer, 161, 207

Raymond, E. T., 303
Reading, Lord, 221, 301
Rechberg, Arnold, 255
Riddell, Lord, 179
Roberts, Lord, 151
Roosevelt, Theodore, 154, 215
Rosebery, Earl of, 67, 151

INDEX

Rothermere, Lord, 44, 45, and *The Times,* 124, and Newfoundland, 134; 350
Rupprecht of Bavaria, Prince, 250
Russell, Alexander, 54
Russell, Hon. Bertrand, 171

St. Davids, Lord, 196
Sala, G. A., 329
Salisbury, Marquis of, 36, 63
Santos-Dumont, 141
Sapt, A., 98–101
Scott, Sir Percy, 286
Selfridge, Gordon, 131
Seton-Watson, 240
Sichel, Walter, 150
Simon, Sir John, 196
Soap Trust, 117
Spring-Rice, Sir Cecil, 209
Stamford Grammar School, 20
Standard bread, 114, 115
Star, 58
Stead, W. T., 7
Steed, Wickham, 174, 186, 212, 240, 340, 345
Steevens, George, 86
Strachey, St. Loe, 344
Stuart, Sir Campbell, 208, 239, 270, 290, 321, 344
Sullivan, Sir A., 86, 113
Sunday Companion, 111
Sutton Place, 89, 156, 207
Sutton, Sir George, 43, 344

Tardieu, André, 230
Taylor, J. H., 347
Teddy Tail, 290
The Times, 119–133, 164; prosecuted, 190; 233, 273
Thomson, "Sandy," 346
Titanic disaster, 113
Tit-Bits, 1–10

Vanity Fair, 29
Victoria, Queen, 36, 68
Von Hutier, General, 253
Von Stein, General, 255

Walter family, 120, 334
War Office, offered to Northcliffe, 236
Watson, Aaron, 28
Webber, Byron, 28
Webster, Tom, 279
Weekly Dispatch, 111, 276
Wells, H. G., 23, 243, 348
What the Public Wants, 349
Whibley, Charles, 344
Williams, Valentine, 327
Wilson, President, 217, 267
Wrench, Evelyn, 344
Wright Brothers, 143, 218

Young, Filson, 345
Younger, Lord, 98
Youth, 27